Restorative Justice, Self-interest and Responsible Citizenship

Restorative Justice, Self-interest and Responsible Citizenship

Lode Walgrave

WILLAN
PUBLISHING

Published by

Willan Publishing
Culmcott House
Mill Street, Uffculme
Cullompton, Devon
EX15 3AT, UK
Tel: +44(0)1884 840337
Fax: +44(0)1884 840251
e-mail: info@willanpublishing.co.uk
website: www.willanpublishing.co.uk

Published simultaneously in the USA and Canada by

Willan Publishing
c/o ISBS, 920 NE 58th Ave, Suite 300,
Portland, Oregon 97213-3786, USA
Tel: +001(0)503 287 3093
Fax: +001(0)503 280 8832
e-mail: info@isbs.com
website: www.isbs.com

First published 2008

ISBN   978-1-84392-334-3 paperback
          978-1-84392-335-0 hardback

British Library Cataloguing-in-Publication Data

A catalogue record for this book is available from the British Library.

Project managed by Deer Park Productions, Tavistock, Devon
Typeset by GCS, Leighton Buzzard, Bedfordshire
Printed and bound by T.J. International Ltd, Padstow, Cornwall

Contents

Foreword and acknowledgements

The cover of the book displays a work of art representing Sisyphus, the tragic hero in the old Greek myth. It was made in 1548–49 by the Italian baroque painter Titian. The versions of the myth differ, but it is told that Sisyphus had the *hubris* (the arrogant recklessness) to defy the gods. They punished him by imposing on him an everlasting burden. Sisyphus is doomed to push a huge rock up a steep hill. But each time the top is almost attained, the rock rolls back down the hill, and Sisyphus must start again, a cycle which will last for eternity.

The myth of Sisyphus has fascinated artists and philosophers throughout human history. It is intriguing indeed why Sisyphus continues his ceaseless and pointless task. One possible answer is that he goes on out of fear of death, which would follow if he did not. The desire for life is stronger than the aversion for the meaningless effort. And, as Camus writes in *Le Mythe de Sisyphe* (1942), by being resigned and continuing the task routinely, without thinking, Sisyphus finds peace.

Another answer is, however, that Sisyphus keeps pushing the rock because of hope. If, deep down, he did not keep some hope that he will ever reach the top, he would accept death. It is typical that all artists, from the ancient Polygnotus to the postmodern Luciano Fabro, represent Sisyphus while he is pushing the rock up the hill, and not in the most frustrating phase, looking at the rock rolling down it, after which he has to walk back to pick up once again the endless effort. The key to the myth is the pushing up the hill.

Both dimensions together are symbolic of the human condition. Positively, we all are driven by the intrinsic unquenchable desire to reach the ideal, while knowing that we never reach it completely. Negatively, we are condemned to keep striving towards the highest possible, because if we did not, deterioration would be unavoidable.

It is a leitmotiv of this book. While trying to combine self-interest with common interest, we know that in the end self-interest always gets the upper hand; scientists continue pursuing objective facts, while they cannot but discover subjectively what is 'out there'; liberals argue for maximal liberties for citizens, but using these liberties unrestrained would lead to catastrophic social relations; philosophers and jurists search for general principles of justice, knowing that justice cannot be but an imperfect human construction, provisional and one-sided. But still, if we did not continue pursuing the ideals, the opposite of the ideal would drown us. If scientists gave up their ideal of objectivity, they would sink into impressionist results with no added value; if rights and liberties were not defended, enslavement would follow; if justice were not pursued, injustice would be the rule.

Restorative justice will be presented as an ideal way of doing justice in an ideal society, while understanding it is a kind of utopia. We need an image of what is at the top of the hill, a utopia, to prevent the human community from dying by cynical selfishness. There is nothing as practical as a good utopia. It is a motivating beacon, a reference to work towards. If some progress is observed, utopia is a source of hope. Without a utopia, there is no hope, and motivation for action and improvement drops.

This book can be considered my tribute to the community of criminologists, and especially to those committed to pursuing scientific understanding of restorative justice and its potential. It was a privilege to meet so many people with great commitment to 'the good', personal integrity and high scientific quality. Reading their publications, meeting them and having discussions with them was inspiring, provoking, questioning, fascinating, stimulating, pleasant, amusing, sometimes even hilarious. It opened up for me prospects of new potentials and hope for a better justice in a better world. These colleagues helped me to develop my utopia and to 'push the rock'.

My special thanks go to Gordon Bazemore, John Blad, John Braithwaite, Paul McCold, Dan Van Ness, Bas van Stokkom and Stefaan Walgrave, colleagues and friends (and one son) who devoted some of their scant free time to read earlier versions of one or two chapters. Even if I did not always do as they suggested, their comments were extremely valuable; they made me reconsider, explain better, or, indeed, modify passages of the book. I also thank my colleague

Willy Clarysse, for the information he provided about the myth of Sisyphus. Patricia Butler was my first language-corrector. Her firm but friendly way of turning my particular English-like language into real English avoided too great a confrontation with my shortcomings in that respect.

Finally, I cannot but thank also my wife, Mieke. For a long time she put up with my absent-mindedness, my hiding away at work, my taking up of time we should have spent together. I promised her that it would be better once this book was finished; I'm not sure that she really believed me. We must see it like Sisyphus: I shall push the rock up to the top of my leisure activities and even laziness, but, unfortunately, the gods may roll the rock back downwards to criminology and restorative justice. What can you do then?

Lode Walgrave
Leuven

Introduction

It is a commonplace that restorative justice is expanding rapidly. From a phrase hardly known, it has become in a few decades a broad and still 'widening river' (Zehr 2002a: 62) of renovating practices and empirical evaluations, a central issue in theoretical, juridical and socio-ethical debates, and a ubiquitous theme in juvenile justice and criminal justice reforms worldwide. No doubt, the boost has to do with the intrinsic social value of the basic ideas and with the quality of the practices carried out all over the world. Probably, the restorative justice discourse also comes timely, in a period of increasing awareness that the current escalation in punitiveness and social exclusion is driving a downwards spiral of lack of safety, discomfort and discontent. Also academic reflection and research are forces which have contributed considerably to the quality and the dissemination of restorative justice practice and theory.

Yet, despite the wide dissemination, there are many conceptions of what is understood by 'restorative justice'. For some, it is a synonym for a particular practice such as victim–offender mediation (in Europe) or conferencing (in Australia and New Zealand). At the other end of the spectrum, others see it as a wide movement to transform the way people live together. The vagueness or even confusion about the concept is a problem for its social credibility and for research.

Well informed critics on the practical, ethical, theoretical and empirical aspects of restorative justice are indispensable in the development of good practice, balanced theoretical insight and socio-ethical understanding. They help to clear out, correct, reformulate, reduce and sharpen insights and ambitions. But the lack of clarity in conception has made restorative justice vulnerable to criticisms which are based on a misconception or a too reduced understanding; some criticisms address practices which do not meet reasonable standards of good restorative practice, or even caricatures of restorative justice. It is difficult to respond to such wrong understandings if the response cannot itself rely on a clear conception.

The lack of clarity is also detrimental for research. If the object of the investigation is not well delimited, you cannot investigate it accurately. If there is no transparent differentiation between socio-ethical options and empirical findings, credibility is lost. If the relation between the mainstream punitive apriorism and restorative justice is not understood unambiguously, they cannot be compared adequately. If there is no view on the variety and complexity of possible restorative justice practices, conclusions based on one type of practice cannot address restorative justice as a whole. If there is no clarity about the objectives of restorative justice, its success or failure cannot be assessed.

Searching for more clarity in concepts and in the socio-ethical foundations

The first aim of this book is to find clarity. I am going to try to distil out of the large and diverse restorative justice literature what are in my view the essentials of restorative justice, and what it should be ideally. In doing so, I hope to propose a clearer distinction between (1) the core of restorative justice as a restricted option on doing justice after the occurrence of a crime, (2) the other practices of resolving conflicts and injustices that are inspired by the same participatory and peace-promoting philosophy, (3) the socio-ethical roots which inspire not only the choice for restorative justice but also many other movements and practices, and finally (4) the social-political or ideological movement of which the restorative justice movement can be a part. While these four areas are mutually closely interdependent and inspirational, they are different things. It is crucial to recognise that, in order to better mark out the objects of our discourses and research. A sharper view allows better scrutiny and better advancement.

Distinguishing restorative justice in the strict sense from its socio-ethical grounds is not meant to smooth over these grounds. On the contrary. A second purpose of this book is precisely to dig up the socio-ethical and ideological layers that inspire the pursuit of restorative justice and other deliberative models of conflict resolution. In my view, the option for restorative justice is not primarily inspired by instrumental reasons (which are important, though), but most of all by socio-ethical intuitions. What brings victims and offenders to agree to meet and to seek together constructive solutions? Why is restorative justice so attractive that many adopt it as a buzzword, even if they have not reflected thoroughly on its content and consequences? Why is restorative justice associated so easily with a social movement which goes far beyond dealing with the aftermath of crime? Again, for reasons of clarity, it is important to disentangle the ethical and the empirical arguments which are all too often mixed up in much of the restorative justice literature.

I will base the exploration of these questions on a kind of introspection. What attracts me in restorative justice? I will explore and make explicit my own socio-ethical intuition and propose it as a separate argument in favour of restorative justice. It is not a neutral argument, but a socially committed one.

Such undertaking holds the risk of yielding a moralising sermon. It might become an exercise in what Pratt has called 'evangelical criminology' (Pratt 2006: 44). If my version of restorative justice were to be locked within the box of beliefs, rejecting external criticism and drifting away from adequate empirical checking, it would be a bad thing. But there is nothing wrong with moral reflection and social commitment by social scientists. I will even argue that it is crucial that social sciences are aware of their social role and play it fully. Purely objective social sciences do not and cannot exist. Hence, the truly scientific attitude is to open not only the 'intra-scientific' methodology for external control, but to explain also the 'extra-scientific' motivations and arguments. While it is crucial to distinguish clearly what we find from what we think and what we hope, all has to be communicated. In that sense, I cannot exclude my 'evangelism', but I can try to keep it under methodological control and make it open for discussion.

Like earlier reforms, the introduction of the restorative justice rationale is a movement depending on commitment and internal motivation, supported by good scientific research. Restorative justice ideas and practices are imperfect, but they add a crucial new dimension: focusing on repairing the harm and suffering caused by the crime rather than on preserving an abstract legal order. Good and committed criminological research can make a crucial difference in the dissemination and the correct implementation of restorative justice.

From juvenile justice to restorative justice in a European continental context

The clarity I am pursuing and the ethical foundations I will seek cannot but be personal. It is clarity for me and the ethical foundations in which I believe. In some respects, they are considerably deviant from mainstream visions of restorative justice. This deviance is marked by my own history in restorative justice and by my European continental roots.

I came to restorative justice via juvenile justice. Until recently, Belgian juvenile justice was one of the most consistently treatment-oriented systems in the world. Its focus on remediating the needs of the child led to neglect of the traditional legal safeguards. But criticising the treatment orientation in juvenile justice entailed the risk of handing over juvenile offenders back to the traditional punitive response (as, for example, in Feld 1999). And that was not my ideal.

Some local practices in Belgium inspired my vision of a possible alternative. In 1981, I wrote an article in a Dutch journal, 'Confronting youth crime with the law: restraint and reparation, but not punishment'[1] (Walgrave 1981). In my view at that time, judicial intervention should refocus on the criminalised act (and not on the needs of the offender), on what would offer the standard for deducing legal safeguards. But the judicial sanction itself should above all consist of pressure or judicial obligation to carry out reparative actions. It would force the juvenile to confront his responsibility, and thereby be more constructively pedagogical and more useful for all. Intuitively, I took a reparative position without knowing of developments in other countries.

It was only in 1991, at an international workshop on Conflict, Crime and Reconciliation (Messmer and Otto 1992) that I heard for the first time the phrase 'restorative justice'. My earlier intuition fitted into the ideas being shared, and the contours became visible of a broader and deeper concept of doing justice. But I still saw restorative justice primarily as a way to escape the unfruitful rehabilitation–punishment dilemma in juvenile justice and as a possible ground for a constructive judicial response to youth crime which would better answer the legal requirements.

Intensive exchanges with colleagues from all over the world in the International Network for Research on Restorative Justice for

Juveniles gradually made me understand how revolutionarily different it is to be focused on repairing the harm and suffering instead of trying to submit the offender to a 'just' response. The importance of the deliberative process came to the forefront. It took a while for me to understand that restorative justice was not so much about a justice system promoting restoration as about doing justice through restoration.

But I did not completely change my mind. So, for example, I straightforwardly use an outcome-based definition of restorative justice, and see voluntary processes only as (crucial) tools to achieve the maximum possible restoration; I include the possibility of imposing judicial sanctions in view of reparation into my restorative justice concept; I am sceptical towards the – in my view – too naive reliance on community, and look for a particular juridical frame to keep restorative justice adequately within the principles of a constitutional democratic state. These and other deviations from the mainstream will become apparent throughout the book.

Probably, these deviant options are mainly due to my European continental roots. Three particularities may explain why developments in restorative justice have taken a somewhat different shape on the European continent (Willemsens and Walgrave 2007).

Common law vs civil law

Restorative justice promotes the inclusion of the direct stakeholders in the response to the offence, which is a challenge to the traditional state monopoly over the reaction to crime. Changing this is more difficult where this monopoly is strongly centralised and consolidated by legal dispositions, as in European civil law regimes.

On the European continent, the *legality* principle prevails, obligating police, for example, to inform the public prosecutor about all cases. The public prosecutor has only limited power not to refer cases to court if there is sufficient evidence. In common law, the opportunity principle prevails granting all agents in the system – police, prosecuting agencies, judges – the *opportunity* to exercise broad discretionary powers in deciding how to act in the 'public interest' and in imposing measures they feel are most appropriate in response to the crime committed. It may bring common law closer to the reality of public life and the attitudes of the 'community', including, however, risks of populist influences and weaker legal safeguards. Civil law provides stricter legal safeguards, but is also more rigid and sometimes unworldly.

The flexibility of the common law system can play an important role in the development of restorative justice. This is true not only because of the space it allows for running experiments, but also because flexibility is a crucial element in restorative practices themselves. It is therefore easier to carry out mediation or conferencing outside of the justice system, within the 'community' for example, or to include these practices in the judicial procedure, as is the case in 'cautioning'. The outcome of the restorative process is not as strictly weighed against legal checks as would be the case in the civil law regimes.

Hence it is not coincidental that most restorative practices have their origins in common law countries, and that Europeans are more concerned with the legal basis for these practices when they are introduced in their countries. More than most common law countries, those on the European continent have legislated detailed procedural rules to implement restorative schemes. From the beginning, legal concerns with restorative justice have been an essential part of the debates on the European continent.

Community vs 'citoyenneté'

Anglo-Americans very much rely on community to explain how they see restorative justice and other social mechanisms working ideally. Europeans are aware that an informal climate of mutual understanding is crucial, but they find the confidence in community naive or even dangerous.

The differences in approach rest on differences in concepts of the relationship between state and citizens (van Swaaningen 1997). Europeans see the authorities as the holders of the *vox communi*. The state is the formalisation of the community, or the community of communities. Most English speakers feel less represented by the state, which is often seen as a bureaucratic taxing machine, an opponent to freedom, located at an unbridgeable distance from real life. Especially in the USA, the shortage of state institutions for education, medical care and social allowances is often partly compensated for by communities based on religion, territory or ethnicity. This may be why many Americans relate to community as opposed to government or state, and are less sensitive to the exclusionary anomalies of many communities, which shall be described in Chapter 3.

Europeans are sensitive to the state's bureaucratic and formalist excesses, but they mostly see it as a tool to be improved. The state is a safeguard against abuses of power by the most powerful.

Citoyenneté, as the French call it – citizenship – is a crucial good, including rights and protections offered by the state, and obligations. Decentralisation does not send matters to the community, as in North America, but to the municipalities (Hastings and Bailleau 2005). Communitarianism often has a pejorative meaning in French society, because it is suspected of promoting the selfish interests of the particular community to the detriment of general citizens' interests. It is not that Europeans love paying taxes; they basically consider it as a contribution to collective life.

This difference may explain why English-speaking scholars see restorative justice more often as an opportunity to extend the reach of community in responding to crime and to push back the interference of formal state power: 'Restorative justice is a form of insurgency because it competes with the state' (Sullivan and Tift 2006a: 5). Europeans are predominantly sceptical towards an – in their eyes – uncritical reliance on informal communities, and are often committed to trying to include restorative practices in a judicial frame while preserving the benefits of informal deliberation.

First Nations and other Indigenous people

Indigenous populations currently have a strong voice in Canada, the United States, Australia and New Zealand. Their traditional practices have energised the debates on criminal justice, and have deeply influenced thinking on and practices of restorative justice.

Unlike other regions of the world, Western Europe has not had a driving and inspiring force toward restorative justice based on the ethnic and cultural diversity of its populations. This is undoubtedly due in part to the rather reduced proportion of non-Western populations. But it certainly also has to do with their status as immigrants. The white population is the 'First Nation' in Europe. White Western society and culture has its territorial roots on the European continent, and that positions ethnic and cultural minorities as 'visitors'. According to the mainstream opinion, those visitors must simply 'integrate' into Western culture, meaning that they must accept Western values and institutions. Muslim or African traditions do not really penetrate European social institutions. They are accepted only in the margins, insofar as they do not challenge the Western model of society. This is also the case for criminal justice.

Furthermore, the centralised civil law system is not flexible enough to be influenced to the same extent as the common law system in Anglo-Saxon countries.

Structure of the book

In Chapter 1, 'Focusing on restorative justice', I explain my own view on restorative justice. It is argued why I opt for a 'restricted definition', addressing only the dealing with criminalisable matters, and not all other practices in schools, welfare work, neighbourhoods, etc. Contrary to most restorative justice writers, I opt for a restricted and outcome-based definition of restorative justice as 'an option for doing justice after the occurrence of an offence that is primarily oriented towards repairing the individual, relational and social harm caused by that offence'. The most important restorative schemes are presented with some comments. The restricted essentialist definition allows for a maximalist option on how to deal with the aftermath of crime. While voluntary dialogue among the stakeholders is promoted where possible, judicially imposed sanctions are also accepted in the restorative justice concept if they are primarily intended to contribute as much as possible to reparation. This acceptance raises questions about the difference between reparative obligations and criminal punishment.

Chapter 2, 'Restorative justice and criminal punishment', argues why restorative justice is clearly distinguished from punishment. The most important difference is that a – possibly painful – obligation to repair is not equal to an intentional infliction of pain. The apriorism that crime must be responded to by an intentional infliction of pain is detrimental for instrumental reasons. I also argue that such apriorism is highly problematic from a socio-ethical standpoint. The need for censuring criminal behaviour and for restoring a kind of moral balance after the occurrence of a crime is recognised. To punitive retributivism, restorative justice is opposed as a model of inversed constructive retributivism.

Chapter 3 is entitled 'Common self-interest: seeking socio-ethical grounds for restorative justice'. The very fact that restoration is given priority over punishment is an expression of a different socio-ethical position. After a review of some ethical approaches to restorative justice, I opt for an 'ethic of social life', advancing common self-interest as the crucial concept. It is self-interest, because I promote community life, not because I am an unworldly idealist, but because I hope to get benefits from being a member of a good community. It is, however, more than self-interest, because we all integrate our self-interest in a project of common self-interest, being to increase the quality of social life. Social life guided by such a project promotes the ethical attitudes respect, solidarity and active responsibility as the most important ones, which are reflected better in restorative justice than in punitive justice. Other values like justice or freedom derive from respect, solidarity and taking active responsibility.

Chapter 4, 'Examining restorative practice', provides a critical review of the available empirical data on restorative practices. The results are encouraging, not decisive. It then tries to understand what makes restorative justice practices function as they do. Several psychological and social-psychological theories provide partial explanations for what happens in a restorative process, but, with a few exceptions, systematic empirical research on explanatory theories is lacking. The chapter ends with a comprehensive programme of empirical questions and methodological issues which, together, make a kind of a map for restorative justice research on micro-social, social and institutional levels. Obviously, restorative justice encounters will fail often, for a diversity of possible reasons. That is why restorative justice must be included in a formal system, which itself should still be oriented towards serving as much as possible reparative outcomes. What such a system might be is the subject of the next chapter.

The aim of Chapter 5, 'Designing a restorative justice system', is to explore how social institutions would look if they gave restorative justice the position it claims, meaning the primary and mainstream response to crime. The republican theory of criminal justice is used as the ground for designing a pyramid of restorative law enforcement. The bottom consists of deliberative conflict resolution in the community, and the top is a small triangle of incapacitation to deal with the incompetent or irrational offender. Between both is a space of restorative justice responses to offences in which the degree of voluntariness is gradually decreased and the (threat of) judicial coercion increased. As restorative justice is another paradigm, the legal principles of traditional criminal justice cannot be transposed unchanged to a restorative justice system. Traditional legal safeguards like equality, presumption of innocence and proportionality are discussed in a restorative justice perspective.

Finally, Chapter 6, 'Democracy, criminology and restorative justice', positions restorative justice into a wider social movement for a more just, more participatory and more inclusionary democracy. The relation between participatory democracy, restorative justice and criminology (and other social sciences) is seen as a triangle of mutually reinforcing dynamics. The working of restorative justice depends on the quality of democratic institutions, but restorative justice philosophy and practice can help to improve the democratic value of these institutions. Participatory deliberative democracy is best served by autonomous high-quality social sciences (including criminology) committed to the quality of social life, but such sciences can flourish best in good democracies. Restorative justice is an opportunity for criminology to return to its roots as an autonomous science focused on improving social life, but restorative justice needs the support of criminological research to develop as a comprehensive philosophy, to improve its methods and to gain empirical credibility. Therefore restorative justice is seen as one of the social forces that can contribute to redressing the current dualisation and weakening of democracy. Its potentials consist of both indirectly promoting the democratic role of criminological sciences and directly contributing to the development of participatory practices and attitudes in the population.

By the end of the book, it should be clear to the reader why I see restorative justice as a most promising path towards a more just and more socially constructive way of responding to crime, but also as one of the social forces that aim at resuscitating participatory democracy. Its potentials are its target of restoring individual and social life if a crime has occurred; its focus on what binds us (common self-interest, dominion, quality of social life) rather than what divides; the reconception of the response to crime from a top-down sentencing machine to a responsive bottom-up problem-solving system; the priority for inclusive deliberation, reducing the use of coercion to the strictest minimum; the expansion of deliberative practices to other fields that deal with conflict and injustice; the chance it offers for citizens to experience the power of respectful dialogue and the benefits of investing in common interest; and its basic trust in the constructive potential of people to take their responsibility actively in crime and justice matters and in other fields of social life.

Of course, I hope to persuade the reader. But if he were convinced completely, no disagreement would be left for discussion. And discussion is what we need for advancement. Hence my greatest hope is that the book might provoke disagreement and constructive discussion.

Note

1 'Recht tegenover jeugddelinquentie: beteugelen en herstellen, maar niet straffen.'

Chapter 1

Focusing on restorative justice

Restorative justice is an unfinished product. It is a complex and lively realm of different – and partly opposite – beliefs and options, renovating inspirations and practices in different contexts, scientific 'crossing swords' over research methodology and outcomes. Restorative justice is, at the same time, a social movement with different degrees of self-criticism and a domain of scientific research with different degrees of methodological adequacy. It is a field on its own, looking for constructive ways of dealing with the aftermath of crime, but also part of a larger socio-ethical and political agenda.

Understandably, it is not easy to define what the concept encompasses. Is it a (series of) practice(s)? Is it a (utopian) view? What is the core, what are the essentials of restorative justice and what is derived or secondary? A generally accepted definition cannot be provided; there is none. What is possible, however, is to try to get a sharper view of the vague contours, to focus the lens. But like a photographer who takes his pictures from a certain position, I can only sharpen the view from my own standpoint, which differs in some ways from the views of other authors. My presentation thus unavoidably includes a number of particular options which will sometimes deviate considerably from the mainstream of restorative justice.

The emergence of restorative justice in modern times

Ancient wisdom

Restorative justice is not a recent invention. Some authors suggest that a reparative response to injustice was for a long time the dominant model in earlier times (Zehr 1990; Weitekamp 1999; Van Ness and Heetderks Strong 2006). It sounds reasonable. One can understand that primitive small communities or tribes could not afford exclusion or enduring conflict in their midst, because the struggle for life needed intensive cooperation and mutual support. The tribes probably tried to find constructive solutions to internal conflicts and to avoid the exclusion of individuals as much as possible. According to this view, it was the centralising of power which gradually shifted the meaning of norm transgression away from harming another individual or the group to breaking the ruler's law. The settlement of the aftermath of law-breaking was taken away from its main proponents, and reparation for the victim became subsidiary to punishment to enforce compliance with the law. From that perspective, the state has done much damage to the quality of conflict resolution in communities. Or in Christie's view, the state stole the conflict from its owners (Christie 1977).

Other authors, however, reject this view as being romantic and based on an unscientific approach. It is 'a kind of foundational myth about the "naturalness" of RJ' (Bottoms 2003: 88). On the contrary, a history of escalating violence and revenge is suggested (Sylvester 2003; Miller 1999). Experienced injustice and damage were responded to by counteractions, undertaken by the victims, their families and their clans. The emergence of central power then gradually blocked this violent private retaliation, replacing it with an increasingly sophisticated, legally ordered system of punishment. Such a view supports Elias' theory on civilisation: violence in communities was reduced and monopolised more and more in the hands of the state (Elias 1994).

As an amateur historian, I draw two lessons from these contradictory positions. First, there may be a problem with the methodology of 'objective' historians. As it is based predominantly on written sources, it may lead to a relative underestimation of restitutive responses. Often, compensation and the associated negotiations were informal and occurred among illiterate people. No authorities or other literate agencies were involved, so that written indications of such resolutions may be scarce. On the other hand, violent settlements probably came more to the attention of the central power, entailing a powerful intervention to stop them. More written reports of such incidents can be expected, so that the number of conflict settlements imposed by central authorities may be overestimated in historians' reports.

Second, the reality was probably not uniform, but mixed and varied, with different degrees of violence and reparative agreements.

Moreover, the way of handling disputes and injustices must have developed differently in different communities and societies (Bottoms 2003). It seems plausible that compensation and restitution have been important ways of responding to injustices, but also that violent settlements occurred spontaneously as revenge or when deliberation appeared not to be possible or no agreement was reached (Schafer 1977). Gradually, rules ordered the amounts and types of compensation and other settlements, and that contributed to reducing the duration of conflicts and violence. But as the state power became stronger and stronger, the scale tipped and punishing the law-breaker overtook repairing the harm. Probably, restitution and compensation have always been practised, but their scope and prevalence in the past is uncertain and probably variable over communities and periods of time.

It is well documented, however, that moral guidelines and virtues that are consistent with the currently advanced principles of restorative justice have been promulgated over time. Texts of the great spiritual traditions – Buddhism, Christianity, Confucianism, Hinduism, Islam, Judaism – promote crucial restorative values such as mutual respect, compensation, apology and forgiveness (Hadley 2001).[1] Practices described in ancient Arab, Greek, Roman, German, Chinese, Hindu and other societies bear witness to restorative values (Braithwaite 2002a; Van Ness and Heetderks Strong 2006). It seems obvious, therefore, that the moral values underlying restorative justice and restorative-type practices are deeply rooted in ancient wisdom, even if their predominance in practice may be uncertain.

Indirectly, this is confirmed through the recent emancipation of native peoples. In New Zealand, for example, Maori tradition inspired the 'invention' of family group conferences (Adler and Wundersitz 1994); in North America, Native traditions grounded the recognition of sentencing and peacemaking circles (Yazzie and Zion 1996; Jaccoud 1998); in South Africa the Truth and Reconcilation Commission and other forms of conflict regulation were based on the Zulu *ubuntu* philosophy (Louw 2006). Whereas the use of these ancient traditions in modern practices is not unproblematic and often based on romanticised visions (Cunneen 2007), their ways of dealing with injustices appear, in many cases (but not all), to be primarily oriented towards objectives such as encounter, community involvement and reparation (Zellerer and Cunneen 2001).

In fact, restorative concerns in the response to norm transgression never disappeared completely, but over many centuries they have been subordinated by the punitive mainstream. In 1900, for example,

Tallack wrote that 'reparation as the chief, and often whole, element of punishment was wiser in principle, more reformatory in its influence, more deterrent in its tendency and more economic to the economy' (in Weitekamp 1992: 84). All this does not mean, of course, that ancient or native practices can simply be copied and applied to our modern societies and cities (Johnstone 2002; Sylvester 2003).

Modern roots

In its modern form, restorative justice reappeared against the background of neo-liberal criticism of the welfare state, which aimed at imposing more responsibility on individual citizens, including those in trouble, and of communitarian objections against state institutions, which were considered alienating and inappropriate to deal with real life. In business regulation, alternative dispute resolution (ADR) was one of the first expressions of citizens claiming space outside of the judiciary to regulate their conflicts informally.

Many interconnected tendencies have influenced the re-emergence of restorative justice more specifically, such as feminism, decarceration movements, indigenous peoples' emancipation movements and options to reconfirm the responsibility of (young) offenders. The most important roots can be grouped into three tendencies (Faget 1997; Van Ness and Heetderks Strong 2002).

Victims' movements, often intertwined with feminist themes, claimed an expanded role in criminal justice (Strang 2002). Initially, they were focused on promoting the victim's rights in his[2] conflict with the offender, and held a strict oppositional view on victims' and offenders' interests. In their 'zero-sum' approach to justice (Strang 2002: 199), the more attention that is paid to the offender's rights and needs, the less space there is for the victim's interests. They strongly support the punitive aspect of criminal justice. While this punitive tendency is still active,[3] many victims' advocates today are oriented towards a broader consideration of the social, personal and juridical needs of the victims. They now understand that simply making a coalition with the traditional criminal justice system is often counterproductive for the victims. More than boosting punishment of the offender, seeking reparation and compensation may result in deeper and continuing satisfaction. Deliberation, rather than enforcement, may contribute to peace of mind (Peters and Aertsen 1995; Dignan 2005; Cario 2005).[4]

Another source of restorative justice is communitarianism. As a reaction to the fragmentation of our postmodern Western societies, some propagate the revival of community as the organic source of informal mutual support and control (Etzioni 1998). Communities are at the same time seen as a means and an end for restorative justice. They are a means in that communities are the 'niches' in which reintegrative shaming and restorative processes can take place (Braithwaite 1989); they are an end, because it is believed that achieving restorative processes in a community is constructive for the revival of community life (Bazemore and Schiff 2001). Within the communitarian agenda, restorative justice has been strongly inspired by religious beliefs (Hadley 2001), as appears from the spiritual basis of the Victim Offender Reconciliation Program (VORP) in Kitchener (Ontario, Canada), which is often mentioned as the roots-project of restorative practices, and through the publications of one of the founding fathers of the restorative movement (Zehr 1990). The communitarian agenda has also been boosted by the emancipation of native people, especially in North America and New Zealand. Their community-based, peace-oriented and deliberation-driven ways of dealing with conflict and norm transgression have deeply influenced restorative practice and thinking (Zellerer and Cunneen 2001).

Especially in the 1970s and 1980s, critical criminology pointed to the counterproductive effects of criminal justice and its incapacity to ensure peace in social life. Critical criminologists partly endorsed the communitarian agenda, but often framed their criticisms in a structuralist, Marxist perspective. Abolitionists argued for the scrapping or phasing out of the criminal justice system, in order to replace it by a bottom-up deliberative model of dealing with conflicts (Christie 1981; Hulsman and Bernat de Celis 1982; Bianchi 1994). Inheritors of this tendency proposed restorative justice-like alternatives (De Haan 1990), or have turned to restorative justice as the mainstream alternative to criminal justice (Blad 1996a) or to youth justice (Walgrave 1995; Bazemore and Walgrave 1999).

Practices have evolved since the early 1970s in the USA and Canada (McCold 2006) and in Europe (Pelikan and Trenczek 2006). Originally, there were a number of isolated initiatives, which did not refer at all to a restorative justice concept. It is only since the late 1980s and early 1990s that restorative justice has really begun to take off. All the tendencies and movements, and a multitude of separate intuitive initiatives, have led to a realm of practices, social movements, theory-formation, ethical reflection and empirical research, which is now referred to as 'restorative justice'. The application of its principles is spreading far beyond criminal matters, penetrating the regulation of disputes and problems of discipline in schools, neighbourhood conflicts, child welfare and protection matters, labour and business regulation, and even the resolution of conflicts involving systematic political violence.

Given its diverse roots, its broad field of implementation and the current variety of forms, it is not surprising that restorative justice does not appear as a clearly defined set of thoughts and implementations, but as a rather confused, seemingly even incoherent, assembly. Adding to the confusion are apparently similar movements, under banners such as transformative justice, relational justice, community justice, peacemaking justice and the like.

In search of the essentials

Different and even competing visions of restorative justice are presented in the literature (McCold 1998; Dignan 2002). Roche, for example, distinguishes between value-based concepts of restorative justice and process-based ones (Roche 2001; see also Johnstone 2004). Process-based concepts focus on the process by which the aftermath of an offence should be dealt with, while value-based concepts underline the broader social values driving the movement for restorative justice, and include non-criminal conflict settlements inspired by the same restorative justice values. Johnstone and Van Ness (2007) present restorative justice as a 'deeply contested' concept, the subject of debates and differences in options and versions. They distinguish an encounter conception, a reparative conception and a transformative conception of restorative justice. While there are overlaps and connections between these conceptions, considerable distinctions also exist. As a consequence, seeking consensus on one single definition is an impossible mission. But clarity is what we seek in this volume.

For a restricted approach

There is a tendency to extend the notion of restorative justice to other deliberative practices in resolving conflicts and injustices, or even to recall it as 'transformative justice', to transform social life through a deliberative inclusionary 'life style' (Sullivan and Tift 2006a). Roche, for example, writes that '… restorative justice consists of much more than just these criminal justice programs' (2006: 217), and he then describes practices in social welfare and in education, alternative dispute resolution in civil matters, deliberative modes of corporate regulation, truth commissions and models of community governance in so called weak states, and restorative justice in diplomacy between states. These practices indeed share 'an emphasis on informal, inclusive deliberation, rather than adjudication, and a determination to find outcomes that minimize harm and strengthen relationships' (Roche 2006: 218). They are guided and inspired by values and visions which also underlie and drive restorative justice. These values will be developed gradually in Chapters 2, 3 and 6. They refer to a conception of social life and democracy, which is for me the *basso continuo* in my pursuit of more restorative justice.

But I do not include them in 'restorative justice'. I opt for a more restricted interpretation of what restorative justice is and focus on the way the aftermath of offences is to be dealt with. In Johnstone and Van Ness's terms (2007), my option is best classified under the reparative conception of restorative justice.

Values are not restorative justice in the strict sense of the word. They are socio-ethical and/or ideological beliefs, over which restorative justice does not have the monopoly. The same values and visions drive and inspire many other movements in social policy and political engagement. They ground practices that use the same deliberative processes to deal with other non-criminalisable conflicts and injustices, in other social contexts. I do not include these 'restorative extensions' in my restricted approach, because they deal with different matters, in different contexts, with different actors and sometimes even with different purposes.

School problems, for example, do not have the same public dimension as offences; the roles of 'victims' and the 'perpetrators' are less pre-established in school than is the case in criminal justice matters (while restorative justice processes often reveal that the official victim is at least partly also an offender and that the official offender has also been victimised); unlike in the criminal justice arena, the actors involved in school problems do live in a close local community; the school context and its interventions are primarily pedagogical, which is not true for a crime settlement; the relationship between students, teachers and school direction is typical and will imbue the whole process. These differences require (slight) adaptations to the underlying philosophy and theory and the practices. These practices are extremely worthwhile as such, because they contribute significantly to the wider socio-ethical movement. School conferencing and family group conferences after offences are mutually inspirational, but they are not the same.

Being clear about restorative justice is crucial, for three reasons.

1 The coercive dealing with criminalisable matters must be kept within clear limits. Such matters are intrinsically different from other injustices and conflicts. Only in criminalisable matters are social interests considered to be threatened to the extent that they may be defended by the use of coercion. Good democracies use coercion very parsimoniously, strictly limited to what is necessary to preserve social life. Whereas restorative justice itself tries to avoid coercion maximally, it operates in a field where the eventuality of coercion is at hand. To mark the limitations of the field clearly, it helps to use distinguishing labels. Therefore blurring the limits of restorative justice is not desirable. Restorative justice operates in a field which is to be kept clearly distinguished from the 'restorative extensions' in other fields.

2 An extended concept of restorative justice loses meaning. The phrase 'restorative justice' is becoming so popular and has attracted so many other movements and tendencies that it has become a buzzword. Restorative justice means all things to all people (Roche 2001: 342). Paradoxically, the notion has been so filled up with meanings that it risks becoming empty of significance. It then becomes vulnerable to misconception and misuse. If you add too much water to coffee, its taste and strength will get lost. The density of an espresso, on the contrary, strongly reveals the taste of the coffee and really makes a difference. Likewise, to keep restorative justice a strong concept which can make a difference, an 'espresso-definition' is necessary, strongly grounded on its essentials.

3 Clarity about restorative justice is also necessary for research. As we shall see, blurred concepts lead to inaccurate research designs, sloppy variables and impressionist results.

Towards a definition

One of the most quoted definitions is that of Tony Marshall: 'Restorative justice is a process whereby all the parties with a stake in a particular offense come together to resolve collectively how to deal with the aftermath of the offense and its implications for the future' (1996: 37). It has two problems. First, it does not mention that the outcome of the process must be reparative or restorative. If the process leads, for example, to the offender's acceptance of walking around a shopping mall dressed in a T-shirt with the slogan 'I am a thief' (as described in Braithwaite 2002a: 160), it is difficult to call this a restorative practice. Or if the victim prefers not to attend a conference and the only outcome is that the offender accepts a drug treatment, the degree of restorativeness is doubtful. Second, Marshall's definition excludes actions that may lead to reparative outcomes without the parties coming together. I shall include, for example, victim support and community service in the possibly restorative justice schemes, even if the communication between the parties is very poor or absent.

Howard Zehr proposed an alternative definition which, more than Marshall's, orients the process towards restoration: 'Restorative justice is a process to involve, to the extent possible, those who have a stake in a specific offense and to collectively identify and address harms, needs and obligations, in order to heal and put things right as possible' (Zehr 2002: 37). While the aim of 'putting things right' adds a reparative dimension to the definition, it clearly remains a process-based definition, excluding (partly) reparative actions that are not based on deliberation.

While not proposing a one-sentence definition, others have tried to grasp the essentials of restorative justice in a few propositions and subpropositions. Zehr and Mika advance three 'critical components': 'Crime is fundamentally a violation of people and interpersonal relationships ...', 'Violations create obligations and liabilities ...', and 'Restorative justice seeks to heal and put right the wrongs ...' (Zehr and Mika 1997: 49–51).

Dignan and Marsh apply the notion of restorative justice to any approach or programme that has the following characteristics: 'an emphasis on the offender's personal accountability to those harmed by an offence (which may include the community as well as the victim); an inclusive decision-making process that encourages participation by key participants; and the goal of putting right the harm that is caused by an offence' (Dignan and Marsh 2001: 85).

Van Ness and Heetderks Strong write:

> ... It is a different way of thinking about crime and our response to it. It focuses on the harm caused by crime: repairing the harm done to victims and reducing future harm by preventing crime. It requires offenders to take responsibility for their actions and for the harm they have caused. It seeks redress for victims, recompense by offenders, and reintegration of both within the community. It is achieved through a cooperative effort by

communities and the government. (Van Ness and Heetderks Strong 2002: 50)

All these definitions point to the essentials of restorative justice, but they add elements that seem unnecessary for an understanding of the concept and which may be confusing. In particular the crucial importance given to deliberative processes risks the exclusion of non-deliberative actions that may also have restorative value. That is why Bazemore and Walgrave proposed a simple and essentialist definition: 'Restorative justice is every action that is primarily oriented toward doing justice by repairing the harm that has been caused by a crime' (Bazemore and Walgrave 1999: 48). It is reduced to the most crucial characteristic, the aim of reparation, and does not mention underlying principles or specific requirements or rights of parties. It may include non-deliberative interventions, such as victim support, or imposed restitution or community service if intended as a symbolic compensation for the harm to social life. This conceptualisation is based on a 'maximalist' version of restorative justice, which includes non-deliberative schemes, and even judicial sanctions with a view to reparation, as being (partly) restorative. This inclusiveness makes it possible to aim at a fully fledged restorative justice system, oriented towards doing justice through reparation and restoration. In the longer term, it would replace the existing punitive apriorism in the criminal justice system.

The maximalist version is controversial. McCold, for example, is strongly opposed to it, and confronts it with his holistic 'purist' version, based uniquely on voluntary cooperation by the stakeholders, rejecting any use of coercion under the restorative justice label (McCold 2000). He refers to Marshall's definition (given above), and considers the deliberative and inclusionary process as the key characteristic of restorative justice.

The opposition is mitigated by the increasing awareness that restorativeness is not a clear-cut concept. Indeed, restorative justice is not an exclusive collection of fully restorative schemes, opposed to all non-restorative schemes. There are no purely restorative practices or actions, clearly distinguishable from all non-restorative practices and actions. Restorative justice is a philosophy, a vision, which may penetrate a range of different actions to different degrees. Between fully restorative responses and minimally restorative ones, gradations of partly or moderately restorative responses exist (McCold 2000; Van Ness 2002a; Zehr 2002a).[5]

I therefore suggest an adaptation of the earlier Bazemore and Walgrave definition, to consider restorative justice as *'an option for doing justice after the occurrence of an offence that is primarily oriented towards repairing the individual, relational and social harm caused by that offence'*. In this version, the focus is shifted from 'action' to 'option'. Restorative justice is not a limited set of actions or programmes but, on the contrary, an option which may inspire to different degrees a variety of initiatives, programmes and systems. 'Restorative justice is a compass, not a map' (Zehr 2002: 10). I also add three categories of harm, to make clear that the harm considered transcends the harm and suffering of the individual victim. Still, the definition remains simple and concise, limiting the key element to the goal to repair the harm caused by crime. All options and actions that aim at putting right as far as possible such harm can be included in the restorative justice concept. All options and actions that do not address these harms are not considered as being restorative justice, though they may be very respectable and worthwhile.

That is why, for example, I do not favour the definition formulated in the third edition of *Restoring Justice* (Van Ness and Heetderks Strong 2006: 43): 'Restorative justice is a theory of justice that emphasizes repairing the harm caused or revealed by criminal behaviour. It is best accomplished through cooperative processes that include all stakeholders.' My problem is that the definition includes an emphasis on repairing the harm 'revealed' by criminal behaviour. Harm that is only revealed and not caused by an offence can be very broad, and may include social exclusion, psychological dysfunction and other direct or indirect causes of the offence. Addressing these elements also as primary goals abandons the strict reactive position of restorative justice and brings it into the deep water of treatment and insatiable preventionism. Though it is important to respond to the offender's social and psychological needs and problems, I do not consider them as a primary target of restorative justice interventions. The relation between restorative justice and treatment or prevention is dealt with in Chapter 2.

Two additional comments

An outcome-based definition

The definition proposed is clearly outcome-based, whereas probably a majority of the 'restorativists' prefer a definition that focuses on the deliberative process as the key characteristic. The UN *Handbook on Restorative Justice Programmes* (2006) does not even provide a definition of restorative justice, only of restorative processes, as if both concepts were identical. McCold clearly reflects this view: 'The essence of restorative justice is not the end, but the means by which resolution is achieved' (McCold 2004a: 15). The communicative potentials of mediation and family group conferences, for example, indeed favour the authentic assessment of the harm suffered and may more easily lead to a genuine agreement on how it can be reasonably repaired or compensated. The offender's acceptance of making reparation expresses his understanding of the wrongs committed and harms caused, and his compliance with the social norms; the recognition of harm confirms the value and recognises the rights of the victim. This is all much more restorative for the victim, the community and the offender than if a sanction is simply imposed on the offender.

Nevertheless, restorative justice cannot be reduced to such a process, for two reasons. First, no process can be defined or evaluated without referring to its purpose. It would be like pedalling in the air. Why do I engage in the process of inviting friends for dinner, for example? Because dining with friends gives me the joy of meeting them, discussing and joking with them, and the opportunity to reinforce our friendship. The joy and the reinforced friendship are outcomes of the process. If the friends did not show up, or if the dinner turned into a heavy quarrel, the process itself would not have been desirable. Likewise, a restorative process is valued, not because of the deliberation on its own, but because of the outcomes it helps to achieve: '... the more common argument is that such processes are useful for achieving a whole range of beneficial outcomes' (Johnstone and Van Ness 2007: 10). A deliberative process is more restorative because the expressions of remorse, compassion, apology and forgiveness which it facilitates may readily yield feelings of being respected, peace and satisfaction. These feelings are outcomes. The 'outcome' is thus to be conceived as much larger than what is explicitly written down in the agreement resulting from a process. It is everything that may result on purpose, directly or indirectly, from the restorative action, immediately or in the longer term. Processes that do not lead deliberately to outcomes that contribute to the reparation of the harm caused by the crime are not part of restorative justice. Conversely, a sanction that is imposed in order to (partially) repair a victim's harm and feelings of safety in the community may under some conditions be considered in a restorative justice perspective.

Secondly, restricting restorative justice to voluntary deliberations would drastically limit its scope (Dignan 2002) and doom it to stay at the margins of the system. The mainstream response to crime would remain coercive and punitive. The criminal justice system would act as the gatekeeper and probably be very selective in its referrals to deliberative restorative processes. Only less serious cases would be presented for (semi-)voluntary processes, excluding victims of serious crimes. And generally, it is these victims who need restoration most badly. Moreover, such a diversionist position gives up the principle of according priority to restoration. A category of citizens would still be handed over to the punitive apriorism, which, as I shall argue in Chapter 2, is contestable from a socio-ethical standpoint and has detrimental impact.

Restoration must be seen as the goal and voluntary processes as tools, though vital ones. Definitions focusing on the process confuse the means with the goal, and limit the possible ways of achieving (partial) restoration. Focusing on the outcome allows for a maximalist version of restorative justice, including all actions aiming at repair. Deliberative processes hold the highest potential for achieving restoration but, if voluntary agreements cannot be accomplished, a maximalist option on restorative justice must be taken. Coercive obligations in pursuit of (partial) reparation have to be encompassed in the restorative justice model. Chapter 5 will present examples of reparative sanctions, such as formal restitution or compensation, fines, working for the benefit of a victims' fund or community service. Such obligations do not achieve the full potential of the restorative paradigm but, as noted above, restorative justice is not a simple black-and-white option. It can be achieved to different degrees.

The maximalist position is a challenge for the way that restorative justice relates to traditional criminal justice thinking and law-making. It is an issue dealt with in Chapters 2 and 5.

Another paradigm
Compared with the punitive or treatment perspective, consequent thinking in restorative justice understands the problem of crime in a different – indeed revolutionary – way and asks different questions. Restorative justice does not primarily ask what should be done to the offender, but how the harm can be repaired. This is what fundamentally distinguishes it from a punitive justice approach, and also from the rehabilitative perspective. Reflecting consequently on this leads us to see other problems that could be solved in a different way, other systems to facilitate the intervention, the involvement of other actors, a different balance in the roles of citizens, communities and the state. Restorative justice needs a switch in thinking, framed by

another paradigm (Zehr 1990; Bazemore and Walgrave 1999; McCold 2000). It offers a distinctive 'lens', in Zehr's term, for defining the problem caused by crime and for solving it. Crime is considered in terms of the harm it causes and not simply as a transgression of a legal order. The primary function of the response is neither to punish nor to rehabilitate the offender, but to set the conditions for repairing as much as possible the harm caused.

By claiming a paradigm status, restorative justice advocates make clear their ambition to present more than a complementary scheme and to challenge the evidence and presuppositions that form the basis of the current criminal justice system. Why the apriorism that offences must be punished? Is censuring behaviour only possible through punishment? Are legal rights only achievable through punitive criminal justice? Are the existing deontological principles of criminal justice unchangeable dogmas, or must they be subjected to examination and adaptation? In the emergence of new ideas, sustaining a dichotomy by the paradigm claim is a necessary constructive method in theory formation, even if correction and synthesis follow. It avoids the all-too-easy coopting of restorative justice into the predominant criminal justice system.

Despite the paradigm shift towards repairing the crime-caused harm, the involvement of the offender's responsibility in the response to the offence remains crucial, not in the first place because something must be done to him, but because his involvement will serve the goal of restoration. Influencing the offender is a secondary objective only, within the frame of the primary restorative goal. The type and amount of obligation are decided by the need for reasonable restoration and not by the need for adequate treatment or proportionate punishment.

A final observation: advancing restorative justice as another paradigm does not mean that it claims to be the only way of responding to all crimes. The definition is 'an option … that is *primarily* oriented towards repairing the … harm …' Priority does not mean monopoly. What is suggested here is a shift from the punitive apriorism to a restorative apriorism: the first concern in responding to a crime must be to assess what the harm is and how it can be repaired as much as possible, not which punishment is to be inflicted on the offender.

Explaining the definition

We now turn to the three main components: the harm, the way of restoration and doing justice.

Harm

The harm considered for (partial) reparation includes the material damage, all forms of suffering inflicted on the victim and his proximate environment, social unrest and community indignation, uncertainty about legal order and about the authorities' capacity to ensure public safety and the social damage the offender has caused to himself by his offence.

Crime-caused harm

The only limitation is that the harm considered by the restorative process has been caused by the particular offence. Restorative justice indeed is a reactive option, 'a way of responding to crimes which have been already committed' (Johnstone 2002: 19). This is particularly important with regard to the harm to the offender. Offenders suffer harm caused by their own offence. They risk further social exclusion and stigmatisation in the family and the community, and being dragged into an escalating process of social degradation in the social institutions. Restorative justice interventions try to avoid or reduce these negative consequences, by offering the offender the opportunity to make up for his misdeed so that he can be reaccepted as a respectable person.

But the offence often reveals problems, related to social exclusion and psychosocial dysfunctions in the offender, which existed before the occurrence of the crime. These are not the primary focus of a restorative justice intervention, which is to repair the harm caused by the offence. For the offender, the bottom line is that the intervention may not inflict additional harm on him and that it tries to avoid further social damage for him. Curing the pre-existing problem is important, but is a matter for social rehabilitation and treatment programmes. In the restricted position I have taken, they are not part of restorative justice, but they may run parallel to it.

Not all scholars accept this limitation. Some consider the merits of restorative processes primarily in so far as they remedy the needs of the offender, the underlying causes of offending (Polk 2001; Weijers 2002). Others consider addressing the pre-existing needs of the offender equally as important as repairing the harm caused by the offence. This is reflected, for example, in the previously mentioned definition of Van Ness and Heetderks Strong (2006). Including the harm which existed before the criminal event to be addressed for reparation is not desirable. It runs the risk of blurring the limits and losing the distinction from the rehabilitative approach. Certainly for juveniles, such programmes might shift from the harm-focused to the offender-focused. The victim would be reduced to a tool for the offender's rehabilitation and not recognised as a party in his own right.

This does not imply that the underlying problems and needs of the offender are absent in a restorative justice deliberation. They are extremely important to an understanding of the reasons for the criminal behaviour, and thus influence the decision-making on what a reasonable and feasible reparation effort might be. They are important in finding out which reparative actions might be meaningful and competency-building for the offender himself. And, as we shall see, restorative justice offers a huge potential in that respect (Bazemore and O'Brien 2002; Bazemore and Schiff 2005). The offender's problems and needs can also be a reason to start a voluntary welfare programme, in parallel or in cooperation with the restorative justice programme.

Public harm

Maximalist restorative justice cannot be limited to settling a tort according to civil law, but deals with crimes, which are considered also as public events, traditionally dealt with by criminal law. In traditional criminal justice, legal order is the public good to be preserved. But this notion cannot be transferred unchanged to restorative justice. 'Legal order' is too abstract and too top-down a value.

Understanding the public dimension of crime and crime-caused harm in restorative terms is not evident. What makes an offence a collective or public event? After a burglary, for example, restitution or compensation for the individual victim's losses could be private, to be arranged by civil law. But we are all concerned that the authorities respond to the burglary. Let us imagine that the authorities did nothing or limited the intervention to registering the crime and identifying the burglar, and then invited the offender and victim to try and find a solution without exerting pressure on the burglar. Probably most burglaries would remain unresolved, provoking private actions to 'make things even', leading to an escalation in mutual revenge and dragging down security in the community as a whole. The uninterested attitude of the authorities would also damage all citizens' trust in public rules, in their right to privacy and property, and in the authorities' power and willingness to preserve order and justice. Not only would peaceful life in the community be lost, but also order and justice in society. 'While the government is responsible for preserving a just public order, the community's role in establishing and maintaining a just peace must be given special significance' (Van Ness and Heetderks Strong 2002: 42). Both order and peace are threatened by the crime and need a public response.

The public dimension of crime lies in the threat and the harm it causes to public trust in norms and norm enforcement. As we shall see in Chapter 5, the concept of dominion, as introduced by Braithwaite and Pettit (1990), helps us understand this. Dominion rests on the assurance that fellow citizens and the state will take rights and freedom seriously. This assurance is indispensable to full enjoyment of rights and freedom.

Crime, then, is seen as an intrusion upon dominion, and more particularly upon the assurance of rights and freedoms. The burglary does not diminish the actual legal rights of privacy and property because they are laid down in legal texts, but rather the extent to which the victim and the citizens are assured that these rights are respected and taken seriously. Public intervention after a crime is primarily needed to enhance assurance: it communicates the authorities' public disapproval of the norm transgression and it responds through action aiming at restoration. It makes clear that the authorities take dominion seriously.

Restoration

Strictly, restoration refers to reparation, correcting or remedying a situation that has degraded. While this simple statement may be true for fixing a broken window, it is mostly much more complicated in the context of restorative justice (Sharpe 2007). The harm to be considered is multilevelled, leaving irreparable consequences (as in lethal crimes, for example); return to the situation before the offence is often undesirable (as in family violence, for example); complete reparation is unachievable for many (deprived) offenders; the type of possible reparation varies between the symbolic, the material and the relational. As a non-native English speaker, I may not fully understand the nuances of words, but I will consider 'restoration' in its holistic significance oriented at the future, and 'reparation' as a partial, often material, restitution or compensation referring to what is damaged in the past.

In principle, restoration addresses the whole person in his community. Often, much less can be achieved. Sometimes, the consequences of the offence cannot be taken away, and restoration is limited to comforting the victim in his life with the consequences of the offence. The restorative process may help him to come off the fixation on what happened, and to look more openly to the future, even if the scars of the wound remain and some wounds continue to fester.

A wide range of processes and procedures may lead to a reparative outcome. But not all processes are equally appropriate for it. The main distinction is between (more or less) voluntary and coercive processes.

Deliberative restoration

The most suitable processes are those that consist of voluntary deliberation between the victim and the offender as the main stakeholders. While such processes cannot be imposed by the court, offenders decide to participate, often under pressure.

Well-conducted restorative processes offer an opportunity for a powerful sequence of moral and social emotions and exchanges (Braithwaite and Mugford 1994; Van Stokkom 2002; Harris, Walgrave and Braithwaite 2004). The 'encounter' (Van Ness and Heetderks Strong 2006) may lead to a common understanding of the harm and suffering caused and to an agreement on how to make amends. It can also enhance the willingness of the offender to fulfil the agreements.

Agreements may include a wide range of actions, such as restitution, compensation, reparation, reconciliation, apologies and forgiveness. They may be direct or indirect, concrete or symbolic. They are aimed at (partial) reparation of the harm done to the victim and at restoration of peace and order in social life. The degree of the offender's willingness to undertake the actions is crucial. His commitment expresses his understanding of the wrong committed and his willingness to make up for it. For the victim, it means the restoration of his dignity and citizenship as a bearer of rights, and possibly also a partial material redress. For the larger community, it contributes to assurance that the offender takes rights and freedoms seriously and will respect them in the future. Even the offender's agreement to undergo treatment can have a restorative meaning, because it expresses his recognition of a personal problem and the fact that he wants to resolve it in accordance with his social environment.

All this may lead to satisfaction for the victim, the reintegration of the offender and the restored assurance of security in the community and of rights and freedoms in society.

Such a sequence is of course the ideal, and is far from always being fully achieved. However, we shall see in Chapter 4 that the reach of restorative processes is further than is often supposed, and that even partial results in terms of satisfaction, procedural justice and reoffending are generally significantly better than those realised by traditional criminal justice procedures.

Imposed reparation

When participatory processes cannot be achieved voluntarily or are judged to be insufficient, pressure or coercion on the offender must be considered. In a constitutional democracy, force may only be exerted through a judicial procedure. And here, divergence among restorative justice proponents becomes manifest. In line with their process-based characterisation (see above), a number of scholars exclude (judicial) coercion from restorative justice. According to this 'purist' view, restorative justice ends when force comes in (McCold 2000).

A maximalist version of restorative justice goes beyond free processes. Maximalists believe that, even if judicial coercion of the offender is considered to be necessary, the procedures should be oriented to obligations or sanctions that primarily seek as much reparation as possible (Claassen 1993; Wright 1996; Bazemore and Walgrave 1999; Walgrave 2002a, 2003). There is no reason to give up the principled priority for restoration when confronted with the offender's resistance. Concerns about the harm caused by the crime also apply if the offender is not cooperative. Victims of non-cooperative offenders are also in need of restoration (sometimes even more so), to which priority still has to be given. The – in that case – coercive social response to the offence must also express those concerns by aiming at the largest possible reparation. The reason for the possible use of coercion remains the harm caused, not deterrence on its own. As we shall develop more in Chapter 5, possible sanctions in view of reparation can take several forms (Dignan 2002; Walgrave 2002a). These judicially imposed obligations mostly yield a reduced reparative outcome, but we have noted already that there are degrees of restorativeness, between full restoration and none.

The difficult relationship between restorative justice and legal coercion will be developed more extensively, especially in Chapters 2 and 5.

Doing justice

Restorative justice is not only about restoration, it is also about justice. There are two ways of considering the notion of justice: moral justice and legal justice.

Moral justice

In judgment in daily life, justice is the outcome of an ethical evaluation. It means a feeling of equity, according to a moral balance of rights and wrongs, benefits and burdens. Basically, the feeling is subjective and biased by self-interest, although embedded in a socio-cultural dimension. In retributive justice, the balance is achieved by imposing suffering on the offender that is commensurate to the social harm he caused by his crime. In restorative justice, the balance is restored by taking away or compensating for the suffering and harm caused by the crime. It aims to achieve 'procedural fairness' (Tyler 1990) and satisfaction (Van Ness and Schiff 2001) for all parties involved. Victims feel that their victimisation has been taken seriously and that the compensation and support are reasonably in balance with their sufferings and losses. Offenders experience that their dignity has not been unnecessarily hurt and that they are given the opportunity to make up for their mistake in a constructive way. All participants, including the community, feel reassured that rights and freedoms are taken seriously by fellow citizens and the authorities.

The best way to guarantee that losses are well understood and that the reparation is adequate is to leave the decision as much as possible to those with a direct stake in the aftermath of the crime: victims, offenders and others directly affected. 'Justice' is what those concerned experience as such. This bottom-up approach is crucial in restorative justice and contrasts with the top-down approach of the criminal justice system. That is, however, not a reason to exclude the state from the settlement of the aftermath of a crime. The state needs to be involved to assure citizens of its commitment to take dominion seriously.

Legal justice

Restorative justice processes and their outcomes must respect legal safeguards. Legal safeguards protect citizens not only against illegitimate intrusions by fellow citizens but also against abuses of power by the state. While this is obvious in coerced interventions, it also applies in voluntary settlements. Informal settlements can be the scene of uncontrolled pressure and even subversive threats to urge unbalanced agreements on the less powerful participant.

How to make sure that rights and balances are observed is a matter of debate among proponents of restorative justice. Some rely fully on the potential of communities (Pranis 2001; Sullivan and Tift 2006a) and try to reduce state control over restorative processes to a strict minimum. They fear the state's power to invade the process and undo its informal, humane and healing potential. Others try to find an institutional context, which allows maximum space for genuine deliberative processes but also offers full opportunities for all parties to appeal to judicial agencies if they feel they are not respected in the process.

In a coercive procedure, all legal guarantees must be observed. In a traditional criminal justice procedure, safeguards like legality, due process and proportionality are evident constraints. The civic interests and rights that they protect must also be protected in coercive restorative interventions (Ashworth 1993). How they have to be translated into legal principles, however, is not evident. The existing legal principles are intended to guide the traditional punishment-oriented system, and Chapter 5 will make clear that how to apply them unchanged in a system premised on restoration is not obvious (Walgrave 2000b).

One of the most fundamental criticisms of traditional criminal justice is that its procedures and outcomes may lead to legal justice, but very often (or even mostly) have lost track of the subjective experience of justice. Many victims undergo a secondary victimisation in the justice procedures and are left with additional frustration and anger caused by the system (Dignan 2005). The majority of offenders feel that they are punished unreasonably severely. Both parties experience a lack of procedural justice, because they feel they are treated disrespectfully, as objects of the investigation and sentencing machine (Tyler 1990). 'The right punishment, according to some retributive theory, will almost always be the wrong solution to the problem. By wrong I mean less just' (Braithwaite 2002b: 158). It is probably the most important ambition of restorative justice to make both justice concepts coincide as much as possible.

Schemes in restorative justice

Restorative justice is not an invention of academics or enlightened policy-makers. It is deeply rooted in the lively field of conflict resolution and response to crime, where creative practitioners have tried to find more satisfying alternatives to the predominant administrative or judicial routine. Currently, a broad range of different practices exists, all of which may express the restorative justice philosophy (McCold 2001). But still, new (versions of) practices emerge, adapted to local circumstances, enlightened by new ideas, invented by intuitive practitioners. Below I present briefly a selection of the most prominent working schemes available today. None of these models guarantees, however, that all practices work fully restoratively.

Victim support

Victim support is a more complete form of helping victims of crime than the victim compensation schemes which focus on material interests. A comprehensive restorative justice model must include victim service and support, being available regardless of whether the offender is apprehended and/or collaborative or not (Peters and Aertsen 2000; Van Ness 2002b; Dignan 2005). That unavoidably results from the paradigm shift in restorative justice, consequently thought through. As the main focus is no longer on punishing or rehabilitating the offender but on repairing as much as possible the harm caused, supporting the victim is the first and most important action in doing justice.

Restorative justice can thus be practised without an offender being arrested. Statistics show that the majority of offences committed do not lead to arrest and conviction. Still, victims of unresolved crimes are in need of restoration. Public security in the local community and far beyond may be deeply affected. From a restorative justice perspective, support for the victim is thus crucial not only for the benefit of the actual victim, but also for the collective assurance that the community and the authorities care about the victimisation and are prepared to do what is possible to repair its consequences. The basic idea is that the occurrence of a crime is a failure of society and community to protect the victim's security, to which he is entitled, so that they must grant as much as possible compensation for or reparation of the harm suffered.

If the offender is not known, not arrested, unwilling or unable to contribute to the reparation, society and the community must contribute directly to the reparation. Victims' funds help to repair or materially compensate harm. Support schemes help to make the mental sufferings bearable and advise the victim as he moves through the justice procedures. Even if the offender is arrested, the authorities must grant that accompanying support or additional compensation will be given to the victim while trying to involve the offender in the next phase of the restorative action.

Currently, the majority of victim support agencies are located at the margins of the mainstream justice system and deal especially with welfare problems linked to the victimisation. This is important, of course, but a consequent restorative way of thinking must position victim support at the heart of the system, not at its margins. Supporting and setting the conditions for maximum possible restoration for the victims must be the first concern of public intervention after a crime has occurred, not an ornamental addendum.

Victim–offender mediation

Victim–offender mediation is generally considered as the original 'archetype' in the re-emergence of restorative justice. The first experiments in its modern form were in the 1980s, as the Victim–Offender Reconciliation Program (VORP) in Kitchener (Ontario, Canada), and later as VORP and VOM (Victim Offender Mediation), especially in Canada and the USA (McCold 2006). In about the same period, Norway and Finland offered municipal mediation opportunities for its citizens, as well as for petty crimes committed by juveniles. Mediation practices quickly spread to Austria, Germany, Belgium and other countries (Pelikan and Trenczek 2006). Whereas the North Americans seem to have been inspired largely (but not solely) by religious and spiritual motives, the first European experiments seem to have been grounded more in academic critical reflection (Christie 1977; Hulsman 1979). In North America as well as in Europe, victim–offender mediation was originally considered on its own. Its recognition as a basis for a comprehensive restorative justice concept came later.

In victim–offender mediation, an impartial mediator invites the two most evident protagonists in the aftermath of an offence to communicate with each other, with a view to finding an appropriate restitution, compensation or reparation for the harm caused by that offence (European Forum 2000). The mediator acts only as a facilitator. He does not make any decision related to the outcome of the mediation. Variations exist in the actual schemes. Mediation can occur through a face-to-face meeting or via a 'shuttle process' in which the mediator acts as a go-between for the participants. Some mediation programmes focus especially on mental healing, while others also include, or even prioritise, material compensation. Some mediation processes are limited to the two most evident protagonists – the victim and the offender – while others include members of the communities of care. The latter form is close to the conferencing model described in the next section.

Some critics of the first practices feared the net widening of social control, addressing very benign misbehaviour only, which would not be responded to at all if mediation did not exist; complained about the focus on the offender in the mediation, to the neglect of the victim's genuine needs and interests; or raised questions about the legal status of the practices. Despite these reservations, the idea was attractive. It aimed at a peaceful community-based settlement and seemed more satisfactory for the participants, more reintegrative for the offenders and more constructive for the local communities.

When restorative justice as a notion began to take off, it was often identified with mediation. This is partly understandable, because in mediation the restorative aspect speaks for itself. Most communication is about the harm and suffering incurred; the outcome aims at restitution, reparation or compensation. All this can be observed and controlled. But as the restorative justice philosophy and practices developed, mediation appeared too restricted in scope. Indeed, victim–offender mediation deals with the dispute between the victim and the offender only, whereas settling the aftermath of a crime should also include concern for its public dimensions. Another limitation of mediation is that it is restricted to voluntary processes. Mediation can thus happen only if both protagonists are willing to cooperate, which reduces its reach drastically to a form of diversion for willing cases. This is not congruent with the increasing ambition to see restorative justice as a comprehensive alternative to the traditional punitive responses to crime.

rencing

dvance conferencing as the 'most restorative practice' (McCold 2000). Especially in the Australasian region, conferencing is even identified with restorative justice as a whole.

In general, a restorative conference is facilitated by an impartial moderator and consists of an inclusive process that brings together the victim, the offender and their 'supporters' in order to find a socially constructive solution to the problems and harms caused by the offence (Hudson *et al.* 1996; Masters and Roberts 2000; Daly 2001; Maxwell *et al.* 2006). The overwhelming majority of conferencing practices address youth offenders.

The original version, family group conferences (FGC), was included in 1989 in the New Zealand Children, Young Persons and their Families Act (CYPFA). According to this Act, the youth court cannot impose any sanction on any youth offender unless an FGC has been tried. The only exceptions are murder and manslaughter, which are referred to the adults' court. Originally, FGC was not introduced from a restorative justice perspective. It was intended as a scheme to bring the response to youth offences more in line with the traditions of the indigenous people, the Maoris, who were over-represented in youth court proceedings. But the huge restorative potentials were soon discovered.

The success of FGC has boosted conferencing practices all over the world, in different versions and with varying scope (Umbreit and Zehr 1996; Prichard 2003; Dignan 2005: 115–21). They have different names, such as 'diversionary conferences', 'youth justice conferences', 'real justice conferences' or 'community conferences', which are now often grouped under a common denomination, 'restorative conferences'. Most conferences are organised as a form of diversion at police level or public prosecutor's level; sometimes they are facilitated by a police officer, as a kind of caution to the young offender; some conferences address the welfare problems of the young offender more than the victim's genuine needs. These variations are important. All in all, one could consider most of these versions as extended mediations including the communities of care in the deliberation. Their plus value is that the involvement of the social network may help to strengthen the positive consequences of the deliberation. But such conferences also have more or less the same limitations as mediation.

The original New Zealand model, however, is different. Family Group Conferencing, as carried out in New Zealand, has particular characteristics which allow it to have a broader scope than most other conferencing models (MacRae and Zehr 2004; Vanfraechem 2006). First, FGC is procedurally located at the heart of the public response to crime. The CYPFA makes it obligatory to try to set up an FGC before the court can impose any sanction. FGC is thus not a diversionary offer but is fully integrated into the court proceedings. Second, police officers are present in the conference in the typical roles of informants and guardians of public order, so that the public dimension of the crime is explicitly represented in the deliberation. This is unique. In other conferencing models, the police act as the facilitator of the conference, which is conceived as a version of police cautioning, or the police presence may be facultative or even not really promoted. Third, lawyers are invited to attend the conference (and the youth advocates mostly do), which offers an additional guarantee for legal safeguards. This is especially important in FGC for serious cases, because they may lead to severe deprivation of liberties.

These particular characteristics enable the original FGC model to deal with serious cases also. Morris estimates that the most serious youth offences – comprising 15–20 per cent of all youth offences – are dealt with through FGC, while the remaining less serious offences are dealt with through cautions or diversion by the police (Morris 2002b). At the beginning, FGC was confronted with a low level of participation by victims. This problem has been partly resolved, but the experience also showed that FGC could proceed in the absence of the victim. If the victim is not present, the police and other participants can draw attention to the victimisation aspects, which is not possible in the case of a single mediation. In fact, the New Zealand practice is one of the most powerful experiences in support of seeing restorative justice as a maximalist option, driving a drastic reform of criminal justice to become a fully fledged restorative justice system.

Healing and sentencing circles

The emancipation of native communities in North America has revitalised a number of circle models to deal with injustices and conflicts in local contexts. The models are deeply rooted in indigenous traditions in Canada and the USA (Stuart 1996; Lilles 2001; Winfree 2002). Circles draw on rituals to connect with the spiritual emotions of indigenous cultures. By and large, two types of circle can be distinguished. Healing circles are meant especially to restore peace within the native community affected by particular problems, such as incest or family violence. Sentencing circles are a kind of community co-judgment in the criminal justice procedure, and take place in the presence of an official judge. Both types involve the local community as a whole in dealing with the aftermath of a crime, are strongly community-based and aim at restoring peace through reparation and healing (McCold 2001; Van Ness and Strong 2002). The deliberative process is very intensive and may take several meetings.

In principle, such circles come very close to the genuine restorative ideals and have greatly influenced current restorative justice philosophy. In practice, sentencing circles appear not only to yield restorative outcomes, but do sometimes lead to very traditional punishments (Jaccoud 2006). Their expansion to modern urban contexts is difficult. The protagonists in many urban crimes transcend by far the local community; the circles presuppose the availability of an active and dense community to be involved in the process, which is more than doubtful in many urban areas; and the circles require an intensive time investment by the participants, which is not evident in our modern hasty context. But such circles actually hold strong potentials in the development of deprived communities and go beyond the dealing with the aftermath of offending. They evolve in the direction of peace committees, described below.

Peace committees

In recent years, interest has been growing in community peace committees, which were first used in Zwelethemba, South Africa. These committees have two missions: peacemaking, i.e. solving particular disputes in the local community, and peacebuilding, i.e. solving more generic problems in the community (Shearing 2001). They have much in common with healing and sentencing circles, in that they are really embedded in local communities, involve extensive participation by community members and proceed in a deliberative participatory way. But there are significant differences. First, they seem to be part of a deliberate strategy to develop local 'nodal governance'[6] of security in a transitional society where government is relatively weak. According to this strategy, the 'peacemakers' are local volunteers who are licensed and must respect a written code of good practice. They are informed by a 'technology, similar to that used in family group conferencing, for mobilising local knowledge and local capacity to engage in both the rowing and the steering of governance' (Shearing 2001: 20). Another difference is the reach of the initiative. Peacemaking forums deal with specific events and conflicts before they are defined as offences by police or the justice system. Peacebuilding forums address more enduring generic problems and conflicts in the local community. Both are involved in a deliberate strategy to sustain processes of peacemaking and peacebuilding over time.

While the model certainly comes within the scope of practice inspired by the participatory and constructive social philosophy behind restorative justice, the reach of peace committees transcends restorative justice practices in the strict sense of the word. Nevertheless, they are an example of how security problems can be dealt with constructively in a social context where crime and deprivation are endemic. The committees not only try to find constructive answers to specific events, they are used at the same time as an opportunity for upgrading a community more generally.

Citizen boards

The American state of Vermont often stands as an example for including in its Reparative Probation Program (1995) so-called community boards composed of citizens (Karp and Walther 2001). The boards meet with those convicted of minor offences to negotiate a reparative contract, which may include letters of apology, community service or treatment. A comparable board is the Youth Offender Panel, established by the English Youth Justice and Criminal Evidence Act 1999, which meets with young offenders appearing for the first time at court and pleading guilty. Two of its three members are volunteer citizens. Its task is to conclude a contract with the offender in a non-adversarial way, according to the principles of restorative justice (Crawford and Newburn 2003). The proponents of such boards believe that this formula involves the community more than if professional judges or probation officers make the decisions, and favours the implementation of the principles underlying the restorative justice philosophy.

Originally, however, this was far from evident. It seemed somewhat naive to believe that boards composed of non-professionals would guarantee that they really represented the community. Most boards do not reflect the heterogeneity of the community they are supposed to represent. Moreover, the original quality of many non-professionals' 'performances' appeared to be 'amateurish, undiplomatic and less knowledgeable than trained mediators' (Karp and Walther 2001: 215). Victim participation was limited or even non-existent. The plan resulting from the meeting was often not primarily oriented towards reparation. Currently, however, a number of boards seem to better achieve the restorative potentials (Bazemore and Schiff 2005). As in most other schemes, the restorative nature of such boards seems to vary considerably according to local situations and practices. But it remains a serious limitation that they are not really deliberative, as they keep the ultimate decision in their own hands (McCold 2004; Dignan 2005).

Community service

Community service is intrinsically different from the models described above. Whereas the previous models involve a communication and decision-making process, community service is an outcome which may be part of the agreement emerging from such a process but which also may be imposed after a traditional judicial procedure. One could call it then a sanction (Schiff 1999).

Community service is not accepted by all scholars as a restorative justice action. Indeed, it is often imposed in a non-restorative sense. Some criminal justice practices use community service as a punishment, deliberately imposing a task that is unpleasant or even humiliating. In other contexts, the service may be part of a treatment or educative programme, intended to influence the offender's attitudes and competencies. In both, the compensatory dimension is secondary or even absent. Another problem is that 'compensating harm to social life' may be too vague and too expansive a notion, which intrudes on the immediate and concrete needs of the victim. It is feared then that accepting the community (or even society) as a fully fledged separate stakeholder in the restorative process would cause a shift back towards the initial position in criminal justice, overriding again the interests and needs of the victim.

However, restorative justice is not limited here to a specific kind of process, but is presented as an outcome-oriented philosophy, an option for doing justice. From a restorative justice perspective, community service is 'unpaid labour done by the offender for the benefit of a community or its institutions, meant as a (symbolic) compensation for the harm caused by the offence to that community' (Walgrave 1999: 139). The harm caused by the crime surpasses the concrete sufferings and losses of the victim, to include also harm to the larger community and society. A credible restorative response to offending should therefore also address these harms and consequent needs. Community service is advanced as the prototype of a compensatory or reparative gesture towards the community (Bazemore and Maloney 1994; Walgrave 1999; Dignan 2002). Several European legislations advance community service (or *Travail d'Intérêt Général* in French) as a possible alternative or addition to victim–offender mediation (Schelkens 1998; Cario 2005).

For some, community service is acceptable as 'restorative' only if it results from a deliberative process. If it is imposed by a court, they call it punishment. I do not agree. Even if imposed by a court, community service can be considered a sanction with a view to reparation. It can have a number of aspects in common with the restorative process:

- a definition of crime as an injury to victims (individual and societal), which is quite different from the traditional penal justice definition of crime as a transgression of law;

39

- an intervention primarily oriented towards reparation of that injury, which is unlike the predominantly punitive apriorism;
- a conception of the offender as being accountable, involving him actively and directly in the restorative action, while the retributive or rehabilitative responses reduce the offender to a passive object of retribution or treatment.

It must be clear that inclusive deliberative decision-making is preferable if possible. But such processes are not always feasible, to say the least. The maximum possible reparation may then be achieved through an imposed sanction with a view to repairing symbolically the harm to social life. Imposed community service will lose much of its restorative potential. But still, I shall argue in the next chapter that such imposition is better than inflicting hard treatment for the sake of pain, as is done under the prevailing punitive apriorism.

Other practices

More practices can be put in a restorative justice framework. One of the most promising is the penetration of restorative justice principles into peacemaking initiatives after gross violations of human rights (Braithwaite 2002a; Sullivan and Tift 2006b; Vanspauwen and Valiñas 2006). The Truth and Reconciliation Commission in South Africa, set up to deal with the aftermath of the apartheid regime, is often advanced as the first example of a non-punitive, participatory, restoration-oriented practice in such a context. Its real impact in South African social life is still debated. It has nevertheless inspired many strategies in states or nations in transition to democracy after war, civil war or systematic violations by authoritarian regimes, such as in Rwanda, the former Yugoslavia or Colombia. These strategies are characterised by attempts to absorb the consequences of what happened by recognising it, by providing as much reparation as possible to the victims and by striving for reconciliation in order to reconstruct a peaceful social life.

It is not possible to include these efforts in one model. Though they are inspired by restorative justice philosophy, they use a mixture of techniques and processes embedded in long-term strategies. They show great variation, depending on local problems, local opportunities and traditions, and available resources. They face many particular problems, such as the tension between the restorative actions and the desire to punish those who are considered the instigators or leaders of the systematic gross violations, the selection of the particular victimisations to be dealt with, and the selection of the responsible or representative individuals to be involved in the processes.

Another important development is the introduction of restorative processes in prison (Umbreit *et al.* 2003; Hagemann 2003; Robert and Peters 2003). Mediation or conferencing is organised with victims and the offenders after they have been sentenced to imprisonment. This is not, of course, another scheme, but its particularity relates to the context. Restorative processes in prison pose problems of qualification. They are not an alternative to, or preparation for, sentencing. They are an addendum to the traditional punitive criminal justice system. And that does not fit with the maximalist view I have in mind for restorative justice. As we shall see in the next chapter, including restorative processes in a punitive context is a significant obstacle to achieving restorative outcomes. Nevertheless, prison mediation can be a good thing in helping the victim (and his family) and the offender come to grips emotionally with the consequences of the crime. It may also be seen as a strategic possibility of having an influence from within the correctional system in a more reparative direction.

Conclusion

The practices described show great variation in operational modalities, scope and context. Some can be considered as being more restorative and others less so. A well known classification of types and degrees of restorative justice practice is presented by McCold and Wachtel (as in 2002). Starting from three dimensions – victim reparation, communities of care reconciliation and offender responsibility – they distinguish fully restorative practices (such as circles and family group conferencing), mostly restorative practices (such as victim support circles, victim restitution and therapeutic communities) and partly restorative practices (such as victim services, offender family work, victim sensitivity training and community service). While the typology may help to clarify the most important dimensions in restorative justice practice, its conclusions cannot be taken too strictly, because they are focused on a limited set of practices. They only indicate what formal schemes facilitate or not, but do not address the huge diversity in practices within the schemes. For example, while restorative conferencing is often presented as the most genuinely restorative process, some conferences can be catastrophic for the participants because they are very poorly monitored. Some community services may be used in a punitive way, but they can also have a highly restorative function if the community really understands it as an expression of the offender's compliance and his willingness to contribute constructively to social life. Citizens' boards may have a deep restorative significance if they succeed in involving the victim and the offender in a constructive dialogue and if the participants are committed to the resulting plan. Once again: restorative justice is not a detailed set of practices, but a philosophy which can penetrate different practices to different degrees.

The restorativeness depends on the degree to which the minimum requirement of restoration is intended and achieved. According to my essentialist definition of restorative justice, the objective of repairing as much as possible the crime-caused harm is the key characteristic. The definition is also restricted, because it focuses on the settlement of the aftermath of crime. Processes in welfare, schools and elsewhere are excluded, even if they are inspired by the same fundamental social and socio-ethical philosophy and operate through comparable action models. While recognising the great value of all these practices, I stick to the restricted definition for the sake of clarity. Overfilling a concept empties it. Because restorative justice practices really seem to work (under some conditions), and because the phrase restorative justice is seemingly attractive and inspirational, it has provoked an enthusiastic tendency to extend it endlessly. Restorative justice is becoming a label for many different practices, beliefs, values and even states of mind. This is a danger. As von Hirsch wrote: 'The literature of restorativism needs not yet greater enthusiasm but more reflection' (1998: 676). Uncontrolled enthusiasm leads to the blurring of concepts and confusion in the aims and limits of restorative justice, poorly thought-out implementation, overestimation of potential, negligence of legal rights and other contextual conditions. As we shall see, a clear and restricted view of restorative justice offers a safe platform for exploring the broader field of social practices later in this volume.

The restricted essentialist definition allows for a maximalist option of how to deal with the aftermath of crime. While voluntary dialogue among the stakeholders is promoted where possible, judicially imposed sanctions are also included in the restorative justice concept if they are primarily intended to contribute to reparation. This acceptance raises questions about the difference between reparative sanctions and criminal punishment. It is the subject of Chapter 2.

Notes

1 It is true, of course, that most of the same spiritual traditions have also produced texts imbued with anger, vengeance and severe punishments against the sinful.
2 Victims can also be female. For practical reasons, I will use the masculine form as the general form. I know that this may be considered politically incorrect, but it is practical.
3 The punitive tendency in the victims' movement seems to be stronger in the United States, which may be due to the generally more punitive climate.
4 This is not to say that there are no problems with victims' interests in restorative justice and victims' advocates. We shall come back to this issue later in Chapter 4.
5 In a comment on an earlier version of this chapter, Gordon Bazemore wrote 'there is a continuum of responses applicable to all crime that potentially vary on a scale of 0 to 10 on different dimensions of "restorativeness".'
6 In nodal governance, the state is conceived as a broker or manager of programmes of governance, for which others must be persuaded to accept responsibility (Shearing 2001: 18).

Chapter 2

Restorative justice and criminal punishment

Originally, most restorative justice proponents emphasised several interconnected differences – even oppositions – between restorative justice and the predominant punitive apriorism in criminal justice (Zehr 1990; Walgrave 1995; McCold 2000; Van Ness and Heetderks Strong 2002):

- Restorative justice does not define crime as a transgression of an abstract legal disposition, but as a cause of individual, relational and social harm.
- In criminal justice, the principal collective agent is the state, while collectivity in restorative justice is mainly seen through the community.
- The response to crime is not ruled by a top-down imposed set of procedures, but by a deliberative bottom-up input from those with a direct stake in the aftermath.
- Contrary to the formalised and rational criminal justice procedures, restorative justice processes are informal, including emotions and feelings.
- The outcome in view is not the infliction of a proportionate amount of pain, but a socially constructive, or restorative, solution to the problem caused by the crime.
- Justice in criminal justice is considered 'objectively', based on legality, while justice in restorative justice is seen mainly as a subjective-moral experience.

In recent years, as the potentials of restorative justice are increasingly being recognised by policy-makers, the judiciary, practitioners, academics and the population, and as restorative practices penetrate the mainstream, the idea of a straightforward opposition between restorative justice and criminal justice is less sustainable. Restorative justice-in-action is confronted with problems, the solutions for which may be inspired by the current criminal justice model.

So, for example, many restorative justice practices actually include the public dimension of an offence insufficiently, or even not at all. But a maximalist perspective must also address restoratively the crime-caused harms to the collectivity. Many questions then arise about the definition of the collective entities (local communities, community, state) and the understanding of their interests and needs; the representation of the collective bodies and the processes and procedures to assess the harms and interests; and the relation between the collective interests and the needs of the actual victim. While traditional criminal justice responses have addressed too exclusively the public dimension, they may offer lessons to be considered in developing maximalist restorative justice.

Voluntary deliberations, as promoted in restorative justice, do not always produce a balanced outcome. If the power balance is unequal, the offender not cooperative, the victim too vengeful, the community too exclusionary and/or the facilitator too interventionist, the outcomes may be clearly unjust. It points to the need for checks and balances based on controllable standards. While the current criminal justice system is too intrusive into the potentials for constructive dialogue at the bottom, it may inspire a model of rights and freedoms to shield restorative processes from abuses of power.

Restorative justice prioritises agreements based on voluntary deliberative processes including all protagonists. Such processes are not always possible, to say the least. That is why the maximalist option of restorative justice also conceives a reparation-oriented form of coercion, raising the possibility of 'reparative sanctions'. In that case, enforcing such sanctions in a constitutional democracy needs a frame of legal safeguards. The traditional criminal justice constraints may serve as a starting point for reflecting on this.

Accepting coercive sanctions may leave no or very few distinctions from punishment. A number of advocates of restorative justice therefore reject any coercion. Criminal justice advocates, on the contrary, consider punishment indispensable, and some reformulate restorative justice as an alternative punishment. It is, however, not evident that the strongest justifications for punishment – censuring unlawful behaviour and restoring the moral balance – unavoidably lead to a need to punish.

As will become clear throughout this chapter and Chapter 5, rejecting the punitive apriorism in the response to crime does not mean that any criminal justice approach is rejected as well. A special category of 'criminalisable' behaviours should be maintained, and a juridical frame for restorative justice practices is needed. Restorative justice cannot simply rule out criminal justice. A number of principles, models and concerns within criminal justice must be taken seriously. The basic question is how to combine the informal flexibility, crucial to the participatory approach of restorative justice, with the formal system of checks and balances needed in a democratic state.

Sceptical scholars do not believe that such a combination is really possible. They recognise the value of restorative practices, but accept them only at the margins of the traditional criminal justice system. In their view, the mainstream response to crime must remain punitive. Two types of arguments are advanced:

1 Crime must be punished on principle or for instrumental reasons.
2 The punishment orientation of the criminal justice system is the cornerstone for building the best possible legal safeguards.

This chapter will dispute the first of these arguments. I will argue that a restorative response to crime is clearly different from punishment, that it is socio-ethically more desirable, and that there are reasons to believe that it is more effective.

The second argument regarding legal standards is discussed in Chapter 5. Rejecting the punitive apriorism does not mean rejecting legal safeguards. There is, however, no consensus on how that should be made concrete. In line with the maximalist version of restorative justice, a model will be presented to modify the currently punitive criminal justice system into a mainly restorative criminal justice system.

Restorative justice and criminal punishment

Restorative justice is not a soft option. In the traditional procedures and court sessions, the confrontation is indirect, impersonal and filtered through judicial rituals. The offender is shielded by the procedures and by his lawyer against facing directly what he has done. Restorative processes, on the contrary, are personal, direct and often deeply emotional. Being confronted directly with the suffering and harm one has caused and with the disapproval of loved ones is a severely affecting burden. Apologising in front of others may be hard and humiliating. Experiencing pressure to make up for the harm is difficult to cope with. The process makes the offender feel a mixture of intense unpleasant emotions, such as shame, guilt, remorse, embarrassment and humiliation, which may have an enduring impact on his further life. Some offenders experience victim–offender mediation and compliance with the agreements as a 'double punishment' (Schiff 1999). The agreements indeed often require serious and unpleasant commitments and considerable investment of time. When imposed by a court, community services are felt as serious sanctions, even when they are imposed in a reparative perspective.

Confusion

The obvious unpleasantness of being involved as an offender in a restorative process has led several scholars to consider restorative justice as 'alternative punishments', not 'alternatives to punishment' (Duff 1992). Duff, for example, considers criminal mediation as a kind of punitive mediation, a special species of penal hard treatment (Duff 2001, 2002). Daly (2000, 2002) is also of the opinion that restorative justice is a punishment, because it leads to unpleasant obligations for the offender. In their view, all hard burdens imposed or accepted under pressure are considered as punishments. This is for them not a reason to reject restorative approaches to crime. On the contrary, they include restorative practices in what they consider to be indispensable in the reaction to crime: hard treatment.

From an opposite standpoint, McCold (2000) criticises the maximalist version of restorative justice. According to him, the acceptance of coercive judicial sanctions (such as community service) as potentially restorative would shift restorative justice back to being punitive. For McCold, all coercive interventions, all obligations to obedience, are equal to punishment, which is, for him, a reason to reject coercion in restorative justice.

Much depends, of course, on how punishment is understood. If every painful obligation following the commission of a wrong is called a punishment, then most initiatives in reparation may indeed be considered punishments. However, this position overlooks some critical differences between punishment and restoration, which in my view are the basis for socio-ethical distinctions.

Intentional infliction of pain versus awareness of painfulness

'Punishing someone consists of visiting a deprivation (hard treatment) on him, because he supposedly has committed a wrong ...' (von Hirsch 1993: 9). Three elements are distinguished: hard treatment, the intention of inflicting it, and the link with the wrong committed.[1] If one of these elements is lacking, there is no punishment. Painful obligations that are imposed without the intention to cause suffering are not punishments. That is the key difference between a fine and taxes. 'Pain in punishment is inflicted for the sake of pain ...' (Fatic 1995: 197).

The crux lies in the intention (Wright 2003). Equating every painful obligation after a wrong with punishment is based on a mistaken 'mental location' of the painfulness. It is the painfulness in the intention of the punisher that counts, not in the perception of the punished. It is the punisher who considers an action to be wrong and who wants the wrongdoer to suffer for it. A number of juveniles, for example, experience the judicial punishment primarily as an important event to enhance their reputation in the peer group. But it still remains a punishment, because it was meant as such by the court. Conversely, juveniles may perceive an obligation to provide reparation as hard and call it 'a punishment'. But actually it is not a punishment if the intention of the judge was not to make the juvenile suffer, but to obtain from him a reasonable reparative contribution.

However, the relation between a restorative action and pain is more complicated than that. Not taking the hardship of a reparative obligation into account could lead to draconian results. Imagine, for example, a deprived youth who is obliged by the court to pay back the full monetary value of the Jaguar car he stole and crashed. This could condemn the juvenile to a lifetime of repayments and poverty. A judge who refers to restorative principles to justify such a condemnation has a mistaken understanding of restorative justice.

Even if there is no *intention* to inflict pain, there must be an *awareness* of the painful effects which must be taken into account. In the restorative justice philosophy, the boy has to contribute to reparation, indeed. But the reparation will transcend the material repayment and focus on relational communication and symbolic gestures. The material restitution will be reduced to a reasonable portion, in view of the boy's financial, mental and social capacities and of his future. The remaining material damage is to be repaid by the insurance or by a victims' fund.

Knowing that something will hurt and taking the hardship into account is not the same as intentionally inflicting pain. In retributive punishment, the painfulness is the principal yardstick, and its amount can be increased or decreased in order to achieve proportionality. In restoration, on the contrary, a relation may be sought between the nature and seriousness of the harm and the restorative effort; awareness of painfulness can lead to a reduction of the effort required, never to an increase. And that is crucial.

Punishment as a means, restoration as a goal

Punishment is a means used to enforce any legal and political system, in democratic societies as well as in the most dictatorial regimes. It is an act of power, intended to express disapproval and possibly to enforce compliance, but it is neutral about the value system it enforces. Restoration, on the contrary, is not a means, but a potential outcome. Restorative justice takes an indisputably consequentionalist approach. It is characterised by the aim of doing justice through restoration. The broad scope of harm amenable to possible reparation inherently demonstrates its orientation to the quality of social life as a normative beacon. As expressed by Cario (2005: 22), traditional criminal justice is 'a tool for social control' (in view of a top down enforced order in any social or political regime), while restorative justice is a 'means of facilitating harmonious social interaction'[2] (leading to deliberative and inclusionary decision-making).

Traditional criminal justice conceives of punishment as the a priori response in order to achieve a variety of possible goals, which, as we shall see, are barely or not at all achieved in reality. In contrast, restorative justice advances restoration in the broader sense as the objective, and chooses among a diversity of social and legal means to pursue it. Punishment, meaning intentional infliction of suffering, is not at all an appropriate tool in the pursuit of restoration. On the contrary, the a priori option of punishment is a serious obstruction. The priority given to the procedure for determining a proportionate punishment often detracts attention from the harm and suffering of the victims; the threat of punishment makes genuine communication about harm and possible reparation almost impossible; the penalty itself seriously hampers the offender's effort to offer reparation and compensation.

Punishment, communication and restoration

The most important function of criminal justice is to be a beacon of social disapproval, to mark clear limits to social tolerance. By declaring certain behaviour as legally punishable, authorities proclaim publicly that such behaviour is not acceptable in their political community. By investigating the crime and prosecuting the offender, authorities make clear that they do not let illegal events happen, and that they are determined to enforce the legal norms. Such censuring communication is needed in all societies. Society at large must see the norm being re-confirmed, and perceive the authorities' determination to enforce it and to protect citizens. Victims must feel support in their victimisation and be reassured in their citizenship. Offenders should get the message that their behaviour is unacceptable.

Censure and punishment

While censure is needed, inflicting hard treatment on the offender is not the only, and not the most appropriate, way to express it. The option for punishment in criminal justice interferes with effective two-way communication (Van Stokkom 2005). Disapproval expressed by the criminal sentence may communicate a clear message to the public at large, but it fails to communicate adequately to the other key actors, the victim and the offender. Good communication needs adequate settings. This is not the case in court, where confrontation prevails over communication, in front of the judge who will at the end decide the kind and degree of hard treatment. The offender does not listen to the moralising message, but tries to get away with as lenient a punishment as possible. He does not hear an invitation, but merely experiences a threat. Punitive sanctions 'are not very effective in deterring offenders, but once the offence has been committed, they deter them from admitting their actions' (Wright 2003: 17). Criminal justice with its commitment to punishment is intrinsically the major obstruction to good communication, because 'it encourages cultures of denial' (Braithwaite 2005: 285).

There is not an intrinsic, inseparable link between censuring the wrong and punishment. 'The penal sanction clearly conveys blame', von Hirsch writes (1993: 9), but this is not always so. Punishment is often seen, not as blame, but as a risk to be balanced against the possible benefits resulting from committing an offence. For some scholars, it is the *de*crease in social blaming in the community that provokes the need for *in*creased penal punishment (Boutellier 1996): because punishment is losing its moral blaming character for increasingly cynical citizens, it is necessary to augment the 'objective risks' of their potentially criminal behaviour by increasing the threat of suffering imposed. Many professional (white-collar) criminals see criminal punishment as a professional risk. For juveniles involved in subcultures, being arrested and condemned often increases their reputation among their peers.

Conversely, do we need punishment to express condemnation of the wrong? Clearly not. Even von Hirsch uncouples blaming from punishment. In his view, censure can also be expressed in other ways, but the punitive way is chosen because of its preventive (deterrent) impact: 'My ... justification would permit the abolition of the institution of punishment were it not needed for preventive purposes' (1993: 14). But relying on deterrence for preventive reasons is not supported by empirical evidence, as we shall see later in this chapter.

What remains is the need for censure, which can be expressed otherwise than through punishment. In daily life, in families and in schools, disapproval is routinely expressed without punishment. Morally authoritative persons without any power to punish are more effective in influencing moral thinking and behaviour than punishment. After a crime has occurred, the settings in support of restoration are more appropriate for communicating moral dis-approval and provoking repentance than are traditional punitive procedures and sanctions. Family group conferences, for example, express intense disapproval of the act through those who care for the offender and for whom the offender cares. As we shall see when we describe the restorative processes internally, most offenders are open to communication if they themselves experience respect and elementary understanding. They can feel empathy for the suffering of their victims, become aware of their contribution to it, feel guilt and be prepared to make restorative gestures. Moreover, they will better understand the social meaning of the norm. Restorative settings position the harm and suffering centrally, present victimisation as the focal concern in the norm and this provides a huge communicative potential (Schweigert 1999).

Punishment, censure and repentance
Recognising the poor communicative potential of traditional courts, Duff tries to combine his retributivist position with punitive com-munication through mediation (Duff 2001, 2002). He remains within the retributivist line of thinking, as he states that '... punishment should bring them to suffer what they deserve to suffer' (Duff 2002: 96). The hard treatment is linked to the offender's 'recognition of his wrongdoing, since that should be a repentant recognition, and repentance is necessarily painful' (Duff 2002: 123). Duff rejects traditional punishments, and looks for ways of 'constructive

punishing' which favour communication with the offender. 'Criminal mediation' and a combination of probation with community service are advanced as prototypes.

This view projects a sequence: communicating censure leads to recognition of wrongfulness, which leads to painful repentance, which leads to possible reparation. Such a sequence is in fact close to what is supposed to happen in ideal restorative justice processes. But it does not fit into the restorative justice philosophy. Three crucial problems subsist.

First, Duff's retributive approach cannot be reconciled with the restorative one because it focuses on what should be done to the offender, whereas restorative justice primarily focuses on how harm can be restored. As discussed above, the obligation to repair is mostly painful for the offender and this painfulness matters, but it is a consequence whereas Duff makes it the objective. His concern is not how the harm and suffering may be repaired but how the wrong can be responded to. This wrong and the way to respond to it are given, not debatable, categories. 'The reactions of others [including the victim – LW], and of the wrongdoer, are … subject to normative appraisal: we must ask not just what they in fact feel, but what they should feel' (Duff 2002: 110). It clearly remains a top-down approach, as opposed to the bottom-up perspective which, as we shall see, is fundamental to restorative justice.

Secondly, the sequence 'censure – recognition of wrongfulness – repentance – restoration' is indeed important, but it may be more difficult to achieve with the apriorism that the process *must* be burdensome for the offender. Repentance is crucial, and experience clearly shows how painful repentance can be for the offender. The hardship is, however, not the intention in restorative processes. On the contrary, in fact: the repentance of the offender is facilitated by the respectful and supportive climate in which it may occur. This climate makes it easier to let the unpleasant feelings of repentance surface, instead of repressing them through machismo and denying victimisation. Rather than promoting repentance, deliberately seeking to make the offender suffer may provoke defiance (Sherman 1993; Braithwaite 2005). In terms of Duff's typology (2001: 115 et seq.): the 'already repentant offender' does not need punishment to comply with apologies and willingness to make up; the 'defiant offender' might become more defiant under the threat of punishment; and the number of 'morally persuaded offenders' will probably be reduced by punishment, because the punishment will turn 'persuadable offenders' into defiant ones.

Thirdly, Duff refers to wrongfulness, as opposed to harmfulness, to consider hard treatment after a crime as necessary. Many retributivists seem evidently to equate legal order with moral order. But that is far from evident. An ethical approach to criminal justice should begin by exploring the ethical quality of penal law itself. Why, for example, is penal law in our Western democracies predominantly geared to public order, individual physical integrity and property, and not, for example, to social peace, solidarity and social and economic equity? Punishments are used to enforce any legal rule, to enforce wearing a beard or a burka in Afghanistan, for example, or to discourage critical journalism in many countries. Leaving enforcement through infliction of pain open to all these possibilities is a dangerous game, as daily events overwhelmingly demonstrate.

Moreover, distinguishing between wrongs and social harms is difficult to accept in the socio-ethics grounding restorative justice. I shall deal with this issue in the next chapter.

Ethical problems with punishment

Most ethical systems consider the deliberate and coercive imposition of suffering on another person as unethical and socially destructive. Punishment 'involves actions that are generally considered to be morally wrong or evil were they not described and justified as punishments' (de Keijser 2000: 7). Nevertheless, criminal punishment for offences is institutionalised, in so far as more justification is demanded for not punishing an offence than for punishing it. Even abolitionists finally appear to formulate in their alternative approaches a kind of 'hidden' penal law (Blad 1996a). Nils Christie (1981), for whom 'reduction of man-inflicted pain on earth' is the central value to strive for, finally accepts that 'absolute punishment' may be needed in some cases in order to express the grief and mourning caused by certain crimes. Punishment of offences by criminal justice is considered as self-evident, while leaving unanswered why the general ethical rule not to inflict pain on others does not apply to responding to offences (Fatic 1995).[3]

Penal theories advance a variety of arguments to justify exempting the punitive infliction of pain from the general disapproval of pain infliction (von Hirsch 1998). They can be clustered as instrumentalist and retributivist arguments.

Punishment is ineffective

According to instrumentalist (or consequentionalist) approaches, penal law is only acceptable if it serves higher social aims. 'All punishment in itself is evil ... if it ought at all to be admitted, it ought only to be admitted in as far as it promises to exclude some greater evil' (Bentham 1823/1995: 24). An exclusively instrumentalist response to crime is potentially 'insatiable' (Braithwaite and Pettit 1990). The aim of rehabilitation, for example, as in juvenile justice, could lead to endless intervention. But juveniles and their families have rights to be respected, regardless of the rehabilitative purpose. Extreme instrumentalism can lead to punishing the innocent or to draconian punishments, in order to increase the deterrent impact. Stated bluntly, implementing the death penalty is the only absolute way to exclude reoffending. But we do not want it and most civilised countries have abolished it for ethical reasons. Hence the instrumentalist justifications of punishment are limited by some (possibly hidden) deontological principles.

Roughly, the instrumentalist aim is purchased in two different ways, by generally deterring those who are considering committing a crime, and by individually deterring or resocialising those who have already committed one.[4] The tenability of instrumentalist theories can be tested by investigating empirically whether the aims advanced are achieved. A long tradition of research leads to the conclusion that punishment is socially not effective for any of these goals (Tonry 1995; Sherman 2003; Andrews and Bonta 2003).

Deterrence research demonstrates the weakness of the general preventive impact of penal law. Even the benefits of incapacitating offenders by imprisoning them are more than outweighed by increased reoffending after imprisonment and by the deterioration in social life in general. There is no indication that harsher or more intensive punishments lead to greater public safety and peace. On the contrary, the more public policy relies exclusively on repression and punishment, the more this will lead to more imprisonment, more human and financial costs, less ethics, less public safety and a lower quality of social life (Skolnick 1995; Tonry 1995; Braithwaite 2005). 'There is widespread agreement over time and space that alterations in sanctioning policies are unlikely substantially to influence crime rates' (Tonry and Farrington 1995: 6). This does not mean that the threat of punishment never has any effect, but it indicates that deterrence has to be looked at in a nuanced way. The general statement that penal law is needed in order to deter (potential) offenders is a doctrine rather than an empirically sustainable theory.

The idea that punishment rehabilitates or individually deters offenders has never been confirmed empirically. Rehabilitation is mostly reflected in the reoffending rate (Andrews and Bonta 2003). Contrary to some penal rhetoric, as in Morris (1981) or Duff (2001), criminal punishments do not morally educate the offender, or only seldom induce in the offender penance and reform. Additional treatment carried out during the period of punishment is in general ineffective. One of the conclusions of the 'what works' research is that 'punishment-based programmes ... on average lead to a 25% *increase* in reoffending rate as compared with control groups' (McGuire and Priestly 1995: 10, my emphasis).

This does not mean that punishment fatally makes offenders untreatable but that punishment is an obstacle to rehabilitation rather than an opportunity to achieve it. Braithwaite, for example, disqualifies the criminal justice system as 'the most dysfunctional of the major institutional accomplishments of the Enlightment' (Braithwaite 2005: 283). The French speak of 'la crise pénale' (Cario 2005). In the actuarial vision, the punitive criminal justice system has even lost its moral function and is thus stripped of any moral and social authority to censure criminal behaviour (Feeley and Simon 1992). Despite a systematic failure to demonstrate the instrumental value of punishing offenders, punishment is still maintained as the mainstream position. Apparently, the instrumentalist illusions are grafted onto retributive emotions.

Punitive retributivism is unethical

Contrary to consequentialism, retributivism (or deontologism) does not primarily ask questions about possible targets or effects of punishment. Punishing the wrong is simply inherent in moral conduct. It is a categorical imperative (Kant). The reasons for inflicting pain are sought in a concept of equality (by rectifying the illegitimate advantage obtained by the crime) or in the expression of blame. Retributivists look for principles in order to implement the categorical imperative in as just a way as possible. They subject penal law to a series of prescriptions such as the legality principle, the due process principle or the proportionality principle.

Like extreme consequentialism, extreme retributivism is untenable, because it would lose contact with real life. A purely principled approach would move the system away from changes in social ethics and beliefs, and would leave no space for human relations, including mutual understanding, apology and forgiveness (Nussbaum 1993).

A deontological theory always hides at least some consequentialist aims. Censuring criminal behaviour, for example, is needed to uphold morality (as in von Hirsch 1993). But why should we uphold morality? Morality is not given by nature. It is a pragmatic social construction, based on civilisation, to keep life in the community livable. Morality itself thus serves a target, and preserving morality through censure indirectly serves the same target.

It is difficult to reflect on criminal punishment without reflecting on targets. If we did not indicate an objective for the criminal justice system, why would we keep it? If we do not expect any positive effect from this very expensive and grievous system, what should we have to fear from abolishing it? Basically, criminal justice must deserve its right to exist through the targets it promotes.

Retributivists advance several arguments to except the punitive infliction of pain from the general disapproval of pain infliction.

From vengeful emotions to retributivist theories
The origins of retribution do not lie in theoretical assumptions (Burms 2005; Mackie 1985). Retribution begins with emotion. Being the victim of a crime or another injustice provokes indignation, feelings of humiliation and anger. It provokes a wish to repay the injuries suffered by inflicting pain on the person who caused them. 'Grievances reveal desires whose only satisfaction is the belief that offenders are being distressed or made to suffer' (Van Stokkom 2005: 166). This is revenge, a 'personal retribution which is typically accompanied by feelings of indignation, anger and resentment for wrongs suffered in one's personal domain of concern' (Barton 1999: 70).

Revenge has both an emotional and a rational dimension. The emotional aspect is the feeling of anger and the search for expression of this anger. The rational aspect is getting even, by trying to restore a balance (whatever it may be). The vocabulary of revenge 'is less about violence than about debt'[5] (Cario 2005: 23). The intensity and the extent of revenge feelings vary according to the degree of injustice experienced. In the Dutroux case,[6] about 400,000 Belgians expressed their indignation and concern in a 'White March' in Brussels. One would be unlikely to find four people to demonstrate about a stolen motorbike (even if it were a Harley Davidson).

However, giving way to personal feelings of revenge may get out of hand. The emotional dimension often overrules the rational balance, at least in the eyes of the one who is the target of the revenge action. For a student, the stealing of his motorbike may represent not just the loss of the monetary value, but of an object for which he has been doing extra jobs during weekends and which allows him to impress his girlfriend. His revenge might reflect these subjective losses, which would not be understood by the thief. The latter may respond by counter-revenge, possibly leading to a spiral of mutual violence.

Anger and indignation in victims are psychologically understandable. But if not channelled, actions of revenge could be catastrophic for social life. That is why the emotions following the occurrence of a crime must be recognised and legally 'restyled' through the authorities' response to the crime. Historically, this process began when central power tried to prevent personal actions of revenge by putting in place a centralised and controllable system to respond to crime. What happens if such a system does not exist or is powerless can currently be observed in the Middle East, for example. Beginning with *lex tallionis*, retributive theories have been developed to justify and orient the central canalisation of personal revenge.

The transformation of revenge into retributivism has, however, reduced or even eliminated the emotional dimension. 'Justice' is reduced to general concepts and procedures, equal for all citizens. It is formalised, and transforms experienced events into general terms, understandable and controllable for all (or their lawyers). Emotions do not fit into this transformation. Moreover, retribution theory focuses more on the public dimension of the crime. It is not the student's losses that count the most. It is the transgression of the general norm forbidding stealing. If the student is interested in getting compensation, it is up to him to engage as a civil party in the criminal procedure. The student's emotional losses are eliminated. Not all citizens work at weekends to pay for a motorcycle. Not all motorcycle owners use them to impress girls. Only the monetary value of the vehicle will be taken into account. Possibly also some 'moral losses' will be translated into a financial amount. As a result, justice may be done in the eyes of the justice professionals, but the student will probably be left frustrated, with feelings of injustice.

Here is where restorative justice has its claim: it tries to address as much as possible the emotional dimensions of crime, and to transform the destructive dimensions in those emotions into constructive motivations. But keeping such process in the frame of a constitutional democracy is, as we shall see, one of the most difficult challenges for maximalist restorative justice. If it succeeds, it may represent a new step in human civilisation. Civilisation is a process of increasing control over spontaneous violence and of bringing violence under state monopoly (Elias 1994). Maybe the next step in civilisation is to reduce state violence itself, by not taking for granted pain infliction after a crime.

A moral obligation?

Retributive theory is grounded in the Kantian principle that punishing wrongdoing is a categorical imperative. It is inherent in morality that wrongdoing must be responded to by imposing hard treatment on the wrongdoer. The offender must be punished because he deserves it. This reasoning in fact turns around the ethical objection to inflicting pain. Not only is punishing wrongdoing exempt from moral objections, it is even morally obligatory. It seems to be what Nietzsche called 'black magic': the morally evil is changed into the morally good by the magic wand of rhetoric (in Van Stokkom 2005: 165).

Retributivism advances two types of arguments. The first is that norm transgression must be censured. Good societies guarantee that rights and freedoms are assured and taken seriously. Good societies therefore must issue clear rules, enforce them and unambiguously disapprove of law-breaking, so as to keep the norm well understood by all citizens and to reduce as much as possible law-breaking in the future. The censuring function thus addresses the public in general. The public must be assured that compliance with the norm is controlled and transgression is not tolerated and sanctioned. But does censure have to include intentional infliction of pain? It is already argued that it does not. Censuring as such, making clear that criminal behaviour is not tolerated, is necessary, but it does not need to be expressed through punishment. I hope to make clear throughout this book that restorative processes offer far better ways of delivering serious and effective censure than does hard treatment.

The second argument of retributivists is the restoration of a moral balance. It is based on a kind of intuitive reciprocity in social life, but it is unclear what balance is meant in actuality. The assumption is that feelings of revenge are legally satisfied by the imposition of an amount of pain on the offender which is in balance with the amount of pain caused by the offence. The grievances are satisfactorily addressed only if it is believed that the offender is also distressed. Others advance that the infliction of punishment erases the illegitimate benefits obtained by the offence. The thief cannot be allowed to take advantage of the illegitimate freedom he grabbed by transcending the norm, or to enjoy the goods he stole. We must therefore spoil his life by imposing on him some pain.

All in all, both arguments are basically negative: in order to satisfy revenge emotions or to balance illegitimate benefits, pain is wilfully provoked and inflicted. Such responses may be understandable in relation to individual emotions, but they are difficult to accept in a considered, rational response by state institutions.

But still, there is the common intuition that 'a balance' is to be restored. It would simply be unjust if we let the offenders get away or if we left the victims alone with their losses and grievances. 'Something' must happen after a burglary, a violent robbery or even a malign act of vandalism. We want the material, mental and social victimisation to be recognised and wiped out. It is basically an intuitive moral balance which has to be taken seriously because reciprocity is a *basso continuo* in our social life. But imposing intentionally hard treatment on the offender is not the only appropriate way to restore this intuitive moral balance.

Proportionality

Proportionality is a 'technical' expression of the balance idea, but it is also advanced as an argument on its own for retributivism. Retributivism is retrospective. Retribution refers to a wrong committed in the past. Offenders are punished because they have offended, not because they might reoffend in the future. The guilt for the crime committed must be proven. The degree of punishment depends on the seriousness of the crime and the degree of guilt. The criminal procedure thus looks backwards, using assessable events and controllable yardsticks to construct proportionality in the degree of pain to be delivered (von Hirsch 1993). One of the main reasons for scepticism about restorative justice is fear that it does not offer satisfying retrospective grounds for legal safeguards (von Hirsch 1998; Ashworth 1993; Albrecht 2002; Eliaerts and Dumortier 2002).

Indeed, the response to crime must be kept within just and reasonable limits. Chapter 5 will devote a section to the proportionality issue, but it must be mentioned here already that the construction of the punitive proportionality is itself highly debatable (Wright 2003). There is no objective indication for relating a quantified seriousness of crime to a quantified degree of imprisonment or fine. It is a matter of convention, which varies in space and time. Moreover, punitive retributivism does not necessarily have a monopoly on providing retrospective yardsticks. Instead of linking the wrongfulness of conduct to the degree of pain inflicted, the seriousness of the harm caused could be related to the intensity of the reparative effort required, for example. Reasons will be advanced to believe that deliberative restorative processes might be more appropriate than traditional criminal justice procedures for assessing a reasonable and just relation between the act and the response.

To conclude provisionally, the survey of possible justifications for the punitive apriorism in the response to crime picked up two elements: (1) in order to preserve the quality of social relations, an intuitive moral balance must be restored, and (2) criminal behaviour must be publicly censured in order to encourage compliance with the norm in the future. It appears, however, that these functions are poorly fulfilled in the current criminal justice system. A more constructive view on retributivism is possible.

Restorative justice as inverted constructive retributivism

Retribution basically consists of three elements: the blameworthiness of the unlawful behaviour is clearly expressed, the responsibility of the offender is indicated, and the moral imbalance is repaired by paying back to the offender the suffering he caused by his offence. Restorative justice in fact shares these components, but in a constructive manner, which may contribute directly to the quality of social life while avoiding the ethically negative apriorism of pain infliction.

Blaming norm transgression

Restorative justice clearly articulates the limits of social tolerance. It intervenes because a crime has been committed and the crime is disapproved of. As will be described later, moral emotions such as shame, guilt, remorse and embarrassment are inherent in restorative processes and result from the disapproval expressed during the process. Restorative justice thus provides the essential elements of censuring. But restorative censuring is distinguished from punitive censuring by the reasons for the disapproval. In current criminal justice, the censure addresses the breaking of a general and abstract public norm. The offender is condemned according to formal criminal procedures because he has transgressed an article of penal law. Restorative censuring, on the contrary, is rooted in social relations. The offender's behaviour is disapproved of because it caused harm to another person and to social life, and he is invited (under pressure) to consider the kind and amount of harm caused. Restorative censuring refers to the obligation to respect the quality of social life.

A problematic aspect may be that the restorative process is, by preference, confidential: the disapproval is communicated only to the participants (Hildebrandt 2005). While public censuring is one of the most important functions of the response to crime, this public message could get lost. Censuring in court indeed conveys the message of disapproval to the public at large. Restorative processes, on the contrary, are internally confidential. But they are organised under a public mandate. The public thus gets the message that the authorities do not let things happen, that they disapprove of the criminal act and are committed to giving a response. An additional message to the public is that the main stakeholders are given a chance to contribute decisively to a response, which should be as constructive as possible to social life. This public address is what Blad calls positive general prevention, contrary to the negative deterrence in punitive justice (Blad 2004).[7]

Responsibility

In terms of responsibility, the offender is considered a moral agent. The person is linked to his acts and its consequences. As in punitive retributivism, restorative justice raises the responsibility of the offender. But there is a remarkable difference. Punitive retributivism is based on a passive concept of responsibility. It is the criminal justice system which makes the relation between the suspect and the act and its consequences. The offender is confronted with his responsibility by the system, and must submit to the punitive consequences imposed on him by that system. He has no active role to play, other than organising his defence as well as possible, to deny (the seriousness of) the facts and to try to get away with the least possible punishment. Passive responsibility is retrospective, in that it is imposed because of an act committed in the past.

Restorative justice relies on a concept of active responsibility. The offender is invited (under pressure) to take active responsibility by participating actively in the deliberations to assess the crime-caused harm and to make active gestures that contribute to the reparation of this harm (Braithwaite and Roche 2001). If this active commitment does not succeed, a sanction will be imposed on the offender, requiring from him an active effort as part of a (symbolic) reparation. Active responsibility is raised because of the act committed in the past, but also oriented towards an action or a situation in the future. Active responsibility, therefore, is both retrospective and prospective.

Balance

The balance principle also is essential in restorative justice, maybe even in a more genuine form than in punitive retributivism. In punitive retributivism, the balance (whatever this balance may be) is restored by paying back to the offender the same amount of suffering and harm he has caused. It is supposed that things are then evened out: both parties suffer equally. The problem is, however, that 'balancing the harm done by the offender with further harm inflicted on the offender ... only adds to the total amount of harm in the world' (Wright 1992: 525). The amount of suffering is doubled, but equally spread.

In restorative justice, the offender's paying-back role is reversed from a passive to an active one: he must himself pay back by repairing as much as possible the harm and suffering caused. The balance is now restored, not by doubling the total amount of suffering, but by taking suffering away. Retribution in its genuine meaning is achieved in a constructive way. *Retribuere* in Latin is a contraction of *re-attribuere*, to give back, and that is what restorative justice seeks to do. One could see in this reversed restorative retributivism also a kind of proportionality. It is based, however, not on 'just deserts', but on 'just dues'. Restorative justice asks the question which 'debt' the offender has and what he owes to pay back reasonably for the losses he has caused.

All in all, restoration and retribution appear to have much in common. They 'may be seen as two sides of a coin, rather than a pair of opposites' (Baehler 2007: 290). Referring to Brunk's work (Brunk 2001), Zehr lists the commonalities as: '... a basic moral intuition that a balance has been thrown off by a wrongdoing. Consequently, the victim deserves something and the offender owes something ... There must be a proportional relationship between the act and the response' (Zehr 2002: 59).

'Because crime hurts, justice should heal' (Braithwaite 2005: 296). In 2006 the grandmother of a three-year-old child killed in a racist shoot-out in Antwerp said: 'Confronted with so much hate, we need a huge amount of love.' Justice should not add more hurt.

Restorative justice does not add more hurt, but tries to take hurt away by inverting punitive retributivism into constructive restorative retributivism. Facing the common concern of both retributive and restorative justice to rebalance the consequences of a wrong helps to indicate more precisely where the fundamental difference lies (Blad 2003): it is the way the balance is going to be restored. Punitive retributivism assumes that intentional pain infliction is indispensable to balance wrongful behaviour and to censure it. That is, in my view, a principle that restorative justice cannot encompass.

Restorative justice and rehabilitation of the offender

Now that the relationship between restorative justice and punishment is cleared up, at least in the way I see it, some comments are also needed on the position of rehabilitative concerns for the offender in restorative justice actions. Several passages of this book touch on this subject.

Whereas it is difficult to find out what rehabilitation really means (Ward and Maruna 2007), it has a connotation with welfare in a social context. Rehabilitated people are reasonably well integrated into their social environment and feel predominantly positive about being so. Rehabilitation is a concern within the current criminal justice interventions, but rehabilitative justice is also an approach on its own, distinct from the punitive mainstream in the response to crime. It is operational predominantly in the response to youthful offending. Rehabilitation-oriented juvenile justice systems suffer less from the socio-ethical drawbacks just described with regard to punitive apriorism. On the contrary, the endeavour to rehabilitate, to treat or to re-educate offenders instead of punishing them is a humane and socially constructive ideal.

But long experience with juvenile justice has revealed other subjects of criticism, on which I have commented extensively in other texts (Walgrave 2004):

- The effectiveness of the treatment-oriented interventions in juvenile justice is generally poor, and often even counterproductive.
- The focus on the needs of the offender and not on the characteristics of the offence removes the grounds for legal safeguards.
- Priority for treatment and support lacks credibility in the response to serious and persistent youth crime.
- The treatment orientation for the offenders neglects the legitimate needs and interests of the victims.

Restorative justice seems to respond fairly well to these objections.

In Chapter 4, it will be documented that restorative processes can also have an impact on the offender's chances for rehabilitation. Measured according to the 'what works' standards, it may be expected not to perform worse in that respect than the mainstream rehabilitative interventions.

Chapter 5 will claim that the retrospective dimension of restorative justice offers good ground for developing particular legal standards, better than that which the purely prospective approach in rehabilitative justice can offer.

A few paragraphs ago in this chapter, I have argued that the restorative approach invokes the responsibility of the offender for his actions, which may be more credible in the response to (serious) crime than the treatment approach which assumes less responsibility and less culpability.

Finally, it seems to be obvious that a genuine restorative justice model is intrinsically more oriented to the victims' needs and interests. But we shall see that it is more complicated than that. Here is where the relation between restorative justice and rehabilitation of the offender is sometimes out of balance. As will be commented on at the end of Chapter 4, it can be feared, especially in the juvenile justice context, that victims may be misused in another agenda. Mediation or conferencing are then seen in a treatment perspective, and the victim's view is subordinate. This is, however, not restorative justice as it is defined in Chapter 1. Restorative justice's purpose is to restore as much as possible, so that adding possible new harm by abusing the victim in an offender-oriented agenda is unacceptable.

Taking care of the offender's rehabilitation by treatment, social reintegration, re-education or support is a high socio-ethical principle, but it must remain subordinate to restorative principles. As Bazemore and O'Brien write, 'doing justice requires repairing the harm of crime' (Bazemore and O'Brien 2002: 32), and 'presenting restorative justice as primarily aimed at reducing recidivism is inappropriate' (ibid.). But within that frame, they state, 'there is great untapped potential in the application of core restorative values and principles to treatment and rehabilitation' (ibid.). Hopefully, offenders will learn a positive lesson from their meeting with the victim, and they mostly do, but the main objective is to restore the victim and to reassure the community. Of course, it is important that the content of the community service contributes to the offender's competency building, but the frame is that it must be seen as a symbolic compensation for the harm caused. In Chapter 4, we will see that restorative processes as such may deeply influence the offender, even if that is not the primary purpose.

Unlike the punitive response, the welfare-oriented rehabilitative approach is not contradictory to restorative justice. Also restorative justice is in fact a welfare approach, but a more complete or balanced one (Bazemore and Day 1996). Justice requires that the restoration of the victim's welfare and of the quality of social life is pursued as a priority, but it does not exclude caring for the offender's welfare. It does, however, exclude a wilful degradation of the offender's welfare, as is the case in the punitive response.

Conclusion

Restorative justice is clearly different from the predominant punitive apriorism in the current criminal justice response to crime. It is neither an alternative punishment nor complementary to punishment. The crucial distinction is in the intentionality. Whereas punishment is an intentional infliction of pain, reparation is an action to undo harm, which may, however, be painful. This distinction in intentionality is far more than mere quibbling over words; it has crucial instrumental and socio-ethical consequences. There is no tenable justification for the apriorism that crime must be punished. The intention of inflicting pain is a major obstacle for effective communication, and it cannot be ethically justified.

Criminal punishment does not work. For society at large, a penal criminal justice intervention offers a strong confirmation of legal order, but public safety is badly served. Pure punishment carries the seeds of more social discord and malaise, and thus of more crime and criminalisation (Braithwaite 1999). Victims are principally used as witnesses and then left alone with their losses and grievances (Dignan and Cavadino 1998). The priority given to the penal procedure and the penal sanction reduces the chances of victims receiving compensation or restoration. For the offender, the sanction has no rehabilitative meaning. It is a senseless infliction of suffering which contributes neither to public safety nor to the victim's interests. On the contrary, criminal punishments have mostly negative consequences for the future social opportunities of the offenders and often, also, of his family.

The ethical justifications, or even obligations, to punish norm transgression do not stand up to scrutiny. Even the necessity for clear censure and the restoration of an intuitive moral balance after a crime does not necessarily imply the intentional infliction of pain on the offender. What remains is the social and ethical rejection of the punitive apriorism, as a counterproductive, ethically highly doubtful intrusion into the offender's freedom. Keeping the punitive apriorism – accepting punishment as the mainstream response to crime – is in itself ethically doubtful.

Despite all this, the punishment paradigm remains strong, for some even stronger than ever. It causes sociologists to question why

(Daems 2007). Sociologists do not try to justify the situation, but to understand and explain it. 'Punishing today is a deeply problematic and barely understood aspect of social life, the rationale for which is by no means clear', Garland writes (1990: 3). For him, the function of punitive justice is symbolic, a display of the power of the authorities. For Baumann, penal criminal justice is part of the 'waste disposal industry' of human waste in modern societies (Baumann 2004). But sociological understanding is not the subject of my quest. I look for a socio-ethical justification of punishment and do not find it.

It is in my view crucial to keep this clear distinction between restorative justice and the punitive apriorism. As shall be seen in Chapter 6, indeed, current societal and cultural evolutions point to more repression and punishment, and the risk is that restorative justice could be co-opted as new punishments rather then as alternatives to punishment (Pratt 2006). But 'The best reform of penal law consists of its replacement, not by a better penal law, but by something better' (Radbruch, quoted in Tulkens 1993: 493). The question now arises whether restorative justice, clearly distinct from the punitive apriorism, could offer that 'something better'. The exploration will take two steps. First, the next chapter will search the socio-ethical grounds of restorative justice and compare it with the punitive retributive philosophy. Then Chapter 4 will investigate the instrumental trump cards of restorative justice.

Notes

1 Contrary to von Hirsch, I do not add the disapprobatory message as another characteristic. Punishment in practice is often administered routinely, and it is experienced as a price to be paid, without any moral reflection at all.
2 '... il importe de passer du droit comme instrument du contrôle social au droit comme moyen de faciliter l'interaction sociale harmonieuse' (Cario 2005: 22).
3 My arguments concern criminal justice punishment only. Punishment in an educational environment, in families or schools, for example, is completely different (see, for example, Walgrave 2001).
4 Incapacitation is sometimes also considered as a possible purpose of punishment. I hesitate to do so. There is a fundamental difference between the preventative aims of punishment and the security concerns in incapacitation. In the first, offenders are locked away because *they* have committed an offence and as an attempt to 'improve' them. In incapacitation, offenders are locked away because *we* are afraid of them.

5 '… son vocabulaire est moins celui de la violence que celui de la dette' (Cario 2005: 23).

6 Dutroux is a Belgian who was arrested in 1996 for kidnapping, detaining, sexually abusing and killing several young girls. The investigation revealed very serious dysfunctions in the Belgian police.

7 Chapter 5 will deal with another problem regarding the confidentiality of restorative processes: that confidentiality does hamper external control of the respect for legal safeguards within the process.

Chapter 3

Common self-interest: seeking socio-ethical grounds for restorative justice

Let me begin with an exercise in introspection. As will appear in the next chapter, the instrumental promises of restorative justice practices are not bad. But imagine that no benefits were found: the victims were not systematically better off, the offenders did not understand better why their behaviour is unacceptable and/or they continued to reoffend as before, and no advantages were observed for community life or public safety. If the effectiveness of restorative justice were exactly the same as the impact of punitive justice, would I then give up the option? I do not think so. Unless its outcomes were significantly worse for the victim, for the offender or for public safety, I would probably stick to the option for restorative justice.

My choice for restorative justice is based primarily on non-instrumental reasons, rooted in my ethical intuitions. In this chapter, I try to make these intuitions more explicit. The reader must be warned. Those who expect a fully fledged ethical tract will be disappointed. I am not a professional ethicist. However, that does not prevent me from being aware that my ethical beliefs and attitudes are crucial in my orientation towards restorative justice.

'Outing myself' ethically is a risky undertaking. Empiricists might find it irrelevant. Professional ethicists could be very critical for my ethical quest, because the process I will follow and the concept of 'common self-interest' which I will position centrally, to my knowledge, do not fit into any of the great ethical traditions and schools. So be it. Understanding thoroughly the option for restorative justice requires exploration of the socio-ethical soil in which it is rooted.

In search of socio-ethical foundations for restorative justice

Ethical foundations or everlasting critical discourse on concrete ethics?

In line with postmodern philosophy, Pavlich rejects general ethical foundations for restorative justice (Pavlich 2002, 2005, 2007). For him, the potential of restorative justice resides in refusing 'a blackmail that commands us to come up with well-founded universal principles or else be condemned as unethical, immoral or just plain irrational' (2002: 2). General ethical principles are expressions of totalitarianism, a form of imperialism over thinking and behaviour. Pavlich states that 'a pervasive – "ambient" – uncertainty has gripped our ethical lives to the extent that we no longer place any faith in reason's ability to formulate universal maxims' (2007: 620). Referring to Lyotard and Derrida, he writes 'there is no such thing as justice *per se*' (ibid.: 621).

Instead, Pavlich presents ethics as indeterminate thinking, based on Derrida's concept of hospitality, by analogy with 'a host welcoming a stranger at the threshold of what will be negotiated ways of being with each other in the immediate future' (ibid.: 622). Thinking and behaving ethically is by definition indeterminate, because it is about making personal choices, taking personal responsibility for being with others. Relying on general ethical rules is not functional and strips behavioural options from personal responsibility, thus from their potential to be ethical. Pavlich does not employ a nihilistic language of 'anything goes'. On the contrary, he imposes 'an immense responsibility upon us for every one of our ethical decisions and actions' (ibid.: 623). The choices are permanently to be submitted to reflection and discourse, holding out the continuous possibility of critical scrutiny. 'Critique is central to the structure of ethical life, as the all-important night watch that must never doze', Pavlich poetically writes (ibid.: 624).

'A restorative ethics could be understood as the critical work performed when subjects gather to name injustice or harm, and address promises of just patterns of being with others that are yet to come' (Pavlich 2002: 5). In Pavlich's view, restorative justice is at risk of losing its critical potential if it abandons this open ethical approach and gives way to what he calls the 'imitator paradox', becoming simply another variant of the traditional justice model steered by the hegemony of the powerful (Pavlich 2005). Comments on this paradox follow in Chapter 5.

It is quite a challenge. Holding indeterminate situational morals, oriented towards being ethically with others, is an attractive perspective. Taking full responsibility for ethical choices based on concrete hospitality for others, while being open for debate and criticism, is probably the highest moral quality one can imagine. However, such morals are probably found only in the most mature, autonomous and self-critical people. Such people seem to combine Kohlberg's ideal moral stage, based on personally integrated principles and ideals (Kohlberg 1976), with Gilligan's ethics of care, based on sensitivity to others' needs and interests (Gilligan 1982). The majority of adults do not reach such a level of perfection, to say the least. If, as Pavlich rightly recalls (Pavlich 2007: 622), advancing general ethical principles could not avoid catastrophes like the Holocaust and other genocides, relying on individuals' ethical maturity would certainly not do better. The ethical maturity promoted by Pavlich is an exceptional state of mind.

Moreover, the kind of open dialogue-based critique that Pavlich has in mind is inspired by Habermas' ethics of discourse, built around the concept of *herrschaftfreie Dialog*, a dialogue free of power and pressure. I do not think that such totally open dialogue is possible in reality. A dialogue about resolving an injustice starts from the observation that an act or a situation actually is unjust and that (some of) the participants will (have to) do something about it. This is not just an intellectual difference in meaning. It is an emotional debate about how a strongly felt injustice will be repaired. Such a meeting is imbued with pressure, either from official coercive institutions in the background, or from participants in the process (Hudson 2006a).

Hence, it may be wiser – in the current imperfect state of affairs – to provide some ethical principles. They are not meant as a system of rigid obligations. The ideal principled man, as promoted by Kohlberg, is probably an insensitive and boring person. Kant's cramped principled judgment, that even if the world would perish the last criminal should be hanged, has been called a 'talionic sophism of a senile genius' (Polak, quoted in Van Stokkom 2005: 165). Well thought out, well documented principles may serve as references to orient judgment in critical ethical situations. While they are never definitively fixed and are not suitable for implementation in all critical situations, they may be beacons for the person who has to take personal responsibility for difficult ethical options and actions.

My understanding of Pavlich's reasoning is that he actually offers such an ethical principle. Imposing upon ethical actors the responsibility to accept reflection and discourse in order to provide a better and more open hospitality to others is a serious burden. Being a good host is an ethical request, even if the concrete quality of hospitality is to be defined through deliberation with the guest. Pavlich's ethical principles may be minimalistic, but they are nevertheless ethical principles. Reflecting on ethics without projecting principles – which may be provisional, transitional, debatable, intuitive or rational – is impossible. It is like pedalling in the air.

It is difficult to conceive of reflection and discourse on ethical decisions without provisional principles as starting points. How can you bring participants together in a dialogue about undoing the consequences of an injustice if they do not share the idea that there is actually an injustice to be repaired? How can you find together a 'just' response if you cannot communicate about why you consider a response is just or not? In the dialogue, you will present your – intuitive – view and argue it. Others will answer by rejecting, nuancing or improving your view, or by proposing a different approach. Principles and interests will be exchanged, moulded, synthesised, interpreted and made concrete, to be applicable and acceptable to all in the specific situation being discussed. The process begins with the opening of ethical (pre-)conceptions for debate.

My quest to explain my ethical drive toward the restorative justice option is meant as a contribution to what Pavlich describes as the everlasting debate on the ethics of understanding concrete injustices and how to repair them.

'Victimalisation' of morals

'It says in the Penal Code what you are not supposed to do, but it does not say why not. In the past, this was a task largely left to the ideological agents', Boutellier writes (Boutellier 2000: 18). In recent years, criminology and criminal justice have increasingly been stripped of moral reflections. In line with cultural postmodernist developments, the concept of crime is 'de-moralised', and criminal policy has become 'actuarial' – managing the problems caused by crime rather than solving them. To avoid further degradation, there is a need for a 'normative minimum' (Boutellier 1996: 19) to underpin and govern social life: '… criminal law will have to constantly find new points of moral departure in a morally fragmented society' (Boutellier 2000: 15). Returning to the earlier religion- or community-based moral systems is neither possible nor desirable, because the progression of individualisation has enlarged the scope of individual freedom. In a pluralistic and increasingly heterogeneous society, solidarity can no longer be based on a common identity or a generally accepted higher order such as religion, nation or community.

Boutellier finds his normative minimum in Rorty's 'are you suffering?' (Rorty 1989): 'the only thing that counts in a secular, liberal society is that people are vulnerable to humiliation and cruelty, pain and suffering; the extent to which we show ourselves to be sensitive to other people's experiences of this kind determines the morality of our culture' (Boutellier 2000: 15). When universalism is rejected in favour of a liberal pluralistic culture, the basis for solidarity is not general, but local and concrete: the shared rejection of observed cruelty and suffering. 'The victim is the central moral denominator in our secularized, pluralistic society ... Solidarity in present-day secularized and pluralistic society is no longer linked to either God or a collectivity of the kind Durkheim has in mind, but to the position of the victim. This is what I call the *victimalisation of morality*' (ibid.: 16). The minimalistic common morals are based on the desire we share to avoid being victimised, and on our spontaneously felt emotional solidarity with those who are suffering. Regarding criminal justice: 'It is not so much the violation of the ideologically embedded norm that needs to be undone, but the concrete individual suffering that justice should be done to' (ibid.: 17). The quotation could have been written by a restorative justice advocate.

But it was not. Concern for the victimised is, of course, central in restorative justice, but victimalised ethics is too narrow an ethical basis for restorative justice.

1 A system of morals based only on fear of being victimised is weakened or even negative. It is as if the common interest is limited to avoiding suffering, while mutual support and solidarity, with a view to achieving together positive growth, happiness, wealth and so forth, have no moral value. I shall argue, on the contrary, that individuals and collectivities are bound by positive values and objectives. The pursuit of more autonomy, more happiness, more wealth, more aesthetic beauty, more pleasure is both an individual and a collective undertaking. It orients the value of behaviour and attitudes, and hence the moral criteria.

2 Advancing victimisation as a pragmatic choice for articulating a moral basis is a weak basis, making victimalised morals extremely 'volatile' (Daems 2007). Human suffering is variable, both in kind and in intensity, and does not always prompt equal solidarity. The theory leaves undetermined the criteria for recognising

victimisation. They may change over time, and depend on power play to determine the recognition or rejection of victim status. Feminist criminology, for example had to deliver a long struggle for some typically female dimensions of victimisation to be recognised. There will be deep disagreement about whether one should include victimisation of entire population groups by social economic injustice (and what this 'injustice' means) or by systematic political discrimination. These are moral questions going far beyond the simple victimalisation thesis.

3   Finally, Boutellier's position that restoring a collective dimension in morals is not feasible, and even not desirable, is highly debatable. Whereas Rorty calls his position 'liberal irony', I would call it liberal cynicism. The approach of both Rorty and Boutellier rests on a traditional liberal concept of liberty, suspecting collective interests and approaches as possible threats to individual freedom. I shall argue that, on the contrary, restorative justice ethics consider community life and individual freedom as mutually dependent.

Ethics of care

In a response to Kohlberg's theory on moral development (1976), Gilligan expressed a 'different voice' (1982), which she called feminine morals as opposed to masculine morals. Whereas Kohlberg considers autonomous justice, based on rational universal principles, as the highest moral principle, Gilligan advances caring, based on empathy and sensitivity to human relations, as the most worthwhile moral attitude. Ethics of care do not refer to universal laws and rights. They are inherently relational and contextual, based on proximity and openness to needs (Gilligan 1982).[1] Emotions and affection are revalorised as opposed or complementary to objectivity and rationality.

Heidensohn (1986, cited in Masters and Smith 1998) used both moral approaches to characterise two models of justice. The (masculine) 'Portia model' actualises Kohlberg's 'ethics of principles', being abstract, rational and rights-based, as represented in the current justice model. The (feminine) 'Persephone model' is inspired by Gilligan's 'ethics of care', and is concrete, contextual, relational and expressive. Masters and Smith (1998) draw on this typology to understand what they call the shift in the ways of responding to crime. In their view, the 'relational justice practices such as victim–offender mediation and FGC [family group conferencing] … are best understood with reference to the feminist "ethic of care"' (ibid.: 8).

Daly (2002) rightly is sceptical of the idea that there would be something like typical female ethics opposed to typical male ethics. But besides that, much of the rhetoric related to the restorative 'encounter', 'meeting the needs of both victim and offender' or 'healing' can indeed be understood as caring interventions. One could even see the ethics of care as an extension of the just-mentioned 'victimalisation of morals': victims are in need of care more than of principled justice (Leest 2004).

But restorative justice is more. It is first of all about ensuring that responsibility is taken for the suffering and harm caused and for the reparation of these consequences. The responsibility in the ethics of care underlines the responsibility of the well-off for those in trouble, of the strong for the weak, of the mother for the child. It is one-sided responsibility. It may lead to a rehabilitative or support approach for the offender, to the detriment of the victim's needs, or to holding the victim as an irresponsible and weak being in need of nothing but care. Responsibility in restorative justice is double sided. Also those who are cared for have to take up responsibility actively. How this responsibility/care balance is made concrete is deliberated in the restorative meetings, which may be hard, include negative emotions such as indignation and anger, and end in serious demands. As we have seen, it may include coercion.

Moreover, restorative interventions deal not only with private conflicts, but also with crimes that have a public dimension. Also the 'generalised other' is addressed. Taking active responsibility, possibly applying coercion to make reparative gestures and addressing the public dimension of the crime are intrinsic parts of restorative justice and transcend the ethics of care. It is difficult to see how such an approach corresponds to the purely caring and particularistic approach of the Persephone model (Van Stokkom 2004). Finally, restorative justice has to be framed within general justice principles, which are difficult to combine with a purely caring approach. Masters and Smith also recognise this danger: 'an ethic of care cannot and should not wholly supplant an ethic of justice' (1998: 16).

Communitarianism

Restorative justice recalls the fundamental *raison d'être* of the criminal justice system. Why is it forbidden, for example, to steal or to commit private acts of violence? Because if it were not forbidden, severe victimisations would occur all the time, which would provoke counteractions 'to make things even', leading to an escalation in mutual victimisation. Constructive social life would be impossible; society would be dominated by abuse of power and fear. Hence, what is logically the first concern of the social response to crime? It is to repair – as much as possible and in an orderly way – the harm done to the victim and the damage to social life.

Instead of the abstract legal order, the quality of social relations and social life in general are (re)positioned as the fundamental reasons for criminalising certain behaviour. The aim is to restore this quality, and not primarily to enforce public order. To achieve this, restorative justice relies mainly on cooperative processes among citizens, and not primarily on coercive intervention by the state. The assumption is that, in appropriate conditions, opponents in a conflict are willing to meet each other in mutual understanding and respect and able to find a constructive solution.

Concern for the quality of social life and belief in the potential of ordinary people to find solutions are not the monopoly of restorative justice. They are central to a much wider political and socio-ethical agenda. Its expression is found, for example, in the earlier mentioned 'restorative extensions' in non-criminalisable matters. While these and other practices operate in different contexts, with (partly) different objectives and with other actors,[2] they are all based on the same fundamentals, considering conflict and injustices primarily as threats to the quality of social life, and responding to them by involving as much as possible the direct stakeholders in inclusive processes with a view to taking action to restore the quality of social life.

Three questions now arise.

1 What is this 'quality of social life'?
2 How can we derive from it a socio-ethical perspective?
3 Is it not naive to rely on the direct stakeholders in conflicts to find constructive solutions?

The third question is, in fact, an empirical question which is dealt with in the next chapter. Here, I set out to answer the first two questions on philosophical and ethical grounds.

From community to communitarianism

The idea of community as a social space 'in which people know and care for one another' (Etzioni 1995: 31), based on shared values, norms and interests, is central in restorative rhetorics (Bazemore and

Schiff 2001; Sullivan and Tift 2006a). This is understandable. Focusing on harm inevitably draws attention to the loss of peace and the social unrest in a community with crime in its midst. A community is more directly victimised by an offence than is the state.

Restorative justice presents community as both a means and an end. It is a means in that community is advanced as the *niche* of shared understanding and interest, where victim and offender can meet and find together a constructive solution. Restorative processes indeed require at least a minimal understanding of a common interest in a constructive settlement after the crime. But community is also seen as an end, in that some locate restorative justice in a broader communitarian agenda, aimed at enhancing community life and avoiding further alienation by the formal criminal justice interventions.

The link between restorative justice and an intuition of community may be important in practice but it is difficult to encapsulate it in a coherent theory. Three problems appear. First, even if it is not a territorial space (McCold and Wachtel 1997) community is presented as a 'web of affect-laden relationships' (Etzioni 1996: 127), or a set of 'dense networks of individual relationships' (Braithwaite 1989: 85). Community suggests an area, delimited mentally, socially or territorially, distinguishing an inside community from an outside non-community. It expands as far as the vague limits conceived by individuals. It is based on 'a sense of community', a 'perception of connectedness' (McCold and Wachtel 1997: 2). But it cannot be delimited. Community appears to be a subjective psychological entity rather than a set of characteristics of given collectivities (Crawford and Clear 2001: 135).

Secondly, building on communities for developing restorative responses to crime presupposes that communities really exist, which is far from evident (Crawford and Clear 2001; Bottoms 2003). It is difficult to mobilise the community to resolve a street robbery in which victim and offender live many kilometres from each other and belong to totally different social networks. Christie admitted that he had only weak arguments against scepticism about community. Of course, local networks of shared values and mutual solidarity do exist and function ('The death is not complete', Christie 1977: 12), but it is not possible to generalise them. Many crimes occur in non-community-like social settings, and solutions have to be found in such settings.

Thirdly, leaving the notion of community as a loose concept exposes it to possible misuse and excesses. Communities are not good per se. 'Communities are not the heavens of reciprocity and mutuality nor are they the utopias of egalitarianism, that some might wish' (Crawford 2002a: 138). The supposed *niche* of community may appear to be a hotbed of suffocating social control within and exclusionism towards the outside world. In the name of community, people are subjected to unreasonable control and stigmatisation. Local communities support repressive police forces and judges and vote for exclusionist politicians. The sharing of values and other social goods is limited to those who are considered to belong to the community. Those who do not are excluded and are often considered a threat. To the outside world, communities based on territory, ethnicity or religion may develop exclusionary tendencies, provoking possibly violent conflicts. This may lead to excessive nationalism and racism. Community contains 'the seeds of parochialism which can lead ... to atrocious totalitarian exclusions' (Pavlich 2001: 58).

In restorative justice, community is an icon, covering the informal, interdependent, respectful social environment in which exchanges can take place in order to repair the victim's harm, reintegrate the offender and restore community relations. But '... there is no necessary reason for the privileged association which now exists between the new communitarian images of community and the spirit of spontaneous collective solidarity' (ibid.: 67). Communitarianism does not, in fact, promote areas, but socio-ethics and values, to orient social life: a form of harmonious living together, based on recognised social attachments, shared values and beliefs, and mutual commitment. It is easy to understand that this spirit or these socio-ethical attitudes are activated more spontaneously towards members of what we subjectively define as 'our community' but they are not the monopoly or privilege of a given area defined by 'community'.

Hence, while there may be doubts about the appropriateness of community to characterise part of social reality, communi*tarianism* as a movement promoting an ideal of community may be a useful label for a socio-ethical movement.

Communitarianism versus liberalism

For communitarians, the awareness of being members of a family, being neighbours, sharing citizenship, having the same culture, believing in the same God, upholding the same values and beliefs, and thus being more likely to understand and support one another makes us deeply rooted in our social context, part of a community that we cannot erase. Our minds think, strive, judge, create, suffer and enjoy on the basis of our experiences in relation to others, with a view to achieving socially situated and valued objectives. We are inevitably bearers of social meanings and live in relation to social values (MacIntyre 1983). Communitarians argue that it is unrealistic and counterproductive to deny this and to promote unrestricted freedom and autonomy in individual choices and actions as liberals do (Bell 1993).

Communitarianism can go too far when it creates the illusion of community consensus 'by the identification of individuals and their interests with a symbolic collectivity and its interests' (Barber 2003: 149). If the view on the individuality of persons is lost, if the self is merged with the collectivity, it is vulnerable to 'all the grave risks of monism, conformism, and coercive consensualism' (ibid.: 150) which I suggested a few paragraphs ago.

We are more than just a part of a group. We have our private lives, needs and goals which we want to satisfy with the largest possible autonomy, free from interference by any person or agency. That is the liberals' point. For liberals, the highest possible value is freedom. Individuals must be given the right to self-determination, to choose autonomously how they will live. The role of the state should be limited to setting the conditions for the maximum possible self-determination by the citizens. State laws are contracts among free rational citizens, guaranteeing each contractor a space of justly divided liberty. Justice as fairness is crucial in such a vision (Kohlberg 1976; Rawls 1972).

However, extreme liberalism keeps up the illusion of totally free and rational individuals, while denying the huge differences between individuals in social, economic, intellectual and other capacities. In fact, the so-called contracts are imposed by the most powerful and influential on the most vulnerable. Liberalism without any correction finally amounts to the right of the strongest to exploit the weakest in society. That is why Rorty (1989), for example, keeps compassion with the suffering of others as grounds for local solidarity, and why Rawls (1972) accepts some state intervention to correct the most severe inequalities in social and economic resources, and launches the idea of a 'veil of ignorance' to reduce the risk of ruthless exploitation by the powerful.

But the highest value of liberalism remains self-determination. Liberalism basically holds a view of an atomic society, composed of lonely individuals permanently competing with one another for more freedom, wealth, power or pleasure. Competition may, indeed, stimulate, provoke creativity and contribute to progress in society.

But if the soil of commonality is too poor, self-determination turns into selfishness, competition becomes combat and competitors change into enemies. The corrections to liberalism are too weak to prevent the current fragmentation of societies towards more selfishness, less mutual commitment and less participatory democracy. 'It is concerned more to promote individual liberty than to secure public justice, to advance interests rather than to discover goods, and to keep men safely apart than to bring them fruitfully together' (Barber 2003: 4). We shall come back to this in the last chapter.

Common self-interest

I am a communitarian because of self-interest. Psychodynamics teach that we are all driven by self-interest. Rather than trying to repress this, we should accept it and include it in our social embedding. Each individual has the desire to shape his own life as he wants it – materially, relationally, religiously, culturally, esthetically and hedonistically. But this shaping is not absolutely free. Obstacles beyond our influence prevent us from achieving all we wish. Also socio-ethical considerations may keep us from going straightforwardly for satisfying our desires. Because we must live together, the options and behaviour of others affect our own opportunities. Inversely, my options and behaviour have an effect on the lives of others. That creates mutual entitlements and responsibilities.

On the one hand, I am entitled to demand an ethical account from others. The drunk driving of one driver is a risk for us all so that we are entitled to stop such driving. The misbehaviour of one professor towards the students reflects negatively on the whole university community, so that the misbehaviour is a matter for all professors and students. In a globalised world, the decision of one government to go to war draws everyone into a situation of increased fear and risk of terrorism and is thus subject to the moral judgment of the whole world.

On the other hand, my personal rights and liberties allow me to make my own choices, and thus I am confronted by my social responsibilities. I can opt for purely ruthless, selfish choices, or I can include the interests of others and of social life in the choices I make. Whereas extreme liberals would stress the right to go for selfish interests (while not always advising to actually do so), extreme communitarians would plead for social pressure or even obligation to opt for the socially oriented choices.

The debate between liberals and communitarians is a socio-ethical debate. Liberties are a crucial good to cherish, but the full use of all legal rights and freedoms is not always ethically advisable. The question how to combine individual freedom and rights with the promotion of high quality in social life cannot be resolved empirically or by new laws and rules. It is a matter of socio-ethical understanding.[3]

Opting for common self-interest

While we have no choice about living with others, we do have a choice about *how* we live with others. Liberals consider the others as competitors, with whom they make minimal agreements on the rules of competition and on guaranteeing one another sufficient space for self-determination. The option then is, in fact, to reduce mutual hindrance. Paradoxically, that will not serve the interests of the competitors. Defining and consolidating the negotiated space for self-determination would imply an everlasting combat for maximum space, yielding winners and losers. Yet the winners also lose, because they must defend themselves permanently against the non-resigned losers and against the losers who develop 'innovative' ways (Merton 1938) of achieving their goals. Consolidating their 'winning position' costs them part of their freedom, by hiding in so-called gated communities, through a reduction in mobility, through the need for security measures, through the price of the criminal justice complex, etc. As we shall see in Chapter 6, neo-liberal policy increases fear of crime and obsession with crime control, to the detriment of the quality of social life even of the rich and powerful. The winners become prisoners of the fear they created themselves.

Instead of considering the others as competitors, I can also bundle my self-interest with that of others. The others then become allies in a common project for more autonomy and my self-interest is integrated in what I call a common self-interest. We try to 'resolve the war of private interests through the creation of public interests' (Barber 2003: 19). Throughout history, human cooperation has made life longer, less dependent on natural elements, more self-determined, more comfortable and more pleasant. But other human achievements have caused new insecurities and threats. To minimise the risks of the latter and maximise the chances of the former, pure self-interest has to be channelled by the socio-ethical understanding that self-interest is best served by integrating it in a common self-interest, a project to achieve more autonomy by promoting a high quality of social life.

The idea of a common self-interest may sound like a *contradictio in terminis*. It merges in one notion the seeming contradiction we are all living in: we are individuals with particular needs, wishes and ambitions, but we also are living with others with whom we cannot but share opportunities and goods. Instead of suppressing one or both elements, the concept of common self-interest actively joins both in orienting self-interest to a project of common self-interest, which is seen in turn to serve individual self-interests.

Indeed, to gain more autonomy, we need each other. The rich need employees in their businesses and factories, construction workers to build their luxury houses, wine-makers for their wines, instrument builders and musicians to make the music they enjoy, police for their security. These workers also need one another, but they also need the rich to set up businesses and to pay taxes, so that the governments can provide the basics for all. At first sight, this may look like a kind of childish Legoland. But it is not.

The underlying idea is that the more smoothly these mutual dependencies operate, based on mutual respect and understanding, the more space there will be for each individual to enjoy liberty and live his life as he wishes. It is in my interest to live in peace, to be part of a community that gives me and the others maximum space, based on respect for plurality and solidarity. It is in my interest also that the other members of the community agree with one another, keeping peace and understanding in our communal life, allowing me to live in peace and to do my own thing. Living in such a community is the common self-interest.

It is self-interest because I invest in such a community for my own profit. I promote such a community life, not because I am an unworldly idealist, but because I hope to get the maximum possible benefits from being part of it. But it is more than self-interest, because I am not alone in going for these benefits. If we all invest in social life, we all profit from its high quality. We do not divide the benefits, together we increase them. The more we share a commitment to the community, the greater are my personal possibilities to enjoy freedom.

What is presented here is not just communitarianism, because without specification, community may lead to the excesses described above. The idea here advances a particular view on the quality of social life as a guiding utopia which recognises my self-interest and my pursuit of autonomy, but combines it with the particular pursuits of others into a project of common self-interest. I would therefore call it 'social life ethics' rather than communitarian ethics.

I am in good company in seeing a version of self-interest as the basic drive in a communitarian political agenda. Chapter 6 will elaborate more on this, but it should be mentioned here that Putnam, for example, writes that our good citizenship is not because we obey 'some impossibly idealistic rule of selflessness, but rather because we pursued "selfinterest rightly understood"' (Putnam 2000: 135). We invest in social life in general because we expect reciprocity from community and the society we are living in. Braithwaite and Pettit (1990) advance 'dominion' as a social conception of freedom. It is the mutual assurance that fellow citizens and the state will respect individual rights and freedoms that increases the individual enjoyment of those rights and freedoms. Barber's quest is 'how to resolve the war of private interests through the creation of public interests, or how to discern in man's social condition the potential for a civic and moral liberty that can transcend the natural and negative freedom of solitary beasts' (Barber 2003: 19). A glimpse of such an idea is even observed in some liberals. As we just saw, Rawls and Rorty, for example, 'season' their self-determination with some social concerns. It is in fact common self-interest, as Boutellier writes: 'Our solidarity is not a value in itself, but is based on the recognition and acknowledgement of each other's possible suffering' (Boutellier 2000: 15).

It is this intuition of having a common self-interest that motivates victims and offenders to meet and to try to understand one another with a view to reaching a constructive solution that can contribute to restoring peace between them and in the community.

Common self-interest as a norm

It is not given by nature that we invest our self-interest in the project of common self-interest. It is ethical advice, as is seen best if the common self-interest is apparently not respected. Obvious disrespect is easily observed. Selfish types straightforwardly pursue uncompromised self-interest in terms of wealth, power and hedonistic pleasure. They force through the self-interests we all have. We may have derogatory thoughts about it because they do not contribute their share to the common interest, but, as long as they do not hinder relations or social life, we do not act severely against it. Some people, however, behave ruthlessly – in business, politics, sports, or private life – to the detriment of others and of the quality of social life. When this occurs we actively reject it, because we consider it an intrusion into our common interest. If everyone behaved like that, social life would turn into a permanent war.

Some will say 'Well, that's life', but I do not want such a life. It is my ethical choice not to accept such a way of life, and I am entitled to do so because of my (our) fate to develop our lives together. In my assumption, inserting my self-interest in a project of common self-interest is both realistic and idealistic. It is a typical Sisyphean position. Giving in to cynicism would be a kind of self-fulfilling prophecy. Resigning oneself to leaving the rock of selfishness at the bottom of the hill is to give up the hope for a better life, to drag it down into an arena of heartless and ruthless struggle for the survival of the fittest. But rejecting cynicism is accepting active responsibility in the everlasting struggle for a better social life while knowing that we shall never reach the ideal. We must keep trying to lift up the perception of self-interest towards more commonality as an essential dimension in our self-interest. Continuously trying to do better is the only way of avoiding degradation into much worse.

At the opposite remove to the selfish actors in the extreme, some people seem to act against their own self-interest to serve others or social life in general. Self-sacrificing behaviour is shown by mothers for their children, by fire fighters for possible victims in a blaze, by soldiers for their country and even by suicide terrorists who offer their life for the religious or political cause they espouse (in the self-interested hope of being happy in heaven). Sometimes there may be some doubts as to whether such behaviour is truly disinterested, but that is not the point here. Such mothers, fire fighters and soldiers are often called heroes, as are the terrorists by their supporters. It expresses admiration for them as exceptional people, who far exceed our own modest capacities. In fact, we praise such behaviour out of fear of the opposite in ourselves: pure selfishness.

Erasing self-interest completely in favour of common interest is not the ideal. Not only is it unrealistic, it would also relegate us to a community with suffocating social pressure and soft control, or bring about a totalitarian regime without personal initiative, progress or pleasure. Examples of such communities and regimes exist, and they are not attractive. To put it bluntly: if everyone sacrificed himself totally for the common interest, nobody would be left to enjoy it.

Sympathy as a ground for developing common self-interest

Sceptics may claim that believing in common self-interest is naive. They will refer to the current hardening of social life and human relations, as is visible through the abuse of power in (international) politics, mercilessness in business, cynical exploitation of legal rights, loss of engagement in community and selfishness in daily life. These developments will be described more extensively in Chapter 6. They seem to leave little hope for common self-interest. But that is not the case.

It is an old wisdom that humans are bound by a basic empathy (see, for example, David Hume and Adam Smith, as in Braithwaite 2006: 402). One of the most striking examples of inter-human empathy was seen recently in the worldwide solidarity after the tsunami in South-East Asia in December 2005. The victims had no obvious connection with our everyday world, and there was no apparent self-interest in helping these people. Still, massive donations and support actions were set up, not only by governments and international organisations, but also by individuals and private groups. The only motive driving this huge movement was compassion with the victims. We spontaneously feel compassion when mass media show the miserable situations of refugees and victims of war, crimes or natural disasters.

At first sight, this observation confirms Rorty's previously mentioned position that human solidarity rests on a common wish to avoid suffering (Rorty 1989). But compassion with a sufferer is possible only through empathy, and empathy encompasses more than just the negative avoidance of suffering. We are also positively moved by the happiness of others, as displayed in movies or in real life (unless jealousy prevents it), and we enjoy the conclusion of peaceful agreements in which we are not directly involved. With people touched by war, we share the hope for peace. Humans are aware of their common self-interest, which is felt emotionally through empathy. It is the basis of their potential for mutual understanding and solidarity, despite differences in opinions and immediate interests. Solidarity goes far beyond negatively avoiding suffering; it is also the ground for constructing together a peaceful and emancipating community.

For several reasons, the potential for mutual empathy is not always activated to the same degree. The intensity depends on the degree of identification: we are more likely to sympathise with family members or fellow citizens than with more distant people. We support the football team of our own country, even if they play badly and brutally. Empathy may be diminished or blocked as a result of experiences in childhood, for example, or because of opposing immediate interests. Sometimes, the luck or success of others is experienced as a threat to our own prestige or interests, so that envy may prevent us from enjoying other people's good fortune. Living conditions and the stress of daily life may cause indifference. War situations lead to dehumanising the enemy. Persons diagnosed as psychopaths are even supposed to be psychologically incapable of feeling empathy. But these are variations and exceptions which do not alter the basic supposition that average people do in general feel empathy with other people.

Such deep human relationships are the key, for example, in the work of the French philosopher Emmanuel Levinas. Duyndam and Poorthuis (2003) open their book *Levinas* with the story of a tragedy as an illustration of Levinas' approach. In April 2002, the German town Erfurt was in shock. A student had walked around his school with a gun, killing 16 students and teachers. He finally faced his seventeenth potential victim, a teacher, in an empty classroom. The teacher called out to him 'Seh mich an!' [Look at me!]. But the schoolboy continued to curse and swear, and aimed his gun at the teacher. The teacher repeated 'Seh mich an!' And then suddenly, the boy dropped the gun and surrendered. What happened? What intangible force was stronger than the gun in the hands of the boy? The answer, in Levinas' words, is 'the face of the Other'.

Levinas' philosophy is not about ethics; it does not prescribe *how* we must behave. Its ambitions are to dig out the source of morals, to find out *why* we are unavoidably confronted with ethical responsibility. The source lies in the relation of the I with the Other. Morals are not, as in Kant, an imposed set of categorical imperatives resulting in absolute rights and wrongs, but are relational and located in life. The relation between me and the other begins with me. I cannot avoid being the centre of my world. The world exists for me only if I experience it. I discover the world and give it meaning. This is what Levinas calls *totaliser* (to totalise): through my observation, actions and giving meaning, I make the world my world.

The relation to another person, the other, is more complicated. I can make him a part of my world and consider him only in so far as he has a meaning for me. If I try to understand what the other feels and thinks, I do this through my own experiences; I consider the other as myself, as an *alter ego* (another I). But I can also consider the other as a fully fledged not-me, recognising the otherness (*altérité*) of the other. In the recognition of the other as an other, I transcend my own world and touch the infinite (*l'infini*). In my relation to the other, I am profoundly caught in a tension between totality and infinity[4] (Levinas 1966). It makes the other vulnerable: he can be totalised and reduced through my interests and meanings, or he can be recognised in his otherness.

Levinas finds a metaphor for this vulnerability in the image of the face. The other offers me his face and, in doing so, invites me to assume my primary responsibility towards him, to care for the other. This responsibility is the basis for all morality. All that can be said about the good life, in terms of norms and values, rights and duties, obligations and proscriptions, or ideals, is deduced from my relation with the other and the invitation it holds to take primary responsibility. This invitation does not follow from the other's intentional actions; it is an inherent consequence of the encounter. But it remains an invitation, not an obligation. I can freely accept the invitation or not. I can concretise the acceptance by assuming my responsibility in my own way. But I cannot escape being invited to take my primary responsibility to care for the other. The more the other is vulnerable and does not or cannot lay any claim, the greater is my responsibility.

Contrary to the social life ethics proposed in this chapter, Levinas does not rely on reciprocity. For him, it is not because of a self-interested hope for reciprocity that I assume my responsibility to care for the other. It is an intrinsic primary invitation with which I, and I alone, am confronted, and which I have to decide to take up or not. It may lead to self-sacrifice, causing some to call Levinas' work a philosophy of holiness (de Saint-Chéron 2006).

One does not, however, have to believe in holiness or in complete self-sacrifice to recognise that people are sensitive to others and to the commonality in their fate. The capacity for empathy and for sympathy is the intuitive ground on which common self-interest can be developed. Whereas the first is a social emotional intuition, the latter is a more cognitive, more socially constructed vision.

Promoting common self-interest

Common self-interest is not a natural condition. It is a social cognitive construction based on the social emotion of sympathy. It is an ethical standard, to be learned through enculturation in upbringing, education, social relations and experiences. It is to be cultivated and encouraged in the community and in state interventions.

According to Kohlberg moral development occurs throughout six stages, classified in three levels, from an 'obedience and punishment orientation' to a 'conscience or principle orientation' (Kohlberg 1976: 376). Children begin at the selfish moral level, avoiding trouble or seeking opportunities for satisfying one's own needs, and ideally end as adults with autonomous moral judgments based on universal and consistent principles. Not all individuals reach the end stage. Development depends on maturity and social learning. The point here is not to discuss Kohlberg's theory but to illustrate the idea that moral development begins with selfishness and that surpassing selfishness is a matter of education and learning.

Let me add another example. In his original version of the social control approach, Hirschi (1969) distinguished four bonds to society: attachment to persons, commitment in a line of activities, involvement in conventional activities and beliefs in social norms and values. In my view, we must understand the emergence of these bonds in a dynamic way. First, children attach to persons, to their caring parents and later possibly to their nursery school teacher. These attachments provide the starting motivation for the children to commit themselves in, for example, education and to become involved in activities which are promoted by the parents and the teachers as conventional. Later, when the commitment and the involvement provide gratifications on their own, the children will also comply more easily with the norms and the values which facilitate these activities and the extended attachment to the 'generalised other'. It is the original intimate and need-satisfying attachment which forms the basis for the development of a more comprehensive, socially embedded moral view.

Likewise, investing self-interested motivation into the project of common self-interest is to be learned and promoted. It begins with selfish children who, like all humans, may feel some empathetic intuitions with their carers. These intuitions are opportunities to make them experience satisfaction in being with others and doing things together with them. During their growing up, children can experience gratification if they contribute to a collaborative ambience in their family, the class room, in their neighbourhood, among their peers. Gradually they (and adults) can be made to understand that their self-interest is best served in a respectful and supportive social climate. The goal is to bring them to recognise that pursuing their own career, wealth and pleasure goes together with doing their share in the pursuit of high-quality social life, that this is not a limitation of self-interest, but a canalisation of it in a social approach to their own opportunities and welfare. The pedagogy of such understanding will focus on promoting primarily the ethical attitudes of respect, solidarity and taking active responsibility, which will be described more extensively in the next subsection.

Obviously, the school is an ideal environment for such pedagogy. Seeing the commonality in the pursuit of self-interest can be favoured through school programmes, the school ethos and in the way school performances are sanctioned positively and negatively. The latter must not only address the individual learning achievements, but appreciate also the socially constructive attitudes and behaviour, such as, for example, a cooperative and supportive attitude towards class mates, the contribution to a constructive class climate, the willingness for deliberation. And of course, using restorative processes in the response to school disciplinary problems is a crucial practice in such pedagogy.

But the school is not alone. Perceiving self-interest in close dependency with common interest is a vision that should be expressed in all social institutions and agencies, and be visible in all politics. It should, above all, speak through the way democracy is practised, as we will argue in Chapter 6.

Ethical guidelines serving common self-interest

The ideal form of living together is a utopia in which each individual enjoys a large margin of self-determination, in harmony with and supported by others who enjoy an equal margin and who cooperate in the quest for enlarging it. The margins and the harmony are not based simply on a negotiated distribution of liberty, but rather on the trust in the common self-interest that reciprocal help and support, when needed, will increase liberty for all. Hence, social life is based on permanent dialogue and participation. The distinction between society and community is meaningless, because the collectivity is governed with a view to individual and collective emancipation, in which autonomy and solidarity are not seen as opposed principles, but as mutually reinforcing. Social life draws its strength not from threat, coercion and fear, but from persuasion and motivation, based on trust, participation and mutual support.

The quality of social life depends on the commitment of the individuals. A collectivity that aims at this utopia promotes the socio-ethical attitudes that serve it. We could call them virtues. Ethicists list a number of welfare-oriented and duty-based virtues, such as hospitality, mercifulness, forgiveness, loyalty, honesty and the like. Each of these individual attitudes is indeed important in developing constructive and peaceful social relations. But they are in my view included in three attitudes which are fundamental in the furtherance of social life driven by the pursuit of common self-interest: respect, solidarity and active responsibility. I shall argue that values, such as justice or freedom, result from these three.

Respect
Respect is an attitude that recognises the intrinsic value of the

other. The recognition may be broad, taking in not only humans, but also nature and objects. It is ethical to respect nature as much as possible or not to destroy objects purposelessly. Respect is more than tolerance, which is a kind of resignation. I endure the noise of a youth party nearby because it would make things worse if I tried to stop it. I tolerate the tabloid press, but I do not see its intrinsic value and I do not respect it. Respect for humans recognises and esteems the intrinsic value of human beings. It is made concrete through the Universal Declaration of Human Rights, for example. The international community recognises that a number of rights are due to all humans, for the simple reason that they are human. Respect is recognisable also in the corrected liberal programmes as presented by Rawls or Rorty.

Respect for human dignity is a bottom-line obligation for all social institutions. Respect is the minimum condition for making living together possible. Respect for persons and groups in the community leads to acceptance of pluralism and multiculturalism. Agnostics, Christians, Jews and Muslims have different beliefs and ways of life, but these differences are not a reason for withdrawal of esteem. On the contrary, they result in deliberation on how plurality can be preserved and contribute to the quality of social life.

Disrespect is actively rejected. Racist political parties disrespect immigrants. Fundamentalist Muslims disrespect non-Muslims. Such groups threaten the quality of social life in our heterogeneous societies. They intrude upon our common self-interest. If persuasion is not effective, they must be confronted actively, and their behaviour may be criminalised and possibly referred to coercive justice interventions (which, as I argued in the previous chapter, are not based on a punitive apriorism). Not that hardened racists will become more respectful by the criminal justice intervention, but it is an important message to the public at large that disrespect is by no means tolerated.

Solidarity

Solidarity is more specific than respect. People do not naturally feel solidarity with objects or with nature. Solidarity presupposes more commitment than does respect, because it includes a form of companionship and reciprocity of support. It draws on the basic inter-human sympathy described earlier, and it is crucial in bundling our individual self-interests into the project of common self-interest. If combined with pluralism (a consequence of respect), solidarity yields more freedom. We depend on one another to preserve our liberties and we are companions in our pursuit to extend our freedom.

The solidarity I have in view is not selective. It is solidarity with all humans, not with peers only. It is easy to deploy solidarity with peers or with equal partners, because the expectation of reciprocity is at hand. But solidarity with the weak, with those who cannot demand or enforce anything, is more difficult to summon. But still, it is necessary. If there is no solidarity with the weak, the exclusive solidarity among the well-off would in fact increase the gap between them and the weak. It would boost the permanent competitive struggle in the pure liberal societies we described above. Solidarity is most easily activated within a particular community, but as common self-interest is not linked to an area, solidarity should also transcend the community level: 'this spirit of solidarity may be regarded as a forever-elusive promise of unpremeditated collective togetherness' (Pavlich 2001: 67).

Solidarity holds crucial added value in comparison with liberalism. It is more than avoiding suffering, as Rorty and Boutellier would say. To respect, solidarity adds the commitment to reciprocity, which contributes to common self-interest.

Unlike disrespect, a lack of solidarity cannot be actively suppressed. We are entitled to *demand* from one another not to degrade social life (through disrespect); we only can (and should) *promote* acting so as to improve social life (through solidarity). A society can exert solidarity and oblige its citizens to contribute to it by taxes and imposed contributions to social funds. But the attitude of solidarity cannot be imposed. Its lack is regrettable, but you cannot oblige people to feel companionship. A respectful relation without solidarity is meagre, but it can be a modus vivendi, a way to survive. It will not preclude living together, but it will yield a poor community life. Hence, a good society exerts solidarity and promotes it among its citizens to contribute to a richer community life.

Responsibility

Responsibility links a person to his acts and their consequences. It confronts the self with its own actions. Two kinds of responsibility exist. In passive responsibility, the person is confronted with his actions by others; this is typical in a top-down situation. Passive responsibility is central in the current criminal justice, where the offender has to submit to his responsibility for his acts, imposed by the system. Active responsibility contains a willingness to act. It is an awareness of the link between the self and the actions, and the behaviour that reflects this (Braithwaite and Roche 2001; Braithwaite 2002b).

Active responsibility is typical in leadership but does not automatically lead to ethically positive actions. Many tyrants and gang leaders probably take active responsibility for their choices and actions. That is why active responsibility must be exerted with a view to ethically desirable objectives.

As we shall see in Chapter 6, the active responsibility of citizens is indispensable to the quality of social life. Indeed, a good society depends on committed participation by its citizens or, in Putnam's terms, on social capital. Participants in social life, or citizens, must take their responsibility and respond actively and autonomously to the obligations of social life. In social-life ethics, active responsibility must be oriented towards solidarity with a view to building the common self-interest. In the ideal situation, members take active responsibility for combating disrespect and promoting solidarity.

Other social values

In a self-interested communitarian utopia, citizens behave according to these three ethical guidelines. However, our societies do currently not function like that and citizens mostly do not behave like that. In the absence of the ideal, we have to do with the achievable. Realistically, we must fall back on less idealistic guidelines to provide a minimum basis for living together. If we do not always take active responsibility driven by solidarity for all, we should at least try to keep as just a balance as possible in our relations, and guarantee for one another space for individual freedom. As long as we cannot summon up enough solidarity to achieve more social freedom for all, we have to divide the available space. It is the lack of these virtues in our current societies that makes it necessary to underline justice and freedom as separate goods.

Justice Justice is for Rawls, for example, the 'uncompromising ... first virtue of social institutions' (1973: 3). Justice suggests a balance of benefits and burdens, rights and obligations, equally spread. It is a situation, not an individual characteristic of a person, not a virtue. Persons can be more or less righteous, meaning that they are sensitive to justice, that they commit themselves to accomplishing justice where they can. The question is whether righteousness (or probity, or integrity) is a separate socio-ethical guideline, on the same level as respect, solidarity and active responsibility. I do not think so. In my view, taking active responsibility in view of expressing respect and achieving solidarity for all will automatically yield situations which are recognised as 'just' by the stakeholders. A community driven by solidarity and calculating less preconceived balances of justice will achieve more self-determination through common self-interest than one which would assure just balances but offer scarce solidarity only. A problem would occur if solidarity were selective and did not address equally all members of the community. We would then indeed have to fall back on an idea of balance called 'justice'.

But according to what principles do we calculate the balance? Is it just that one citizen lives in a villa in a Brussels suburb and possesses a yacht in Saint Tropez and a chalet in the Swiss Alps, while another citizen living a few kilometres away in a deprived neighbourhood can barely feed his children? Conversely, one might cynically observe that the university professor has to earn his living by getting up early every morning and working hard till late at night, while the unemployed can sleep as long as he wants and still receives his weekly allowance.

Religious, naturalistic, formalistic, utilitarian and care-oriented ethical systems propose different particular visions of how to consider the balance. Rawls' theory of justice (1973), for example, is based on a 'veil of ignorance', the assumption that all members of society are uncertain about their future social position, which keeps them from unjustly abusing their current position. However, research does not confirm the existence of this veil of ignorance. On the contrary, most people have the realistic awareness that their future social position depends largely on their current one.

Out there, 'there is no such thing as justice per se' (Derrida, quoted in Pavlich 2007: 621). The justice balance can take different shapes. Liberals advance justice as the crucial value, and then try to impose their view on how justice has to be understood. It prevents them from having to consider seriously the value of solidarity. Their distributive approach sees benefits and burdens to be divided through confrontation and negotiation of competing interests. It also yields conflicts and abuse of power. In societies based on a distributive concept of justice, conflict is endemic.

That is why I argued to frame the justice ideal in the concept of solidarity. The justice balance is then based on mutual care and partnership, not on formal rights. 'Where there is sufficient community peace, there will be relatively little need for order. Where there is little peace, more order will be needed' (Van Ness 2002: 142). In Duff, we read: 'If people are bound together by strong bonds of mutual affection or concern … there may be less need and less proper room for contractual definitions of their respective rights and obligations' (Duff 2001: 37). It is the lack of active responsibility for maintaining respect and solidarity which forces collectivities to fall back on formal justice. It is in the interest of the powerful to keep it like that. Hence the current position of justice as a separate and crucial ethical rule. In principle, it should not be like that. If citizens and institutions took their responsibilities for ensuring respect and solidarity for all, justice would follow automatically, but in a different shape.

Freedom   Liberal freedom is understood as a situation exempt from constraints. In such a conception, my freedom ends where the freedom of others begins. It is as if the amount of freedom is fixed, to be distributed among citizens. Others are rivals in my struggle for the maximum possible amount of freedom. If freedom is an individual good, it includes the freedom of the strongest to exploit the weakest and to bend the rules of justice to one's own interests. But unframed freedom leads to abuses. In Russia, for example, the collapse of the communist regime created space for a wild and uncontrolled capitalism. It resulted in a wide gap between, on the one hand, a few very rich 'plutocrats' who used the margins of deregulation to build their fortunes on fraud and corruption and, on the other hand, the rest of the population which remains poor and powerless. The commotion in April 2006 provoked by the Danish caricatures of Mohammed is illustrative of how unframed freedom of speech can breach the obligation to respect the sensitivity of others.

That is why absolute individual freedom cannot be a fundamental good. It has to be limited by norms that contribute to the quality of social life. Freedom is a social good which needs to be seen through more fundamental principles of respect and solidarity. By intrinsically respecting fellow citizens as they are, you grant them the possibility to be different and to behave accordingly. Furthermore, solidarity will lead to support for others to express their differences freely. Christians help Muslims to build their mosques. Adults help to create space for the young to express their youth culture. The rich help the poor to put their lives back on track. It will lead to more mutual respect and a larger margin for self-determination to live the differences.

Of course, being different and having different interests can raise conflicts. Conflict can be stopped by a powerful intervention, leading to frustration and continuous discontentment. A conflict can also be an opportunity for deliberation about how individual self-interests can be respected and related to the common self-interest. If it is embedded in a climate of mutual respect, there is a considerable chance that negotiation will lead to peaceful solutions. And expressions of solidarity will contribute to finding constructive outcomes. Freedom is not the result of a struggle for selfish interests; it is what we grant to one another.

Wrong against common self-interest

The quality of social life is advanced as the common self-interest. As a consequence, a wrong is what harms the quality of social life.

Are other wrongs imaginable? We have seen in the previous chapter that Duff, for example, distinguishes wrong from harm. In his view, criminal punishment sanctions not so much the causation of harm but the commitment of a wrong (Duff 2002). What could such wrongs be? The death penalty, killing in war, abuse of power to impose harsh living conditions on entire populations, torture of prisoners (suspected of terrorism) – all these actions could be called intrinsically immoral, but they are committed in and by self-declared 'model democracies'. In political and professional life, lying and cheating are common. In sports, committing so-called 'professional faults' is normal. Hence it seems that moral rules and attitudes to them are framed according to the interests they serve. Freud argued that our morality is basically a psychodynamic construct to keep our libido within socially acceptable channels. For Durkheim, the function of morality is to preserve cohesion in society.

Fundamentally, morality and social norms are pragmatic, to preserve self-interest and social life. Evil is not an abstract moral category, as opposed to another abstract category of good. Evil is what hurts or threatens my human dignity, my physical integrity, my social and material territory and comfort, and my common self-interest. Rejection of a wrong is less inspired by an intrinsic attachment to right than by a pragmatic aversion to what our community sees as a threat to our personal and social lives and comfort. 'Crime injures feelings only in a secondary and derived way. Basically, it is the interests which it hurts.'[5] Fortunately, self-interest is mostly well understood as common self-interest, in terms of living in a harmonious collectivity, in a good social life (Putnam 2000). It is difficult to imagine a moral wrong that would be beneficial to social life,[6] or a moral good that would be detrimental to social life. Socio-ethical wrongs and social harmfulness coincide almost entirely.

We are discussing here *socio*-ethics in a self-interested communitarian perspective. Our *individual* ethics may cover a wider realm than the social. Moral judgment is partially a personal affair based on personal criteria. But socially, the only touchstone is common self-interest. Some behaviour may be considered ethically reprehensible but be irrelevant for the quality of social life. We may find excessive gluttony or spending of money on senseless luxury decadent or even immoral, but it is difficult to forbid it. Men may wear a beard and women dress in a burka to please Allah. Others cover their head to express their attachment to Jahweh. Still others feel obliged to attend a religious service every week to pray to God. They do so because of personal religious beliefs. A good society must facilitate religious activities out of respect for plurality, but it cannot impose religious obligations on those who do not believe in Allah, Jahweh or God. That would degrade social life into an absolutist regime with no freedom of thought or speech. It is what happened in Afghanistan under the Taliban's rule. The achievements of the Enlightenment guaranteeing personal rights and freedoms would be lost. A Talibanised society is not what we want. The public rule is not pleasing God but participating constructively in social life. The quality of social life is the ultimate value in the quest for socio-ethics.

A society that serves the quality of social life will limit enforcement of public order and norms to what is needed to ensure this quality. Why, for example, is there a debate about whether criminal justice should intervene in some types of sexual behaviour among consenting adults or in the use of drugs? While there may be a large majority which considers such behaviours undesirable or even unethical, there is no agreement on whether they are so harmful to other people or to social life that they justify the authorities' intrusion into individual rights and freedoms. Authorities cannot interfere coercively in our lives unless it serves to prevent harm to fellow citizens or to public life.

This harm principle is found in many propositions (Feinberg 1991). Von Hirsch and Jareborg (1990) distinguish four types of 'damage to standards of living' to decide on the blameworthiness of a crime. Braithwaite and Pettit (1990) speak in terms of 'intrusion upon dominion'. Boutellier (2000) advances 'victimalisation' as the 'moral minimum' to underpin a commonly acceptable criminal justice system. They all consider harm or damage to others or to collective life as the reason to criminalise behaviour. Of course, behaviour may be harmful by accident whereas wrongfulness lies in the *intention* to cause harm. But still, wrongfulness depends on *the harm* intended, and the degree of wrongfulness on the degree of harm intended.

That brings us back to the core business of this book – responding to crime. If harmfulness is the reason for criminalisation, should the social reaction not aim primarily to repair the harm rather than to punish the wrong? This theme has been developed in the previous chapter and we now clearly see the logical inconsistency of defining crime in terms of harm, as the reason for prohibiting behaviour, and responding to it by punishing, making reparation of the harm more difficult.

Comparing ethics in restorative justice and in punitive justice

At the end of the previous chapter, the punitive apriorism in the current criminal justice system was rejected. We can now test this apriorism against the guidelines for an ethics oriented towards common self-interest. At first glance, advancing respect, solidarity and active responsibility as the basis of socio-ethical behaviour may seem to be mere rhetoric. Who would object to these virtues? Let us examine whether they also guide the current criminal procedures.

Is respect an ethical guideline in the punitive apriorism in criminal justice? Respect for the victim is absent, because he is not included in the punitive reflections. The victim can, of course, ask for compensation according to civil law, but this procedure is subordinated to the public criminal procedure. Punitive retributivism is focused on the offender. Considering the offender as a moral agent and treating him in a just way recognises him as a competent responsible human being who understands right and wrong and is able to make free choices and decisions, and as a citizen with guaranteed rights. Retributivists consider it an expression of respect when they state that offenders have the right to be punished. But the respect is not complete. The offender is not respected as a whole person with personal interests and interpretations, possibly including a willingness to make up for his misbehaviour. In the end, the offender has to submit to a proportionate punishment. Once a crime has been committed, respect for the person is withdrawn. The offender is judged as a moral agent to be considered guilty, but not as a morally and socially competent citizen who might be motivated to contribute to a constructive response to the problems caused by his crime.[7]

I do not see solidarity – companionship and mutual support – in the punitive apriorism. The response does not support the victim. The suffering and harm of the victim are registered only to assess the guilt of the offender, not as needs that are important per se. Support for victims is located at the margins of the criminal justice system and allowed only in so far as it does not impede the criminal justice investigation and procedure aimed at imposing a proportionate punishment on the offender. That does not help the victim. On the contrary, the punishment usually hampers possible reparation. In restorative justice, principled solidarity with the victim is evident, though we shall see that practice sometimes fails in this regard. Solidarity with the offender appears through the attempt to avoid social exclusion. On the contrary, the offender is encouraged to make up for his conduct in order to preserve his position as an integrated member in social life.

Responsibility is central to retributivism. Current penal justice holds the offender responsible by imposing on him the obligation to respond for his misconduct, but again the responsibility is incomplete. Responsibility only means being forced into criminal procedures and accepting the negative consequences. It is a passive, retrospective form of responsibility to which the offender is submitted by the criminal justice system. He is not supposed to take active responsibility in order to try to find a constructive solution to the problems he created. The victim, equally, is considered only as a passive object of the victimisation. His only responsibility is to contribute to the criminal procedure by reporting the crime and acting as witness. Current criminal justice in fact burdens its agents with a crucial form of active responsibility: they must censure criminal behaviour and impose proportionate punishments, and do so according to legal procedures and other standards. As we have seen, restorative justice largely relies on active responsibility. The offender's active responsibility includes the obligation to contribute actively to the reparation of the harm. The victim is encouraged, but not obliged, to assume the general citizen's responsibility for trying to find peace-promoting solutions. Restorative justice also stands for responsible collectivities, bound by obligations to search for socially constructive responses within the rules of law.

This brief comparison demonstrates that socio-ethical attitudes or virtues, such as respect, solidarity for all and active responsibility, are more clearly inherent to restorative justice than to the punitive apriorism. Hence restorative justice is more likely to contribute constructively to social life and relations. The priority for the quality of social life, as expressed in the communitarian utopia, underlies the bottom-up approach in restorative justice. It appears through a priority for informal regulations, as opposed to imposed procedures and outcomes. The point of departure for restorative justice, as in social life ethics, is that solutions must primarily be sought through the human and social resources in social life itself. This is opposed to the top-down approach in traditional criminal justice, where decisions are imposed according to strict rules, leaving restricted room for the views and interests of those directly concerned.

Conclusion

This chapter is based on two observations: (1) we all are pursuing self-interest in a broad sense, directly or indirectly; and (2) we cannot but be influenced and channelled by our inescapable living with others. From these observations, it follows that we can demand from one another that we do not hamper one another, and socio-ethically advise that we at least partly merge the achievement of our self-interest in a project of common self-interest, which is investing in the quality of our social life. Common self-interest expresses the intrinsic permanent tension between a tendency to satisfy our self-interest uncompromised and the ethical norm of channelling the achievement of our self-interests through a common self-interest. It may be seen as a paradox,[8] but it is a fundamental condition of our human existence. As for Sisyphus in the Greek myth, there is a permanent tension between the ideals we are pursuing and what we actually can achieve. An ideal community, as an area of shared values and interests, of mutual understanding, and of an emancipating balance between support and control, does not exist; it would be counterproductive to believe that it does. But still, we understand intuitively, based on partial and temporary experience, that such a community is a valuable ideal. We need this tension as a source of hope that things can go better than they currently do, and as a motivation to keep trying.

The majority of victims are not captured by anger or a need for revenge. What they want is repair, an explanation and the possibility of going on with their life in peace (Strang 2002). Most offenders understand that they have committed an unlawful act and that they risk a sanction for it, which they hope to keep as low as possible. That is probably a realistic estimation of how the two most prominent protagonists begin a restorative process. They hope to get something from it for their own sake. During the process, both begin gradually to understand that there is more. The victim becomes aware of the benefits he gets from the reparative actions by the offender and appreciates the restorative value of a well reintegrated offender; the offender realises the harm he has caused and understands that his social prospects will be better if he assumes his responsibility by making up for the harm he has caused. Both recognise that they have interest in finding a constructive solution, so that they can live in peace in a supportive social climate. Their self-interest is integrated in the project of common self-interest.

Common self-interest is the glue of social life. Promoting common self-interest is its drive. As we shall see in Chapter 6, it is observable in social movements and a multitude of social, political, educational and problem-solving practices focused on enhancing the quality of social life. The socio-ethical basis explored in this chapter encompasses more than responding constructively to crime. It is about how citizens participate decisively in the way society and community are governed through social, economic, welfare and cultural policies, and about how they are committed and interact in daily life. Restorative justice, in the restricted version presented in the first chapter, is part of this social movement, is largely inspired by it and aims to contribute to its development, but it does not encompass the whole of this view. Restorative justice does not aim to change the way we live, but the way we deal with crime.

It is now time to take the next step in our quest and look at restorative justice from the feasibility standpoint. In the next chapter, a survey of the available data will help us to find out whether, and to what extent, the ambitions of restorative justice are achievable in reality.

Notes

1 In the same sense, Nussbaum (1993) contrasted the old Greek concepts 'dikê' (Plato), the strict retributive approach which 'knows neither equity nor grace, but only cares for strict and simple justice' (Nussbaum 1993: 219), with 'epieikeia' (Aristoteles), which recognises 'imperfect human efforts and complex obstacles to doing well' (ibid.: 219), and leads to equity, mercy and more constructive ways of responding to crime. Nussbaum also called this 'good feminist thought' (ibid.: 248).

2 So, for example, conferencing in welfare issues or in school contexts may, more than conferencing in criminal matters, be seen through the ethics of care.

3 The moral relationship between pursuing self-interest and acting for the good of others is the subject of Bloomfield (2008). As this appeared after this manuscript was sent to press, I could not give it the full attention it deserves.

4 *Totalité et infini: essai sur l'extériorité* (1961) is considered the first grand opus by Levinas.

5 'Le crime ne blesse les sentiments que d'une façon secondaire et dérivée. Primitivement, ce sont les intérêts qu'il lèse' (Maxwell 1914, cit. in Debuyst 1990: 357).

6 Some would not agree. They may suggest that, for example, torturing a prisoner in order to extract information about criminal or terrorist networks may be ethically reprehensible, but beneficial for preserving safety in social life. It is not my view. The ethical rejection of inhumane and cruel treatment is not an abstract rule but based on a fundamental human right which is meant to safeguard a minimal quality in the way people and states interact. Moreover, one can doubt whether authorising torture really is constructive for social life.

7 This objection applies less to Duff's approach to punishment (2001), but the problem remains the punitive apriorism.

8 As Dan Van Ness wrote in a comment on an earlier version of this chapter: 'It is as though a person has articulated all the reasons to disbelieve that there is a God but then proposes living according to Christian values.'

Chapter 4

Examining restorative justice practice

While certainly not all current restorative justice practices are based on an elaborated socio-ethical approach, as developed in the previous chapter, the majority of them are inspired by similar socio-ethical intuitions. They are based on a belief that restorative processes and objectives are 'better', 'more constructive' or 'more just' than the punitive apriorism and formalism in the current criminal justice system. But do restorative justice practices actually achieve what they promise? Brilliant ideas may indeed turn out badly in practice. A systematic check is needed of what restorative practices bring about in reality. In this chapter, I take stock of what is currently known so far.

Restorative practices are being implemented for an increasingly broad range of crimes, including the most serious, all over the world. A growing number of countries and states provide dispositions in their legislation that favour responses with a view to reparation. International organisations have recently issued statements and recommendations endorsing a restorative approach to offending. At first glance, this expansion alone suggests that restorative justice practices are indeed a feasible response to crime, and that they are attractive to an increasing proportion of the population, justice officials and policy-makers. But that may be too simplistic a conclusion. There is a need for a deeper and more nuanced exploration. We shall begin with an examination of the available empirical assessments.

Empirical research on restorative justice practice

Regular consultation of the several websites on restorative justice and restorative practices reveals an almost daily increase of empirical assessments. They range from small local tests to broad international comparative projects. Today's conclusions are likely to be out of date tomorrow. The following brief survey is based on several good quality surveys and meta-analyses, with a particular focus on victim–offender mediation and conferencing (Latimer *et al.* 2001; Kurki 2003; McCold 2003; Bonta *et al.* 2006; Sherman and Strang 2007). They all mention serious methodological shortcomings, which is for McCold one of the reasons[1] to conclude that 'research on restorative justice practice is a mile wide, but only an inch deep' (McCold 2003: 106).

Research to evaluate human interventions is always precarious. This is true not only for research on restorative justice practices, but also for evaluations of traditional punishment, prevention and treatment programmes. The meta-analyses in the 'what works' research tradition, for example, list a number of methodological shortcomings in many evaluations (Sherman *et al.* 1997; Andrews and Bonta 2003), including unclear indication of measurable programme objectives, invalid instruments, absence of or inadequate control groups, doubtful external validity, problematic measurement of reoffending, over-optimistic interpretations by committed believers and lack of attention to undesirable side effects. In addition, the evaluation of restorative justice is confronted with a few particular challenges (McCold 2003; Bazemore and Elis 2007; Hayes 2007), as will become clear in this chapter.

A preliminary empirical question is whether restorative justice processes actually take place. Not all offences reported to the system are referred to restorative processes. The 'system selection bias' is caused by the referring agencies which screen out cases that they consider – rightly or not – inappropriate for such a scheme. A 'self-selection bias' occurs between the referral and the encounter. Some programmes do not accept all cases referred because they seem not to match their criteria or capacities. For several reasons, invited stakeholders may choose not to participate. Sceptics expect that a voluntary meeting between victim and offender will take place in only a minority of cases, mostly involving benign offences among acquaintances.

To check the feasibility of restorative processes and to estimate the external validity of the empirical investigation, the several steps in the selection must be charted. Registered crimes are filtered by the system for referral to a restorative process; referred cases are filtered by practitioners and by the refusal of potential participants; not all cases processed lead to successful conclusions. The differences between the groups at each selection stage reduce the scope of the research results.

McCold found that 'approximately half of the cases referred to programmes never reach a hearing' (McCold 2003: 89). The rate varies between 10 per cent and more than 90 per cent, and depends on many variables, such as type of programme, type of crime, target group, the previous relation between the victim and the offender and the social context of the programme. If the meeting takes place, the agreement rate varies between 72 and 100 per cent, and the rate of compliance with the agreement varies between 38 and 96 per cent. Several systematic factors influence these scores.

Victims

Consistent with the paradigm shift in restorative justice, we look first at the possible impact of restorative practices on victims. Surveys indicate that between 20 and 80 per cent of victims are willing to participate in mediation or conferencing. Most programmes report over 50 per cent willingness. The participation rate depends partly on the nature and the seriousness of the offence, but surviving family members may also participate after murders (Umbreit et al. 2003). Victims' participation rates also depend on offender characteristics. They are higher with juvenile offenders than with adults, lower if offenders belong to an ethnic minority.

Of crucial importance is the process by which the victims are invited. Reasons mentioned for non-participation are fear of being confronted with the offender (and his family), apprehension about losing control over one's own anger and unwillingness to spend more time on the case. Principled rejection of the restorative approach is found rather seldom. Maxwell and Morris (1996) found that only 4 per cent of victims explicitly wanted a punitive judicial procedure. In a sample of 45 victims, we found only one who advanced reasons of principle for refusing to attend the conference (Vanfraechem 2003).

The satisfaction of the participants is one of the most researched variables in assessments of restorative justice. While this may seem too superficial and general a concept, it is an important one (Van Ness and Schiff 2001). Because restorative processes put the decision on how to repair the harm in the hands of the direct stakeholders, it is logical to look for subjective criteria that express their feelings.

Satisfaction means that the participants acquiesce with the conference or mediation and its outcome. It does not mean that they are completely happy or enthusiastic. Satisfaction is to be understood in relation to what they expected. Sometimes, satisfaction is a kind of relief, because the event went better than they feared. Moreover, satisfaction is a container concept that covers a broad diversity of feelings and subjective evaluations.

Satisfaction is one of the most general and stable findings. Victims who participate in mediation or conferencing are significantly more satisfied than those who go through a traditional judicial procedure (Strang 2002; Dignan 2005; Sherman and Strang 2007). They perceive a high degree of procedural justice, appreciate the communicative value of the encounters, and find the outcomes more just than traditional judicial sanctions. Victims also suffer less post-traumatic stress after a conference, and have less fear and anger and more sympathy for the offender (Dignan 2005; Strang and Sherman 2005; Strang et al. 2006). The great majority of victims are of the opinion that all victims should be offered an opportunity to attend a conference (Vanfraechem and Walgrave 2004).

Nevertheless, not all victims are equally satisfied (Daly 2005a), and a small percentage are even more in distress after the process than they were before (Maxwell et al. 2004). Still, this proportion is significantly lower than among those who go to court. Most of the dissatisfied victims had been involved in poorly monitored conferences (Strang 2002).

Our conclusion must remain cautious, however. The high satisfaction scores are found in a selected group, i.e. those who were prepared to participate. One can expect that satisfaction would be lower among those not participating. Moreover, in conferencing victims meet with an offender who has already confessed which is certainly not always the case in court sessions. And the confession of the offender is crucially important for the victim's feelings (Daly 2005a). Therefore it only appears that those victims who are willing to participate are not disappointed. There are also indications to suggest that many of those who did not participate would have been more satisfied if they had.[2]

Offenders

Among offenders, willingness to participate in a restorative process is also high. For example, Strang et al. list participation rates between 100 per cent and 58 per cent in their survey of several conferencing applications (Strang *et al.* 2006). The offender's motivation is not clear. Probably many of them simply hope to come out better that way than if they went to court. That is not necessarily a problem. As long as it does not lead to secondary victimisation for the victims, one can realistically expect and accept that the offender begins a meeting with some calculation. We would all do the same. We shall see that the process during the meeting itself makes most offenders understand what they caused and to become increasingly emotionally involved and less rationally calculating.

Satisfaction rates among offenders are very high. Bonta *et al.* (2006) mention an average expression of satisfaction of 87.7 per cent. McCold (2003) found more feelings of fairness and satisfaction in the programmes characterised by the highest degree of stakeholder participation. He also found that the correlation between victim satisfaction and offender satisfaction was high, so that the pursued win–win situation seems to be achieved.

As reoffending is a peculiar subject creating great public interest, it is a matter for a separate subsection.

Reoffending

'Evaluating a new paradigm by the criteria of the old paradigms is inappropriate' (McCold 2003: 95). Restorative interventions are not a new treatment programme. They express another paradigm, in which repairing the harm is the primary objective. While reoffending is not the first concern of restorative justice, the bottom line is that restorative justice interventions should not provoke more recidivism than traditional interventions. If they did, the effect would be negative for public safety, causing additional harm to peace and safety in the community. Moreover, increased reoffending after restorative processes would be detrimental to the public and political acceptability of restorative justice.

Despite the many methodological difficulties, to which I shall come back later, the available results are not unequivocal and do not lead to triumphant conclusions. Sherman and Strang (2007), for example, conclude from their survey of randomised controlled trials that the (mostly police-led) conferences significantly reduced repeat offending among violent offenders under 30 years of age in Canberra, but produced little or no difference among violent males under 18 years in Northumbria. A significant reduction was found among male property offenders under 18 in Northumbria, but little or no difference among property offenders under 18 in Canberra.

A few restorative justice schemes seem to increase reoffending compared with traditional criminal justice sentencing (Latimer *et al.* 2001). It is not always clear why but some hypotheses can be advanced. Sherman and Strang (2007), for example, noted more rearrests among young Aboriginals for property offences in Canberra, and refer to comparable (but non-significant) observations among young Hispanics in Bethlehem (Pennsylvania) (McCold and Wachtel 1998). My hypothesis is that the increases were a direct consequence of the police facilitation of the conference. If ethnic minorities have poor relations with police, which is often the case, police-led conferences may provoke more defiance than compliance.

Bonta *et al.* (2006) used methodological requirements to select 39 studies of restorative justice programmes, broader than just conferencing, for meta-analysis. The overall effect was about a 7 per cent lower rate of repeat offending compared with traditional criminal justice handling of cases. There was little variation in the mean effect across samples (adults/juveniles) and types of intervention. Studies published after 1996 reported greater effects than those published earlier, and this was attributed to the higher intrinsic quality of the projects. The schemes yielded little effect if they were contextualised within criminal justice sanctions. Those outside the criminal sanction system produced up to a 10 per cent reduction. Better results were achieved in programmes targeting mostly violent offenders, which is in line with other outcomes reported for violent crimes (Sherman *et al.* 2000; Hayes 2005) and serious crimes (Sherman 2003). This is paradoxical when one observes that conferences are applied mostly to divert rather benign youth offences from court. Better effects are also achieved with low-risk offenders (violent offenders do not necessarily have a higher risk of reoffending).

Retrospective studies confirm that the best predictor of reoffending is not whether there is a conference but rather prior life experiences and offending and the social prospects of the (young) offender (Maxwell *et al.* 2004, Hayes and Daly 2004). One can indeed imagine that a single intervention may have more influence on a young person who still has intensive bonds to social life than one who has drifted far away from social norms and values. It is probably in the same sense that we must understand why more young offenders desist after conferencing than older ones (Hayes and Daly 2004).

Many of the above-mentioned studies and surveys compare restorative justice practices as a whole with current criminal justice. They do not differentiate sufficiently among the various modalities and versions, while Maxwell *et al.* (2004) and Hayes and Daly (2003) have shown that the quality of the conference matters. 'Good outcomes depend on good practice', Maxwell summarises (Maxwell 2007: 65). Less reoffending was observed after family group conferences that were experienced as 'fair, forgiving, allowing to make up for what they had done and not stigmatising or excluding them' (Maxwell *et al*. 2004: 214). When the offender expressed remorse and a consensus was reached, conferences were more effective (Maxwell and Morris 1999; Hayes and Daly 2003). It is not clear, however, whether remorse is provoked by the quality of the conference or is part of a compliant attitude of the offender which existed prior to the conference.

An important element is the follow-up after the conference. If the conference is followed by systematic support or treatment for the offender, the risk of recidivism is much lower (Maxwell *et al*. 2004). A well conducted conference is an excellent opportunity to start such support. Daly (2005b) found, for example, that sexual offenders were more likely to accept treatment after a conference than when they had been given a punitive sentence. 'It may be not the role of restorative justice facilitators to deliver treatment programming; yet it would be useful if they would recognize the need for treatment and the type of programming that would assist in reducing offender recidivism, and make the appropriate referrals for treatment' (Bonta *et al*. 2006: 117). This is not contradictory to the particular restorative justice objectives, but may be seen as complementary to them.

All in all, the results regarding reoffending are complicated and sometimes contradictory. Restorative justice interventions are not a magic potion to eliminate recidivism. There is a tendency to reduce reoffending, but a few studies report more. One of the main reasons for the confusion may be the lack of differentiation in the independent variables. Restorative practices differ in the technical quality of the facilitating process, in the type and version of practices, in the (absence of) judicial context, in target groups, etc. (McCold 2003). All these variants may influence outcomes, including reoffending. For example, one cannot deliver recommendations on restorative justice for ethnic minorities in general on the basis of data from police-led conferences only. Equally, there are reasons to believe that the characteristics of family group conferencing in its original New Zealand context, described in Chapter 1, are more able to deal with serious offending than the police-led diversionary conferencing schemes. Such differences matter, and should be included more systematically in assessment research.

Parker (2005) concludes that there is no proof that restorative justice reduces recidivism. He points to the so-called 'what works' research to indicate what should be done. 'What works' refers mainly to a series of meta-analyses of earlier evaluations of treatment and prevention programmes aimed at identifying the characteristics that might be effective in reducing recidivism. Bonta *et al.* (2006), for example, list three principles for effective rehabilitation: (1) the intensity of the intervention must be in proportion to the offender's risk of reoffending; (2) the programmes must target the direct criminogenic needs rather than indirect non-criminogenic needs; (3) the programme must be tailored to the learning style of the individual. Cognitive-behavioural programmes that appeal to the active responsibility of the offender are more effective than other treatment or punitive approaches (McGuire and Priestly 1995). No programme is infallible. The reductions in reoffending are always limited and do depend on the kind of the intervention, on the characteristics of the target groups and on many factors beyond the scope of the programmes (Loesel 2007). In fact, the 'what works' tradition should be renamed as 'what works sometimes'.

Actually, restorative justice practices do offer an excellent basis for implementation of the principles just listed (Bazemore and Bell 2004). Well conducted restorative mediations and conferences focus on direct relational needs, go straight to the crime and its consequences, appeal to the offender's active responsibility and offer a cognitive reparation experience in a 'no-nonsense', well structured way, which is perfectly understandable for all participants.

One principle, however, deserves special attention in restorative justice evaluation. Bonta states that the intensity of the intervention must be in proportion to the offender's risk of reoffending. Most evaluations have measured the reoffending after the restorative meeting, in isolation from the after-care. It may be naive to expect that a conference of a few hours could on its own change a life course that is sometimes going wrong from birth. But we just saw that the meeting is an excellent opportunity to begin treatment and other social support afterwards. A well conducted restorative encounter offers more than the traditional judicial procedure: an opportunity for the offender and his family to recognise that things are going wrong and should change. They may be more ready to accept treatment afterwards. For the reoffending issue, the quality of the follow-up is at least as important as the conference itself and should be included in the evaluation studies.

Despite the partial congruence of restorative justice practices with treatment in the 'what works' style, a profound contradiction subsists. Whereas restorative justice views the offender as a moral agent, capable of taking responsible and constructive options if adequate conditions are fulfilled, the 'what works' approach does not. 'What works' sees the offender as a bearer of risks and examines what kind of treatment is to be applied to him. The offender is viewed as the passive object of the intervention, in the same way as the machine to be repaired is viewed by the engineer.

In that respect, the Good Lives Model in offender rehabilitation, as presented by Ward and Maruna, is more in line with the restorative justice philosophy (Ward and Maruna 2007). The Good Lives Model 'begins from the assumption that offenders are essentially human beings with similar needs and aspirations to nonoffending members of the community' (ibid.: 24). The best possible chance for offender rehabilitation is the offender's motivation. 'Yet, without their support, no one will ever save rehabilitation' (ibid.: 176). The great majority of offenders aspire to leave their socially marginalised lifestyle and to become respected law-abiding citizens, but many of them are unable to make that turn on their own. Without a realistic hope that the aspiration can come true, they will not commit themselves to an enduring effort to surpass the crime-prone situation. Appropriate help can foster such hope. That is why Ward and Maruna call their approach 'what helps' instead of 'what works'. Restorative justice fits well in this view. As described earlier in this chapter, a restorative process is an opportunity for the offender to discover positive ways of being somebody. Being offered the possibility to make up for the harm caused and to feel respect for that may open the window on a more socially integrated future and thus be a major motivation in the offender's quest for rehabilitation.

Still, having an impact on the offender is not the primary aim of restorative justice programmes, though it can be a part of the 'balanced' reparative goal (Bazemore and O'Brien 2003; Bazemore and Bell 2004). Even if research on restorative justice does not convincingly demonstrate a general positive impact on reoffending, the overall results are encouraging. The participation rate is higher than sceptics would expect; victims and offenders report that they are better off after such a process; and there is evidence that recidivism is no worse. And that is what matters in the coherent restorative justice approach. How can these results be explained? The next section examines the possible theoretical understandings of a restorative justice process.

Trying to understand restorative processes

A constructive meeting between a victim and an offender would not seem likely. Victims and offenders would seem by definition to be opponents. Mostly, their initial view of what happened would be contradictory, and it would seem difficult to find any common ground on which to base a fruitful exchange. As will be explained in Chapter 6, the current hardening of social life probably does not make things easier in that respect. Yet the fact is that people do come together to find peace-promoting solutions. And the practice is spreading fast. How can that be explained?

First, the socio-ethical assumptions, outlined in the previous chapter, appear to be confirmed in practice. Restorative justice philosophy rests on a belief that, despite their contrasting roles and initially contradictory views of the incident, victims and offenders have reasons to be motivated to try to find a constructive solution. And it happens, indeed. If the appropriate conditions are shaped, both victims and offenders are usually brought to understand that they share a common self-interest in an authentic dialogue, with a view to a constructive settlement and the social peace it facilitates. In terms of the Levinasian philosophy on human relations, a restorative encounter brings many victims and offenders to look each other in the face, to see each other's vulnerability and to feel invited to assume responsibility towards each other.

Theoretical models

'Research on restorative decision-making must be viewed as in the stages of relative infancy' (Bazemore and Schiff 2005: 326). So far, most research on restorative justice has tried to find out *whether* such processes work, rather than *why* or *how* they may work. The volume of empirical work to explain how restorative justice practices work, according to which mechanisms and emotional dynamics, is relatively small. But hypotheses can be advanced, based on a rich fund of theories on human and criminal behaviour and its treatment. Many of these theories are supported by empirical data, some of which are collected in restorative settings. Braithwaite presents a number of them to explain why restorative justice processes might be effective and speculates about why restorative justice might work better for prevention, rehabilitation and deterrence (Braithwaite 2002: 73–136). Bazemore and Schiff categorise possible theoretical explanations along three core principles: repairing harm, stakeholder involvement and community/government role transformation (Bazemore and Schiff 2005: 43–95; Bazemore and Elis 2007). These authors import theoretical explanations from other social contexts for use in restorative justice. Harris (2003), on the other hand, uses restorative justice theory to identify four 'procedural aims' to steer restorative processes towards positive outcomes: empowerment, restoration, reintegration and emotional resolution.

I will not draw up a new list but describe briefly the theories I see as most relevant. First of all, restorative justice processes seem to avoid some deficiencies inherent in penal justice. In Chapter 2, I mentioned the scarcity of communication in traditional criminal justice. The formalised settings and the threat of punishment make authentic communication of what happened and why almost impossible. This dramatically reduces the potential for a positive impact on the stakeholders. Restorative justice processes, on the contrary, offer ample potential for authentic communication.

Sherman (1993), for example, opposed his defiance theory to the traditional deterrence expectations in classical penal theories. In his view, the extent to which offenders experience sanctions as arbitrary or illegitimate will affect their resistance against the authorities that imposed the sanctions. The day-to-day functioning of the criminal justice machine provokes defiance rather than compliance.

Among the positive theoretical hypotheses as to why and how restorative justice processes function as they do, a crucially important theory is reintegrative shaming (Braithwaite 1989). The core of it is, in Braithwaite's words, '(1) that tolerance of crime makes things worse; (2) that stigmatization, or disrespectful, outcasting shaming of crime, makes crime worse still; and (3) that reintegrative shaming, or disapproval of the act within a continuum of respect for the offender and terminated by rituals of forgiveness, prevents crime' (Braithwaite 2002a: 74). If shaming is stigmatising, as in most court interventions, the risk is psychosocial identification with non-conformism and further offending. If, on the contrary, shaming is focused on the behaviour and not on the person, and is followed by gestures of reacceptance, it is a powerful emotion that can lead to desistance from reoffending. This theory was boosted in criminology in the 1990s, and has been predominant in the restorative justice literature. Restorative conferences were seen as an ideal scene of 'successful reintegration ceremonies' (Braithwaite and Mugford 1994).

Since then, several criticisms have challenged the original version of the theory. First, the centrality of the shame emotion in restorative encounters has been nuanced and completed. Other (moral) emotions

111

and dynamics, such as guilt, remorse and empathy, seem to play an equally important role (Walgrave and Aertsen 1996; Morris 2002a; Karstedt 2002; Van Stokkom 2002; Faget 2006).

Secondly, it has been recognised that shame, as such, does not necessarily lead to compliance (Scheff and Retzinger 1991). Being submitted to a shaming experience can lead to reintegrative gestures, but also to disintegrative reactions. It can provoke a kind of defiance, comparable with what Sherman (1993) suggested after court interventions, expressed through denial of responsibility or anger at the shamer. It thereby becomes a very destructive emotion. That is why later versions have completed the reintegrative shaming concept: it is not shame as such but 'acknowledged shame' that is the constructive emotion which may lead to accepting responsibility and being prepared to comply. 'Shame acknowledgement involves the discharging of shame through accepting responsibility and trying to put things right. The opposite is a resistance to accepting responsibility and making amends. Shame displacement means displacement of shame into blame and/or anger towards others' (Braithwaite and Braithwaite 2001: 12).

Thirdly, reintegrative shaming theory was developed originally to orient the prevention of crime and reoffending. It was only later that conferencing was 'discovered' as an excellent process to make shaming work reintegratively. But it still focuses on what happens to the offender. Because restorative processes are focused at least as much on emotional and other benefits to the victim, reintegrative shaming is too limited in scope. Some (Umbreit and Zehr 1996; Dignan 2005) fear that programmes relying too much on reintegrative shaming theory risk being less restoration-oriented and using the victims as 'shamers' or 'props' instead of focusing genuinely on the victims' needs.

It is, however, difficult to avoid an offender feeling shame if he is personally confronted with the rejection of what he did as in conferencing or mediation. To reduce the risk that shame remains unacknowledged, the social emotional climate of the experience is crucial. Here is where the theory of procedural justice comes in (Tyler 1990; Tyler and Huo 2002). This theory opposes the punitive model of enforcing compliance with the law to the procedural justice model. In their contacts with the police and justice system people are more concerned with the way they have been treated than with the outcome of the procedure. Procedural justice focuses on the subjective sense of being treated fairly with respect and equity, being taken seriously and being listened to by the authorities. The basic assumption is that when people are treated with procedural justice, 'they view law and legal authorities as more legitimate and entitled to be obeyed' (Tyler 2006: 308). Procedural justice is crucial for belief in the system's legitimacy, for both victims and offenders. It brings about a shift from the motivation to avoid punishment by an external power towards an internal motivation to comply with a legitimate authority. The characteristics of a restorative justice meeting offer better conditions for the stakeholders to feel such procedural justice than traditional court proceedings (Tyler 2006). The empirical assessment mentioned earlier confirmed that both victims and offenders feel fairly and respectfully treated in a conference. It is probably the main reason why they acquiesce with the process and with what is agreed. It is a crucial (but not sufficient) basis for both to begin to (re)construct their lives as (re)integrated citizens.

In addition to being treated fairly, the support and confidence of the loved ones provides a strong platform for a new start. Bazemore and Schiff (2005) refer to Cullen's idea of social support as a crucial concept in understanding what happens in conferencing and its aftermath. Victims and offenders who can rely on ongoing relationships of informal control and support will benefit in a conference. These 'natural helpers' are empowered in a conference to provide ongoing guidance and assistance, and to support healing and adjustment in the aftermath of the crime and the conference. The idea recalls Hirschi's theory of social bonds (1969), especially the attachment bond. There are indeed reasons to believe that a successful conference may help tighten social bonds, so that they are an informal social platform for reparation and for social reintegration afterwards.

If participants experience procedural justice and feel supported by their informal network, shame can be acknowledged and can become reintegrative. For offenders, it may be the starting point for reconstructing their identity in a more socially conformable way. Maruna (2001) found that desistance from further criminality depends most of all on the opportunity to 'make good', meaning to reform the conception of the self as a social-norm-compliant person. External events may provoke a relatively sudden awareness that life can and must be changed (Laub and Sampson 2001). Sherman (2003) suggests that restorative encounters may facilitate such 'epiphanies' (as he calls them). Maruna also presents restorative conferences as redemption rituals, and sees the opportunity to repair what has been done wrong as a major chance to build a new identity. In terms of the Good Lives Model presented briefly above, a restorative justice encounter can be very helpful for the offender to turn the page and start the journey towards social rehabilitation.

Finally, as argued above, well monitored restorative justice processes offer an excellent context in which to implement the principles of effective correctional treatment, as advanced in the 'what works' research tradition (Bazemore and Bell 2004).

Except for the procedural justice theory, the theories mentioned so far focus mainly on the offender. Strang *et al.* (2006) advance a theoretical approach concerning the victim. Cognitive behavioural therapy indicates that 'victims may extinguish their fear by repeatedly reliving their trauma or confronting people involved in trauma in safety and far from the fearful place where the event occurred' (Strang *et al.* 2006: 285). Moreover, cognitive behavioural therapy offers the victims an opportunity to be shown that they were not responsible for what happened to them. Restorative justice encounters obviously present a context wherein the victim can relive and confront the victimisation in a safe and respectful climate, which may help to reduce the post-traumatic stress.

Strang *et al.* also refer to Collins' theory on interaction rituals (Collins 2004), which may help to understand the socio-emotional dynamics of a restorative conference. In this theory, interaction rituals are meetings characterised by four features: (1) participants are physically present and influenced by proximity; (2) participation is clearly defined as distinguished from non-participation; (3) all participants focus on a common target; and (4) all participants are moved by a common emotional mood. Restorative encounters clearly respond to these characteristics. Interaction rituals may provoke 'collective effervescence', a high emotional intensity which concentrates the emotions on the common goal. It can be applied to the intensive emotional dynamics in a restorative process and help to explain why they so often lead to constructive and satisfying outcomes, including apologies and forgiveness.

A sequence of moral emotions

Let me try now to bring some sequential order to the above, based on a theoretical ideal sequence of moral emotions suggested by Harris *et al.* (2004).

We think that most offenders will begin the session with embarrassment as they are exposed to possible blame. Probably, many offenders also feel at the beginning some vague shame and guilt: they understand that they have misbehaved, disappointed their parents and caused trouble or harm. These unpleasant and disempowering feelings can provoke some defiance, initiating a process towards unacknowledged shame. Most will hope to get through the process in the least uncomfortable way possible. Victims' emotions at the beginning are linked directly to their victimisation: the offence has caused harm and was humiliating. They feel shame and possibly embarrassment over the humiliation they have undergone (Strang 2002), but also want this suffering 'made right', because they know the intrusion was unjust. Victims probably hover between two ways of making things right: punitive retribution, which would consist of inflicting an equal humiliation and suffering on the offender, or restoration, which would be requesting reparation or compensation for the prejudices caused by the offence.

These emotional starting points can orient the rest of the conference. An unremorseful or defiant offender can immediately cause greater dismay and additional indignation in the victim and others, provoking escalation of the conflict, stigmatisation and secondary victimisation. It is therefore crucial to create a secure climate of respect and fairness, and to make sure that procedural justice is experienced from the beginning and support from the 'natural helpers' is clearly felt. Many offenders will then be able to take a vulnerable position and accept responsibility. In such a climate, victims will also understand more easily that the conference cannot respond to their expectations from the very beginning.

Then the victim tells his story of harm and suffering, fear and anger. In doing so, the victim shows the suffering to which he has been subjected and invites the participants to 'look at me', in a Levinas-like sense. Most offenders, confronted with that, will be touched by compassion and begin to sense the invitation to apologise. It is an important transformation. The initial shame, focused on *one's own discomfort* under the regard of the other, will be completed by compassion, which is focused on the *discomfort of the other*. Previously, I argued that most people, including offenders, have a potential to feel empathy for other humans, and especially compassion for those who are suffering. Not all feel the same degree of empathy in all circumstances. In our expectation, most offenders will not remain indifferent to the suffering of their victims, even if they were indifferent initially. Victims will appear to them as being more than 'an object with a handbag' or some anonymous owner of a car, but a concrete human being with needs and emotions. If the conference goes well, the offenders will understand the suffering.

But it is not only compassion they will feel. They will recognise that their own behaviour has caused the suffering. The wrongfulness of their behaviour now appears clearer. Guilt may emerge and its grounds become more concrete than at the beginning: the reason for the norm is clear and even emotionally felt. Moreover, offenders also feel shame, especially because their wrong-doing is exposed to those who care about them and who are important to them.

This is crucial to the conferencing process. The ideal sequence relies very much on empathy to induce remorse or guilt and shame. The offender must recognise the suffering of the victim and accept responsibility for it. Both aspects can go wrong. Empathy in the offender for the victim's suffering is possible only if the offender himself experiences empathy. If he is disrespected, he is likely to become fixed in a defensive, defiant attitude, and to close his mind to the suffering of the victim. If he feels respect, despite rejection of what he did, and experiences that participants try to understand who he is and how he came to do what he did, he is more likely to open his mind to the suffering of the other.

Still, shame and guilt are unpleasant feelings which one wants to be relieved of. Acknowledging responsibility only adds to the pain. And that can also make things go wrong. The direct confrontation may provoke in the offender a defensive reaction, denying the suffering or rejecting the responsibility for it. But shame and guilt may also be accepted and resolved through acknowledgment and reparation. If the offender experiences support and gestures of reacceptance, he is more likely to risk a weak position and accept responsibility for what happened. To be relieved of the unpleasant feelings, the offender will then be inclined to make positive gestures in a restorative sense, including an apology.

Apology is crucial in a restorative process. It can, as Bottoms suggests (2003), 'be plausibly represented as a generative social mechanism that can potentially lead to the restoration of prior social relationships in a community' (2003: 94). The offending act, the victimisation, cannot be undone, but the very fact that the act has been committed and that it is unjust must be explicitly noticed. An apology is a crucial part of the sequence: the call by the victim for an apology – the apology itself – forgiveness. An apology, 'no matter how sincere or effective, does not and cannot undo what has been done. And yet, in a mysterious way and according to its own logic, this is precisely what it manages to do' (Tavuchis 1991: 5, cited in Bottoms 2003: 95).

In an apology, the offender recognises guilt. He expresses an understanding of the wrongfulness of the norm transgression, and confirms his recognition of the victim as a bearer of rights. 'I have done it to you, and I should not have done it.' While recognising guilt, the apologising offender asks the victim to 'ex-cuse', literally to 'de-accuse' him, to undo him from guilt. The offender takes the vulnerable position by submitting to the victim, placing his fate in the hands of the victim. The victim may refuse or accept the apology, possibly under certain conditions. The roles are reversed now. Whereas the offender exercised power over the victim in the offence, it is now the victim who has the decisive power. The willingness of the offender to undertake material actions to secure restoration underlines the truthfulness of the apology and concretises the recognition of the harm he has caused. But still, the offence and the injustice done to the victim are not undone. It is as the novelist Ivo Andric writes: 'Injustice, once committed, can neither be corrected, nor annihilated. Attempts to rectify or remove it only create new injustices ... And if there were no forgiveness and forgetting, injustice would cover the world and turn it into hell' (Ivo Andric, cited in Fatic 1995). We must hope that the next step in the sequence is taken. It is facilitated by the offender's apology.

In a successful sequence, most victims now feel restored in dignity and in citizenship by the apology. The victim's desire for revenge fades. Whereas revenge emotions are a drive to respond to humiliation by counter-humiliation, there is no object for this any more: the offender has in fact removed the humiliation through his apology. To a certain degree, he has 'humiliated himself' in the eyes of the victim. Moreover, the offender's apology is amplified by the other participants' support, which adds to the vindication of the victim. At this stage, the basic empathy between all humans is also activated in the opposite sense, so that the victim can feel some sympathy for the offender. This opens the way to forgiveness and dialogue, aimed at a constructive solution.

Forgiveness is more than accepting that the compensation is in balance with the harm suffered. It is a highly moral act to decide to put an end to the conflict while the act and its consequences are not undone (Tutu 1999; Dumont 2000). Forgiving is a gift by the victim to the offender, because it conveys to him the victim's trust that he will refrain from causing further harm and opens hope for constructive relations in the future; it is also a gift from the victim to the community as a whole, because the community will benefit from the elimination of enduring conflict and unsettled accounts in its midst. Genuine forgiveness transcends the common self-interest and hope of reciprocity, because it is a one-sided step, though it may lead to a better reciprocal dialogue. In its most authentic meaning, it recalls the high moral standard in Levinas' work, which some compare to 'holiness'.

We must be clear by now. Genuine apologies and true forgiveness are favoured by the context and the process in restorative encounters, but they cannot be primary objectives. They are beneficial effects, not explicit goals. If they were delivered under pressure or even ordered, they would lose their meaning. It is the fact of being offered freely as a gift which constitutes their emotional and relational strength.

The offender's public expressions of remorse and apology and his offer to make reparation also bring him respect, because he had the courage to face his responsibility and is willing to make reparation. The acceptance of the offer by the victim and the approval by the loved ones are expected to have an impact on his ethical identity as a basically respectable person. There is a chance that he will be able to leave the offence and its consequences behind him (after meeting the conditions) and that he is not fixed in the role of 'irredeemable criminal' (Maruna 2001).

The whole process in a non-adversarial respectful and supportive climate may facilitate the offender's and his family's awareness that things have been going deeply wrong and that something must be done to stop the negative development. It may be the occasion to search actively for treatment or help, or to accept such an offer.

This outline of the emotional dynamics represents an ideal situation. Reality is, of course, much more complicated. Each conference is different, depending on the nature of the crime, the people involved, the way the process is prepared and facilitated, and many other specific circumstances. Moreover, the outline has focused on the two main stakeholders only, victim and offender, whereas the impact by and on other participants is also of crucial importance. Despite strong recommendations to include parents and other members of the community (of care) in the encounters, research on their participation is scarce. So, for example, only a few studies (for example Prichard, 2003) have explored systematically the parents' role in conferencing.

But the outline may make it easier to understand the potential of restorative encounters to generate satisfaction and feelings of procedural justice among the participants, and why they are more likely to comply with the agreements than after a judicial procedure. It also argues for recognition that parents may experience more respect and support, and feel empowered to take up their parenting tasks again; they may also be more open to seek or accept external assistance and treatment afterwards.

The outlined sequence also points to the central importance of empathy as the gate-opener in the process. Empathy and compassion are indispensable 'intermediate emotions' to make guilt emotionally felt, triggering the rest of the process. Therefore the contextual climate is crucial to make empathy possible. Empathy and respect are possible only if the person himself experiences empathy and respect. They are the key to understanding the communicative and interactive added value of restorative processes. It reminds me what an experienced conferencing facilitator told me: 'Conferences bring out the good in people'.[3] It is the absence of such a supportive climate in traditional criminal procedures that makes it almost impossible for the offender to be open for compassion. The offender then gets locked into feelings of embarrassment and disempowerment which favour unacknowledged shame and defiance rather than an open dialogue.

And now we face a paradox. Although we noted a number of theories and arguments as to why restorative justice should be more effective, the empirical assessment so far does not convincingly confirm our expectations. In particular, the theoretically based expectations with regard to reoffending are not clearly sustained by the available evidence. Why is that? Several suggestions are possible. The theories may be too naive or too one-dimensional; practices may reflect poorly the theoretical promises; the research projects may not be differentiated enough to focus on crucial factors and mechanisms. A combination of these elements is probable. On top of this, the most plausible explanation might be found in the Good Life Model. As we have seen, this model states that there is no magic treatment to rehabilitate the offender; rather, the motivation of the offender himself is crucial. To succeed in his rehabilitation efforts, the offender must be helped (by his 'natural helpers' and by professionals), and he needs a minimum of favourable social conditions and prospects. The main reason why restorative justice processes reduce reoffending less than might theoretically be expected is probably that such processes may help the offender to find the appropriate motivation but cannot really change the social conditions of the offender's life.

Anyhow, disentangling the impact of restorative justice processes takes, in my view, large and comprehensive research programmes. In the next section, I sketch out such a research programme, keeping in mind the methodological pitfalls mentioned earlier.

Charting empirical research on restorative justice practices

Restorative justice is a philosophy covering diverse practices and influencing them to different degrees. Schemes are located at different levels of intervention and address dissimilar groups and problems. The (multiple) targets are often unclear. Some relate to immediate outcomes, others long-term effects. Some are core objectives, others can be considered as secondary, but still meaningful, benefits. Success and failure depend on a great variety of variables and mechanisms, from the personal to the societal. In my view the most comprehensive study so far is what has been presented by Bazemore and Schiff (2005). They present a survey of restorative group conferencing with juveniles in the USA, oriented by an accurate theoretical analysis of fundamental restorative justice principles and based on quantitative and qualitative data. But they do not differentiate between the very different schemes of restorative group conferencing, and they do not assess causal relations between processes and outcomes.

In my view, one research project cannot cover all versions, dimensions, mechanisms, factors and causal relations. Grasping empirically the entire scope of restorative justice and its practices in one single project is a mission impossible. What can be done, however, is to try to construct a theoretical frame in which to locate all factors, dynamics, mechanisms and elements – most of them interdependent – that may play a role in empirical observations of restorative justice practices. Such a construction has four levels:

1 a description of the diverse legal and institutional preconditions in which restorative processes are carried out;

2 an observation of the practices themselves (which are multiple and varied), including the particular potentials, limitations and risks of each;

3 a differentiated registration of the possible outcomes – these may have a broad range of aims related to different actors, different levels and different time perspectives;

4 the conception of an adequate research design, which is able to attribute the possible outcomes of the practices to the intrinsic characteristics of the restorative practices rather than to other variables.

Differentiation of the process preconditions

It is not possible to draw conclusions about restorative justice in general from empirical data only on police-led conferences. One cannot include victim–offender mediation, family group conferencing and peacemaking circles in one restorative group conferencing notion without losing crucial information about essential differences. It would be like carrying out 'what works' research on the effect of treatment without distinguishing between the many varieties of psychoanalytical, behavioural, cognitive and other approaches, differences in duration, differences in target groups, etc. The original 'nothing works' conclusion, based on surveys of treatment programmes, was the result of using categories that were too roughly drawn. Later, the greater accuracy of the 'what works' surveys gave a more precise indication of elements of possible treatment success or failure. Likewise, restorative justice is in need of a differentiated 'what helps' tradition, exploring, however, different fundamental objectives: it is not the degree of reoffending that is the basic criterion, but the degree of reparation achieved.

Differences in setting may have a great influence on effects. The following list of potentially influential elements is not meant to be exhaustive.

- *Institutional and legal context.* Some restorative processes are seen as forms of diversion, others are located at the heart of the procedure, and still others take place in prison and are carried out in addition to traditional punishment. Some programmes enjoy the full cooperative support of justice professionals, others have to cope with indifference, lack of understanding, and even open or subversive scepticism and boycott. There is a great difference in types and seriousness of cases targeted or reached. Research on restorative practices must register and report these and other distinctions in their legal and institutional context, because they can all have a decisive impact on the reach of the cases.

- *Type of scheme.* In Chapter 1, I briefly surveyed a great variety of practices that can be included in the restorative justice concept. With a few exceptions, the differences have been insufficiently researched. Empirical assessment cannot decide on restorative justice as a whole, but must indicate clearly what kind of scheme, in which version, is being explored. Indirect shuttle mediation is not the same as face-to-face encounters; the original New

Zealand model of family group conferencing differs from the so-called Wagga-Wagga conferencing model in several essential characteristics, which can have systematic consequences for reach and outcomes.

- *Positioning of the restorative justice agencies.* We have seen that autonomy of the agencies can affect their ability to get the right cases and to be able to deal with them in an uncompromised restorative way. Some agencies work with highly sophisticated professional facilitators, others prefer volunteers. The training and follow-up of the practitioners are very different in intensity and content. Needless to say, these elements influence how practices are carried out and their quality.

Intensive description of process

Even when conditions are comparable, actual practices can be very different. And these differences affect what happens and why.

- *The preparatory phase* between the referral and the start of the encounter functions as a filter for hidden or open, intentional or unconscious, coincidental or systematic selection. It also sets the direction for the remainder of the process. How do selection and orientation work and how do they affect what happens later in the meeting? To determine the external validity of the findings, it is crucial to investigate which cases finally come to a meeting, which do not, and why.

- *The encounter* itself must be closely observed. First, the intrinsic technical quality of the process must be checked. As in any profession, there are brilliant performers and bunglers among facilitators; some meetings may go wrong because of unexpected or unsystematic events. It is therefore important to observe the responsiveness of the facilitators, to what extent they remain focused on restoration, whether they are attentive to all aspects of procedural justice and how they manage the emotional socio-dynamics of the meeting. Secondly, attention to the dynamics may help to document the theoretical suppositions mentioned earlier. Observation of participants should focus on the psychosocial dynamics and their sequence, such as: expressions of mutual understanding, sympathy, support, solidarity and social pressure; indications of moral and other emotions, such as regret, remorse, shame, apology, forgiveness, anger, rejection and embarrassment;

the quality of the social climate in terms of authenticity and respect. Special attention should be paid to the participatory calibre of the meeting and the impact of the persons of confidence. If relevant (in family group conferences, for example), the role of the police or advocates must be carefully investigated, as this is a matter of debate among restorative justice practitioners. Such careful observations, which are predominantly qualitative, will make a crucial contribution to an understanding of whether restorative processes achieve their procedural aims and their impact on later outcomes.

- *The actual agreement* reached at the end of the encounter is a formal expression of the immediate outcome. As we shall see, there are other outcomes, which are probably even more important than the formal agreement. Nevertheless, the completion of the process by a formal agreement is an essential indicator. The content should be noted. If possible, the reparative, reintegrative and (indeed) punitive dimensions should be disentangled. It is important also to notice what arrangements are made for follow-up. All these elements depend partly on the process conditions and characteristics described above, and may themselves have consequences in the aftermath of the meeting.

- *The follow-up* after the conference is crucial. Is it carried out as agreed? Unexpected events may disturb the original plans; crucial actors, such as parents, social workers, victims and teachers, may not do what they promised; the school may respond in a less reintegrative way than was hoped; the treatment accepted may go better or worse than intended; the offender may be seduced by other (positive or negative) opportunities; the victim may face new opportunities or setbacks. All these and other elements can have a great impact on the follow-up and on the final results of the restorative process.

A broad spectrum of possible outcomes or consequences

All the above can be seen as variations in the independent variables. They form a much-differentiated complex of interacting factors and dynamics which affect, often decisively, the outcome of mediation, conferencing or other restorative justice actions. We now turn to what can be classified as the dependent variables.

Many potential beneficiaries of a restorative justice process can be identified, such as the victim, the offender, the parents, other individual stakeholders, the (local) community, public security, the public at large and even the justice professionals. For each of these stakeholders, the expected benefits are different, ranging from satisfaction with the process, material reparation and psychological healing for the victim and reintegration for the offender, to more peace in the community, public security and enforcement of norms. Some of the outcomes can be measured immediately after the meeting; others will be seen at a societal level in the longer term.

Another distinction is between outcomes related to core objectives in restorative justice and others that are not primary objectives but beneficial side effects. In the vision presented in Chapter 1, all outcomes that address reparation in the strict sense of the word are core objectives. That is why material reparation and the 'satisfaction' variable, in all its dimensions, are so important, for example. On the other hand, as previous paragraphs have made clear, the reduction of reoffending is, in my view, not a core objective by principle, but a beneficial side effect. For strategic reasons, however, it may be added to the core objectives.

Examination of the outcomes of restorative processes should not only focus on possible beneficial effects, but must also look for possible undesirable side effects, such as loss of legal rights, distress among participants, more reoffending and dissatisfaction among the public.

Like Bazemore and Schiff (2005), I classify the broad range of possible outcomes to be checked as immediate, intermediate and long-term outcomes.

- *Immediate outcomes* are measured immediately after the meeting and reflect how the participants view the event. The broad scope of satisfaction among the victims, offenders and their respective persons of confidence is an important indication of the quality of the process and its immediate reparative value. Aspects include the experiences of procedural justice, of support and of being listened to and a sense that rights have been respected. The participants' evaluation of the informal and formal results of the encounter include the recognition of apologies and forgiveness, remaining emotions of anger, fear, sympathy and compassion, understanding of the formal agreement and confidence that it will be complied with. All these immediate outcomes are related directly to the quality of the process mentioned in the previous section, and assess how the kind and quality of the process influence the direct outcomes of a restorative justice meeting.

- *Intermediate outcomes* are observed some time after the encounter. It is difficult to decide exactly how much later this observation should take place, but my suggestion is for an evaluation phase when the agreements are supposed to be fulfilled. The intermediate screening focuses partly on the same issues as the immediate screening. The impressions immediately after the conference are given in 'hot' emotion, under the direct influence of the intensive encounter. But it has to be checked later if the feelings were deep and enduring or only superficial impressions. In addition to requestioning, other issues to be looked at are whether the agreement has been completed, if so under what circumstances, and if not why not. How the follow-up has been carried out should also be examined. The longer-term impact on the participants can be checked as well, for example: the victim's feeling of being restored; signs of post-traumatic stress syndrome; the offender's belief in social values and institutions; indications of integration; possible reoffending; and the quality of parents' parenting practice. It is now also possible to begin investigating the impact on other actors, such as satisfaction among professionals (participating police officers, referring justice officials), which may become clear through an increasing number of referrals or the referral of more complicated and serious cases.

- Finally, the *long-term outcomes* still focus on the direct stakeholders, but also include broader objectives at the level of the community and society. Continuing and increasingly systematic implementation of restorative justice schemes may have an impact on public familiarity with the approach, on public feelings of security and even on crime rates. In the development pursued, restorative justice should occupy an increasingly important place in mainstream justice.

Ensuring comparability with other schemes

Assessing well all the above would add considerably to the understanding of what goes on, but the explanatory potential would be weak. In order to attribute the outcomes of restorative practices to typical restorative characteristics, they must be compared with those of non-restorative practices. Moreover, the development of good practice in restorative justice would benefit considerably if the different restorative justice models were compared. The best way to organise such comparisons is through an experimental or a quasi-experimental research design.

The independent variables should be defined more clearly than is currently the case in most projects. In line with what is described above, the legal and institutional context, the selection stages in the access to the process, the model of restorative process used, the quality of its implementation, the definition of what is considered successful, the inclusion and the quality of the follow-up – all these variables are important in getting a clear insight into what happens, and what can possibly have an impact on the outcomes.

Likewise, the dependent variables have to reflect more accurately the restorative objectives as primary targets and specify clearly a realistic time perspective for their achievement.

It is naive to consider causality as a simple linear relation between one independent and one dependent variable. Between the moment of referral of a case to a restorative process and, ideally, the achievement of restoration for the victim, reintegration and less reoffending for the offender and peace in the community, a chain of mutually interactive variables is at work. As described above, the independent variables are a complex of mutually interacting factors. Circular causality must thus be expected. Practices that cream the easy cases may offer impressive results while intrinsically better practices may 'adventure' more into difficult cases and therefore present less blatant successes. Referral criteria will influence the reach and mobilise the skills needed in the agencies; in turn, skilled and well located restorative justice agencies can influence the system's referral criteria. The referrals, the model and the technical quality of the actual process affect decisively the immediate outcomes; the types of cases processed, the immediate outcomes and the quality of the follow-up affect compliance with the agreement; this will largely determine intermediate consequences. If this chain of interdependent variables mostly goes well, it will enhance confidence in the referral system, increase community support for extending the reach of restorative justice and lead to referrals of more delicate and serious cases. But that again will require the restorative justice agencies to develop competencies to deal with more difficult cases. If, on the contrary, the restorative process fails too often, confidence in the referral system and the attractiveness of restorative processes will be reduced and the whole development may stop.

Perhaps the most difficult task in evaluative research is to compose an adequate control group. The most appropriate way of doing so is by random assignment of similar cases to either the restorative programme as the experimental group or to a non-restorative pro- gramme, as the control group. It is then chance, rather than any intentional intervention, that decides the composition of both the experimental and the control groups. If the groups are large enough, one can ascribe any observed differences to the experimental programme. Random assignment requires a large study group, a sophisticated research design and the cooperation of referring agencies. Latimer *et al.* (2001) performed a meta-analysis of 13 studies that included a control group. Sherman and Strang (2007) examined 36 direct comparisons, not all of which were based on adequate random assignment.

But random assignment does not resolve all problems. First, selection bias cannot be eliminated completely. Avoiding systemic selection bias needs the cooperation of the referring system – usually the police or the judiciary – which is far from evident. Avoiding self-selection bias is also difficult, because participation in restorative justice processes requires a voluntary choice, which is, of course, not so for judicial interventions. Self-selection bias can be circumvented by first asking offenders and victims if they are willing to participate and then randomly selecting the experimental and control groups from those who accepted. Such a procedure is possible only if the total number of referred and willing individuals is large enough. Moreover, it raises deontological problems: it is indeed a delicate matter to exclude willing victims and offenders from the possible benefits of restorative justice simply for reasons of experimental research design.

Second, voluntary participation by the offender suggests that he at least does not deny guilt. This is certainly not true for those who go to court. The control group will thus contain a number of court cases who claim not to be guilty. This has a huge impact on the victims' experience. For them, confronting an offender who confesses is much more satisfying of their need for vindication than having to face someone who denies the charges. And, of course, the voluntarily participating offenders in the restorative process make up a more compliant group than those – deniers and confessors – who go before the court.

Third, even where a restorative programme is adequately compared with a traditional criminal justice intervention or a treatment programme, it is not necessarily the case that only those programmes are being compared. Most restorative justice schemes are carried out in a pioneering phase. The very fact that they are being subjected to systematic empirical assessment is often an indication of a personally committed attitude in the programme leaders and practitioners and a supportive environment. Many evaluated programmes are in fact 'demonstration projects' (Dignan 2005), i.e. experimental initiatives undertaken in privileged circumstances, for which the generalisability is doubtful. It is uncertain how restorative justice processes would function if they were used routinely, as are the criminal justice interventions with which they are compared.

Conclusions on the impact on individual stakeholders

Empirical research on restorative justice is a long, complicated and difficult undertaking. Often, evaluation research must contend with research designs and measurements that are less rigorous and reliable than the ideal. Satisfactory solutions to these problems cannot always be found because restorative research does not occur in a laboratory. It is done in real life, deals with real problems in real people and groups with particular interests, needs and rights. While restorative justice processes are based on certain principles and rely on specific skills, they do not always operate along strict scripts; their reparative objectives are broad and may be interpreted differently by the different stakeholders. All this makes restorative justice processes susceptible to a huge variety of factors, dynamics and mechanisms which are impossible to control.

Yet critical empirical assessment of restorative justice practices is badly needed. Compromises with the practical and ethical obligations of real life are unavoidable, but we must know what and where they are. While not all possible variables can be controlled, they can be mapped to see where and how social and psychological factors and mechanisms can affect the results. With that in mind, research designs can be completed and the degree and type of unavoidable methodological compromises can be estimated. The results of evaluation research always have to be read with realistic common sense. Empirical modesty must prevent us from claiming that the added value of restorative justice practices can be proved scientifically and beyond any doubt. Such misplaced claims are seen all too often with regard to treatment programmes.

But still, research methodology must be continuously improved so as to be able to collect the best possible data on restorative justice practices in relation to traditional criminal justice interventions. It remains the best possible safeguard we have to avoid restorative justice becoming part of 'evangelical criminology: the fervour with which it [RJ] is pursued ... can blind its followers to its implications' (Pratt 2006: 45). Restorative justice would degrade into a system based on belief, and the restorative justice movement into a sect of believers driven by a 'crusading zeal' (ibid.: 49). Again, the Greek myth of Sisyphus is illustrative here. Just as Sisyphus could never reach the top of the hill with the rock but had to continue trying, restorative justice research will never reach definitive evidence, but must continue trying to improve the scientific empirical data of its practices.

Investigating the public dimension of restorative justice

The research reported so far has focused on how restorative processes function and how they affect the direct stakeholders. But crime is also a public event. Hence the possible public impact of restorative justice must also be addressed. How would the existence and (mainstream) implementation of restorative responses to crime in general affect the public and public security?

Restorative justice proponents hold that it would contribute to building stronger communities, better than the existing criminal justice practices (Braithwaite 2002a; McCold 2004b). They point to the satisfaction rates among community members participating in conferences, to the increased community orientation and decreased reoffending rates among offenders, to the benefits for school communities and workplaces that have implemented restorative responses to norm transgressions, and also to the few historical occasions on which restorative-like processes have influenced peacemaking in larger communities. The impact of restorative justice on a community is anticipated by the increasing community involvement in restorative practices. This, it is said, is beneficial for cohesion within the community, which in turn improves informal social control and decreases feelings of insecurity. Counter-arguments have been advanced by those who consider that restorative practices are too soft on crime so that they do not have a sufficiently deterrent effect on offenders. Sceptics fear that a systematic restorative approach would provoke an increase in crime.

All in all, there are few empirical data on the real impact on communities (Kurki 2003). Reasons for that may be: (1) the difficulty of defining what a community is and the consequent difficulty of measuring empirically the impact on it; and (2) the lack of systematic implementation of restorative practices in specific communities so that its impact on social life in general is hard to observe.

The most systematic implementation of restorative justice schemes is in New Zealand, where since 1989 family group conferencing for all serious youth offences is a mainstream response under the

Children, Young Persons and Their Families Act. While New Zealand, like most other developed countries, may have been suffering a wave of increasing intolerance and feelings of insecurity, the statistics on youth offending do not show an increase (Morris 2004). On the contrary, Maxwell *et al.* (2004) calculated that the number of arrests fell from more than 8,000 in 1987 to less than 2,000 in 1990, and then rose gradually to just under 3,000 in 2001 (ibid.: 264, figure 12.1). The number of young offenders in court fell from 400 per 10,000 young people in 1987 to fewer than 200 in 1990, and then rose to 240 in 2001 (ibid.: 267, figure 12.2). The number of convictions fell from 1,318 in 1987 to 269 in 1990 and 234 in 2001 (ibid.: 281, figure 12.5). The number of custodial sentences imposed by adults' courts on waived youths fell from 295 in 1987 to 104 in 1990. In 2001, there were only 73 (ibid.: 282, figure 12.6). I am inclined to call such developments spectacular and beneficial for public safety.

Other empirical data on impact on public life are scarce and fragmented. Guarino-Ghezzi and Klein (1999), for example, describe two local restorative justice programmes which involved the public and seemed to enhance public safety.

There are data to indicate that public acceptance of restorative responses to crime is good. Research on public attitudes towards crime and justice suggests that the public attitude is not as straightforwardly punitive as is sometimes claimed. In research in London and the east of England, Maruna and King (2004) found that one-third of 941 respondents could be considered punitive, while one-third took an opposing view. Based on a survey of public attitudes to punishment, Roberts and Hough concluded that 'the public is unlikely soon to abandon the notion of punishment', but they also found dissatisfaction with the traditional punitive system and support for 'more creative, non-carceral alternatives' (Roberts and Hough 2002: 6). They also write that 'restorative (non-punitive) responses carry considerable appeal for the public, particularly for the young and non-violent offenders' (ibid.). Moreover, Roberts and Hough rightly observe that public opinion is not cut and dried but that it can change over time.

Samples of lay respondents in New Zealand (Galaway 1984), Great Britain (Wright 1989), Germany (Sessar 1999), Canada (Doob *et al.* 1998) and the USA (Bae 1992) have been presented with options on how to respond to crime. When reparative alternatives were included and presented realistically, a majority preferred such responses. As might be expected, the type of crime influenced the degree of preference. One of the most significant studies was by Sessar (1995).

He presented 38 dummy cases, ranging from theft from cars to armed robbery and rape, to a large sample of inhabitants in Hamburg. Respondents could choose from five possible responses:

- voluntary victim–offender regulation without any official intervention;
- victim–offender regulation monitored by an official mediator;
- possible reparative agreements to be prepared and confirmed by the criminal justice system;
- criminal punishment, which may be reduced if the offender is willing to make amends;
- criminal punishment, not influenced by possible reparation.

In all cases, a majority opted for the reparative options, mostly outside (41 per cent), but sometimes also inside the system (17 per cent). Of those who opted for punishment on principle, only 21 per cent chose the last, purely punitive, response. The modalities outside the judicial system were seldom chosen for burglary or rape, but even then, a large majority preferred reparative possibilities under judicial supervision. Notably, the possibility of reoffending did not change these preferences. Sessar concluded that '... the conception of the public's strong punitive sentiments is a myth' (Sessar 1999: 301).

Despite the scarcity of reliable empirical data, the communitarian rhetoric of many restorative justice advocates has so far not been refuted. Communities and the public at large might find benefits in more systematic implementation of restorative responses to crime. There is no reason to believe that this would be detrimental for safety and safety feelings – on the contrary. There is no empirical indication that the restorative justice option would be blocked by a so-called general public punitiveness. While simplistic repressive outcries may sound the loudest in the media, it is far from evident that they are the mainstream. Such an attitude seems rather to be a myth, boosted by a simplistic media and extreme-right politics. Kurki writes: 'Restorative justice processes carry great potential to turn incidents of crime into positive opportunities of creating new relationships, building communities, and strengthening grass roots democracy. The potential is as yet unrecognised by most criminal justice agencies and researchers, and as a result, largely unrealised and unstudied' (Kurki 2003: 310).

Conclusion: exploring the limits of restorative justice practice and beyond

This chapter has offered theoretical and empirical reasons to believe in the potential of the restorative justice approach to crime. Not only is it desirable, as I argued in Chapter 3, but it now appears also to be feasible and effective. Additionally, the restorative potential seems to be recognised by the public. Hence it is not surprising that restorative justice practices are spreading fast, and in increasingly differentiated versions, all over the world. Restorative justice is increasingly seen as another paradigm, offering in the longer term a fully fledged alternative to the traditional responses to crime. Empirical research so far has produced no reason to scale down these ambitions. But the results must be read with care. Due to methodological inadequacies, most of the research data are illustrative but not conclusive. Most of the practices evaluated were restricted in size and scope, and often implemented in privileged circumstances.

Nevertheless, restorative justice is developing from being an interesting track to be explored towards a clear possibility or even an indispensable part of the mainstream response to crime. Development must go hand in hand with more and better research, moving beyond the blunt general question of whether restorative justice works or not to address detailed questions on which restorative justice programmes help best for what purposes, for which kind of cases, under which conditions, how and why. The new generation of research on restorative justice will need, among other things, to be oriented more by theoretical explanations, to pay more attention to the emotional dynamics in the processes and include more qualitative research strategies.

The status closer to the mainstream raises explicit questions about the limits of restorative justice. Several possible limits must be considered.

Serious crimes

Arguments have been advanced to exclude serious crimes from restorative processes. Some suggest that people who commit serious crimes cannot be beneficially involved in a restorative process. This indicates a naive view of the aetiology of crime, as if the seriousness of a crime directly expresses the social callousness of the offender. Serious criminals can also be sensitive, can feel deep remorse and may be willing to make up for what they have done.

Retributionists say it is a matter of principle to respond to serious crimes with punishment. I have already rejected the principled apriorism for punishment. Offending, and a fortiori serious offending, must be responded to with a possibly coercive public reaction, but it should still aim primarily at possible reparation and not at making the offender suffer.

The media, policy-makers and justice professionals co-opt victims' interests in their punitive agenda and refer to the so-called retributive feelings of the victims. Research has not documented a general call from victims for punishment. On the contrary, as this chapter has made clear, many victims of serious crimes accept participation in restorative processes and draw more benefits from such participation than from traditional penal justice procedures. Rather the *idéologie victimaire* (Salas 2005, cited in Daems 2007: 368) instrumentalises the victim as an argument in the penal populist tendency.

An important reflection is that fewer risks can be taken with those who have committed a serious crime because their possible reoffending could lead to serious revictimisation. One ought not indeed run headlong after restoration if this gives space for more harm, suffering and social unrest. The principled priority for restoration may need to face up to the need to preserve public security. In a few cases, incapacitation of negatively defiant offenders will limit the potential for reparation.

All in all, seriousness of crime cannot be an a priori argument to exclude offenders and victims of serious crimes from restorative interventions. On the contrary, the restorative justice paradigm makes the amount of harm and suffering caused by a crime an essential argument in favour of actions with a view to restoration. Victims of serious crimes and communities where these crimes occur probably suffer more hurt than those involved in trivial offences. They are more in need of restoration. This may seem difficult in practice, but it is contradictory to restorative principles to exclude victims of serious crimes a priori from restorative actions.

Respect for victims' interests and needs

At first sight, it seems evident that justice responses inspired by restorative principles meet victims' needs better than traditional criminal justice does. Empirical assessment so far confirms this expectation: in general, victims' satisfaction after participation in restorative encounters is significantly higher than after being involved in criminal procedures. Yet the position of the victims in restorative justice practice is less clear than it may seem.

Victims and victims' movements do not compose one homogeneous group (Dignan 2005). Victims respond very differently to victimisation. While their advocates originally held a predominantly oppositional view of victims' and offenders' interests, this is changing (Strang 2002). It is increasingly understood that victims have much to lose in an uncritical coalition with the criminal justice system. Despite recent efforts to improve their position and experience in traditional criminal justice, they still often risk secondary victimisation (Dignan 2005). Whether restorative justice might bring a fundamental improvement is still to be examined.

Daly (2002 and 2003), for example, found that 40 per cent of restorative conferencing in South Australia took place without a victim present, and that one in five of the participating victims were more or less upset after the conference. Surely, these negative outcomes may be partly due to implementation failures. As argued above, not all restorative justice implementers do a good job. But there are also more fundamental risks.

So far, the large majority of restorative justice processes are implemented within or mandated by justice systems which are basically offender oriented. Hence the continuous, often inarticulate, pressure to focus on the offender. Genuine respect for the victim's interests and needs may become subordinate. This is especially true in the juvenile justice context, with its strong rehabilitation tradition. Mediation or conferencing is then sometimes seen in a treatment perspective, subordinating the victim's view (Davis *et al.* 1988; Acorn 2004). Social pressure may be exerted on the victim to participate, to be 'moderate' in his claims or to accept agreements that are primarily focused on the treatment needs of the offender. The victim's story is then used as a 'pedagogical means' to motivate the offender for treatment rather than as a decisive indication to determine appropriate reparative actions.

Abusing the victim in an offender-perspective is contrary to restorative justice principles. To reduce this risk a strong relation must be kept between restorative justice practices and theoretical reflection on the essentials, as proposed in Chapter 1: the essentials of restorative justice are not in the process but in the purpose to restore, so that any risk of secondary victimisation is unacceptable (Walgrave 2003b). Yet, the pressure to keep an offender focus will remain strong as long as restorative justice practices are included in the traditional justice systems. That is why the maximalist vision of restorative justice is promoted, reorienting criminal justice towards doing justice primarily through reparation, leaving its obsession of doing something to the offender. If not, one must fear that the more restorative justice becomes embedded in criminal justice, the more 'it is forced to absorb external priorities that may have little to do with restorative principles' (Green 2006: 185).

Another possible problem for victims is, paradoxically, the opportunity they are offered to be heard and to play a crucial role in the aftermath of the offence; it may turn into a moral obligation or even a duty. Whereas most restorative justice advocates promote intensive stakeholder commitment from an emancipation perspective, it may become too heavy a burden. Garland (1996), for example, indicates that the state's interest in restorative justice may be inspired by its tendency to shift its responsibility for citizens' security onto the citizens' shoulders. Contemporary states are no longer able to fulfil their mission of assuring safety to all citizens in all circumstances, and try to load part of the charge on the citizens themselves. From that perspective, developing restorative justice would mainly help to unburden the criminal justice system, but instead burden the stakeholders, especially the victims.

In traditional judicial procedures the victim is positioned as the one to whom something is due. The judicial institution and the lawyers have the initiative and shield the victim from direct responsibilities. Restorative processes seem to take away this relatively 'comfortable' position. The encounters begin from an impartial position, leaving the offender/victim role more open, and set the scene for a direct confrontation. Not all victims can cope with that. The offence has been traumatising, and it is feared that the process may cause additional trauma and reiterate the power inequalities that existed already between the victim and the offender before the crime occurred (LaPrairie 1995), which could be detrimental, especially in family violence (Stubbs 2002).

I do not see any guarantee to exclude this risk totally. Indeed, the unavoidable corollary of awarding rights and opportunities to victims is to burden them with responsibilities. In principle, the fact of being victimised is not a reason for ceasing to be a fully fledged citizen, including rights but also responsibilities. We must theoretically hope that victims, like other citizens, are also committed to common self-interest through socially constructive solutions to their victimisation and the social unrest caused by the offence. But the emotional consequences of the event may make that (provisionally) impossible, and that has to be respected. Hence facilitators must be fully aware of the victim's feelings, respect his possible refusal to participate in a restorative meeting and pay intensive attention to keeping the victim's feelings respected if they do. Moreover, as will be described in the next chapter, a restorative justice system should provide first-line support for all victims, and such support could add safeguarding the respect for victim's rights and emotions.

Besides that, the only remaining question is whether victims in general are more at risk in restorative justice than in other responses to crime. Based on what we know now, we can answer it with a clear 'no, on the contrary'. The perfect system, satisfying fully all victims' needs and interests, does not exist, as it does not exist for any purpose. But we must keep trying. Remember Sisyphus.

Naïvety of restorative justice presuppositions?

Some will argue that the potential of restorative justice is seriously limited by its reliance on voluntariness and goodwill in the stakeholders. I have dealt with this earlier in the chapter. If adequate conditions are fulfilled, the great majority of stakeholders appear willing and able to find constructive peacemaking solutions to crime and other conflicts. Despite their contrasting roles and initially contradictory views of the incident, both victims and offenders find their common interest in a constructive settlement and in the social peace it facilitates. I argued my view that it rests on a fundamental human empathy and a quest for common self-interest.

It remains a vulnerable position, because it is grounded in a belief. It is easier to impose passive responsibility on an offender than to call on his – uncertain – readiness to take active responsibility. In Foucault's words (1975), punishment can discipline the body but not commit the mind. Restorative justice addresses the mind. It tries to involve the offender actively through cooperation. And that is not evident in the current punitive mainstream. Most offenders seek to get away with the least possible punishment and are not committed to constructive social relations in the community. The previous chapters have, however, provided theoretical and empirical reasons to ascribe this defensive resistant attitude mainly to the punitive context itself. A deliberative respectful climate, as in restorative practice, will deconstruct the 'culture of denial' (Braithwaite 2005) and uncover the desire for constructive social relations which is present deep down in the great majority of offenders. Such an approach does not always work, to say the least: some will not respond to a respectful call to take active responsibility.

The question is how to approach the offender initially. Do we suffocate the potential for sympathetic encounters beforehand through legal procedures and threats of punishment? Or do we give solidarity and inter-human sympathy a chance by acting first as if the offender is able to take part in an encounter? Putnam mentions psychological evidence that people who are treated as if they are trustworthy act in a more trustworthy way. If people are given active responsibility, they will assume it constructively. If people are approached with positive sympathy, they will respond to it equally sympathetically. 'In that sense, honesty, civic engagement, and social trust are mutually reinforcing' (Putnam 2000: 137). Therefore, beginning by relying on interhuman empathy is not naïve but a well considered option. It is in line with the definition of restorative justice in Chapter 1: '... an option of doing justice ... that is primarily oriented towards repairing the ... harm caused by that offence'. It is not naïve to give *priority*; it would be naïve to give *exclusivity* to repairing the harm.

Sometimes this approach will fail because of refusals by the stakeholders, or it may appear to be impossible because of justified concerns for public safety. 'In a society of fallible humans, what kind of assurance can each of us have in the good faith of others? A legal system, complete with courts and law enforcement, provides a strong answer' (Putnam 2000: 136). That is why restorative justice must be included in a formal system. But the system itself can still be oriented towards serving as much as possible reparative outcomes.

What such a system might look like is the subject of the next chapter.

Notes

1 The other reason is the lack of theoretical depth of the restorative justice research.
2 We presented the outcomes of the conference to eleven of the non-participating victims in our sample. Nine of them called the outcome 'just' or 'very just', and seven of them found that 'maybe they should have participated' (Vanfraechem 2003).
3 Allan MacRae (2000), at that time a youth justice coordinator in Wellington.

Chapter 5

Designing a restorative criminal justice system

So far in this book, restorative justice has been considered a particular paradigmatic option for doing justice after a crime has occurred, clearly distinguished from the punitive apriorism in traditional criminal justice. Socio-ethical arguments have been advanced as to why a restorative apriorism is more desirable than the currently predominant punitive apriorism; experience and empirical data also show that systematically giving priority to restorative responses to crime is a realistic option. The next step is to propose how a maximalist restorative justice concept, as outlined in Chapter 1, could take shape in a constitutional democracy. Such an exercise abandons the safe field of imagination and enters the real world of institutions.

The most demanding challenge is that common self-interest, as promoted in Chapter 3, is far from being reality. The reality is pervaded by abuse of power and populated by citizens of whom many are purely selfish. While justice was advanced as a derivative value in the ethics of social life, in current non-ideal societies it is a value in itself. Indeed, it is very often impossible to achieve a deliberative solution in the aftermath of a crime because the ideal niche of mutual respect, solidarity or active responsibility is far away. Respect and solidarity risk being subordinated to self-interest and abuse of power. Hence we must rely on a system of rights and duties to check processes and outcomes. We must look for a system that combines the widest possible scope for decisive inclusive processes with mechanisms of coercion, while safeguarding essential individual rights. But these mechanisms and rights must themselves express as far as possible the socio-ethical guidelines described previously.

There are many examples of how restorative processes are implemented and located in relation to mainstream legal systems (Miers 2001; Miers and Willemsens 2004). It is generally agreed that the New Zealand juvenile justice system is the most deeply imbued with the restorative justice philosophy because of the central position of family group conferencing in the procedures: except in cases of murder and manslaughter, youth courts cannot impose any sanction without such a conference being attempted (Morris 2004).

On a more abstract level, the most far-reaching conception of a restorative justice system is provided in the RJ-city project (www.rjcity.org/the-city 2007). This project tries to imagine how an American city of about one million residents could replace its criminal justice system by a restorative justice network and a system that would consequently respond to crime in terms of a restorative justice philosophy. The report provides a detailed account of such a network and the institutions needed to respond, in principle, to all crime with a primary view to restoration and reparation. The network is based on intensive community involvement but works in a particular relationship to judicial coercive power. The project demonstrates the feasibility in principle of orienting the mainstream response to crime primarily to restoration and reparation, but also reveals that, at certain points, compromises have to be accepted. However, the structure proposed in the RJ-city project is very detailed and clearly focused on a typical American approach. Some of its characteristics are hardly imaginable in a European context.

My purpose is different. It is not to work out a very detailed system, because such a system cannot but be local, embedded in local traditions and institutions. The ambition is to present a comprehensive model of institutionalisation, based on principles and theoretical reflections.

Thinking of institutionalisation risks perversion of the original restorative justice philosophy through cooptation and instrumentalisation (Aertsen *et al.* 2006). Inaccurate articulation of the concepts, insufficiently grounded through reflection, makes them vulnerable to being undermined by bureaucratic or professional interests and incapable of coping with punitive apriorism. In the desire for implementation, some restorative justice advocates anticipate possible cooptation and resistance by politicians and the judiciary, and try 'to enhance the attractiveness of RJ for policy-makers in the criminal justice system' (Aertsen *et al.* 2006: 288). They accept, for example, the traditional deontological principles, such as proportionality or right to a defence, as the frame for including restorative processes in the criminal justice system or try to demonstrate the utility of restorative justice practices in the ongoing rhetoric about the need for more safety. Restorative justice is then easy prey to instrumentalisation in the state's attempts to regain legitimacy, for example through selective attention to the victim, or by reformulating the responsibility aspect into a hardliner's newspeak towards (young) offenders. The perversion of the restorative justice philosophy is then at hand.

Nevertheless, thinking about institutionalising restorative justice is unavoidable, and can only take place in the context of an imperfect society. The risks depend mainly on where the process begins. If 'restorative justice becomes institutionalized within a socio-political agenda rather than a legal-conceptual framework, the development ... will serve co-optation by the state' (Mackay 2006: 212). If, on the contrary, institutionalisation starts from a strong conceptual framework of socio-ethical, theoretical and legal principles, and is supported by empirical assessment, there is a greater chance that a balance can be found 'between the ethical and the political', as Hudson writes. 'Without the political/conditional, justice would be based on abstract, unchallengeable principles; ... Without the ethical, ideals of justice would not be present to provide any restraint to the politics of risk, ..., the politics of exclusion and elimination of the different or risky' (Hudson 2006b: 278).

The institutionalisation model proposed here is grounded in the theoretical and socio-ethical foundations developed so far. It can be a guide to help to prevent co-optation, corruption or perversion of the genuine restorative justice philosophy in the unavoidable process of institutionalisation. But it remains a tricky undertaking. That is why I will, at the end of the chapter, come back to the desirable balance between the ethical and the political, checking my options against what Pavlich called the 'imitator paradox' in restorative justice developments (Pavlich 2005).

Dominion

The notion of dominion, as presented in Braithwaite and Pettit's republican theory of criminal justice (Braithwaite and Pettit 1990), synthesises the legal institutional dimension (the objective rights and freedoms that are legally defined) and the informal relational dimension (the subjective assurance that others will respect these rights and freedoms). It offers an excellent basis for developing legal and institutional theory on restorative justice (Walgrave 2000).

Dominion (or 'freedom as non-domination')[1] can be defined as the set of assured rights and freedoms. It is the mental and social territory which we have at our free disposal, guaranteed by the state and by the social context in which we live. The assurance aspect of rights and freedoms is critical. 'I know that I have rights, I know that others know it, and I trust that they will respect them.' I am assured only if I trust my fellow citizens and the state to take my rights and freedoms seriously. Only then will I fully enjoy my mental and social domain.

The assurance element marks the decisive distinction between the social concept of 'freedom as non-domination' and the liberal concept of 'freedom as non-interference'. In the latter, the rights and freedoms of the individual citizen end where the rights and freedoms of the other citizens begin. The set of rights and freedoms is conceived as a stable given which must be distributed as justly as possible. All other citizens are possible interferers in my freedom and rivals in my struggle to expand my freedom. Such a concept also opposes the individual citizens to the state. State intervention is pushed back as far as possible and strictly limited to what is vital to preserve individual liberties. Justice and jurisdiction are settlements of conflicts of interests between citizens, and between citizens and the state.

In the republican view, on the contrary, rights and freedoms are a collective good. Dominion is not a stable given but a value to be promoted and expanded by individual and collective action. Fellow citizens are allies in trying to extend and mutually assure dominion as a collective good.

Restoring assurance in dominion

A good state, Braithwaite and Pettit write, must promote dominion. Dominion is thus not an enclosed field but a value to be promoted. Interdependency can be raised between the republican theory and the pursuit of common self-interest, as described in Chapter 3. The utopia of a collectivity driven by solidarity and active responsibility can be achieved only in so far as the state and the citizens mutually assure respect for rights and freedoms, as accorded in dominion. Inversely, the assurance of rights and freedoms is achieved only to the degree to which citizens take up their responsibilities in view of respect and solidarity. We all have an interest in respecting and developing dominion. Dominion is the political frame for a high-quality social life, and is thus the political translation of what I called common self-interest.

The citizens and the state seek to extend and deepen dominion by promoting equality through more participation in democracy, more education, equitable socio-economic policy, welfare policy and the like. Criminal justice is the defensive institution. Its aim is not to extend or deepen dominion, but to repair it when it has been intruded upon by crime (Walgrave 2000). The intrusion most hurts the assurance of dominion. In the case of a burglary, for example, it is not the legal right of privacy and possession that is lost because these rights remain legally defined. What is lost, or at least shaken, is the *assurance* that fellow citizens respect these rights. The victim is confronted with the fact that, despite the legally guaranteed home safety, he did not enjoy this safety.

But, contrary to the position taken in the 'civilisation thesis', the impact of the burglary goes beyond the individual victim. In the civilisation thesis, criminal law is replaced by a system of – legally monitored – compensatory mechanisms to settle 'difficult or unpleasant' situations among citizens according to civil law (Hulsman 1982). In that view, the restitution or compensation of the victim's losses could be strictly private, to be arranged as a tort in civil law. If the victim and the burglar then agree about restitution and compensation, all is settled. However, that would mistakenly neglect the public side (Johnstone 2002; Bottoms 2003). The burglary damages not only the individual victim's trust that his privacy and possessions will be respected by his fellow citizens. The particular victim stands as an example of the risk run by all citizens. If the authorities did nothing against the particular burglary, it would undermine all citizens' trust in their right to privacy and possession.

Hence public intervention after a crime is not primarily needed to redress the balance of benefits and burdens or to reconfirm the law, as traditional penal theories suggest. It is needed first of all to enhance assurance by communicating the message that the authorities take dominion seriously. The intervention must reassure the victim and the public at large of their rights and freedoms, and restore these rights and freedoms into a fully fledged dominion. This is done through clear public censure of the intrusion and through public actions involving, if possible, the offender in reparative actions. As seen in previous chapters, voluntary cooperation by the offender is more effective in restoring assurance, but it is imperative that it is backed by public institutions. The reassurance comes not only from the offender's repentance and apologies, but also from the authorities' determination to take the assured rights and freedoms seriously.

The aim of restorative justice as a public intervention is to restore the assurance of rights and freedoms, which is crucial for restoring the intruded-on dominion. Dominion, in which we find our common self-interest, is the ultimate criterion for evaluation of restorative processes and values (Braithwaite 2000a).

Respecting rights and freedoms in dominion

Dominion is not only a value to be promoted; it is based on a hard core of legally defined rights and freedoms. They provide touchstones for limiting and channelling public responses to crime, including restorative justice interventions. All responses to crime must aim to repair dominion, i.e. the assurance of rights and freedoms. They must therefore themselves fully respect these rights and freedoms. Braithwaite and Pettit (1990, 2000) list four principles: parsimony, checking of authorities' use of power, reprobation of crime and reintegration of victims and offenders.

Parsimony is central in the search to combine informal processes with the need for formal controls. In the republican theory, criminal justice must strive for satiable goals (repairing the intruded dominion) and is bound by the pursuit of parsimony in using its coercive power. Parsimony is more restricting than satiability. We can eat until satiation, but we can parsimoniously do with less to survive. Satiability includes the obligation to set an upper limit, as required by the proportionality principle in traditional criminal justice theories. Contrary to proportionality, however, parsimony does not set a lower limit. Parsimony requires an active search for non-coercive ways of restoring dominion. The more voluntary restorative processes can lead to satisfying and balanced outcomes, the less appeal is needed to coercive judicial interventions and thus the more parsimony is achieved. A coherent restorative justice system should fulfil its parsimony obligation by leaving space for, and diverting to, voluntary processes, in which victim, offender and collectivity can together seek an agreed settlement of the aftermath of a crime with a view to restoring dominion. The parsimony principle is not new. It reformulates the long-existing subsidiarity principle, according to which criminal justice should be activated only when other social systems appear to be incapable of responding adequately to the offence.

The 'checking of power' principle is part of the assurance aspect in dominion. Citizens must be assured that they cannot be subjected to arbitrary power by the powerful and the authorities. Possible abuse of power is best avoided in two ways: (1) by decentralising the top-down power of the courtroom as much as possible towards bottom-up deliberative meetings with those most directly concerned; and (2) by developing rules to hold the authorities accountable (Roche 2003), and to check that dominion has not been unnecessarily intruded on for the offender, the victim and other stakeholders. Checking of power is largely comparable with the traditional deontological principles guiding criminal justice. We shall see, however, that these principles need to be revised in order more adequately to frame a system oriented towards restorative justice.

The other two principles can be combined. According to the 'reprobation' principle, the intervention must clearly reject the criminal offence, but 'reintegration' means that the intervention must avoid as far as possible stigmatisation or other forms of social exclusion of both the victim and the offender. On the contrary, the interventions must facilitate the offender's social reacceptance. This can be done, for example, by giving him the opportunity to regain social valorisation through making up for what he did wrong. In the republican theory, indeed, dominion must be maximised for all, including victims and offenders. Contrary to maximising dominion, as requested by the republican theory, the punitive apriorism in the traditional criminal justice approach leads to many unnecessary limitations of rights and freedoms and frequently provokes further social exclusion of the offender (and even of the victim).

A pyramid of restorative law enforcement

Several authors have presented outlines of a restorative justice system (Van Ness 2002b; Braithwaite 2000a; Dignan 2002). I have myself described elsewhere how the Belgian juvenile justice system could be reformed to be primarily oriented to restoration (Walgrave 2001b). The models presented are highly comparable, which suggests some agreement on the contours of what might be a comprehensive restorative justice system. They all start by giving priority to voluntary deliberative processes, then provide several variations of coercive interventions by courts while keeping opportunities for (partial) reparation, and finally allow for incapacitation of some 'dangerous' offenders for security reasons. The levels roughly represent different degrees of restorativeness, as described by Van Ness (2002b), for example.

Braithwaite's regulatory pyramid includes restorative justice in a republican system of criminal justice aimed at preserving dominion

(Braithwaite 2002a: 32). The bottom section consists of participatory restorative processes which, it is assumed, will regulate the great majority of offences. A more reduced space of punitive deterrence is located above the restorative space, to deal with offenders who are not intrinsically motivated to participate in voluntary reparation, but who calculate rationally the benefits and burdens of their behaviour. On top of the pyramid is a small triangle of incapacitation, to deal with incompetent or irrational offenders. Braithwaite writes that 'restorative justice will often fail ... and in such cases the safety of the community requires escalation to more punitive approaches' (Braithwaite 2002b: 166). He adds, however, that 'restorative justice values should be given as much space as possible within the punitive institution' (ibid.: 166). In Braithwaite's view, the longer-term ambition is to enlarge the bottom and reduce the top, and to include restorative values as much as possible within the punitive justice institution.

Dignan has adapted the proposal in his 'enforcement pyramid' (Dignan 2002: 181, 2003: 147). The main difference is that Dignan includes the judicial sanctions in the middle space more explicitly in restorative justice. What Braithwaite called deterrent punishment is, in Dignan's model, replaced by two components, a larger one for court-imposed restoration orders and a smaller one for court-imposed presumptive restorative punishments.

The pyramid shown in Figure 5.1 is largely inspired by these two designs. The levels are not conceived as closed boxes, but as constituent parts of a dynamic system which are mutually dependent and reinforcing and between which cases can circulate. Moving a case a level up is admissible only if it is necessary; moving a case a level down is required whenever possible.

Deliberative conflict resolution in the community

The bottom level of the pyramid is not included in the practices covered by my restricted definition of restorative justice. It does not deal with criminalisable matters, but with frictions, conflicts and incivilities, which, if they last too long, can erode the quality of social life in families, neighbourhoods, schools or workplaces. The capacity to resolve such tensions through respectful inclusive deliberation is vital for community life. But it also provides a fruitful soil for developing restorative justice practices, described in later sections.

In daily life, conflicts between people emerge because of misunderstandings, conflicting interests or wounded pride. Neighbours continue to annoy one another, even after they have forgotten the

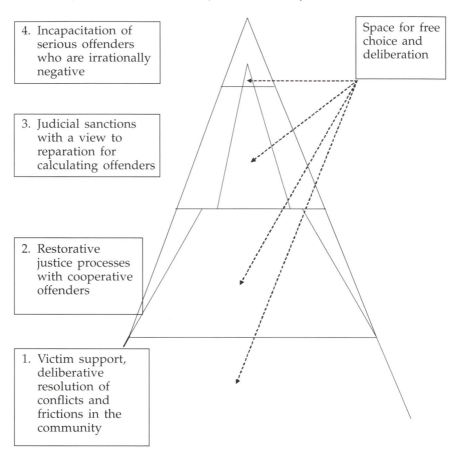

Figure 5.1 Pyramid of restorative law enforcement

incident that originally caused the problem; loitering youths cause irritation and feelings of insecurity; colleagues develop deep mutual aversion for vague reasons; slumbering tensions or open quarrels in families degrade relations; incidents in schools escalate into enduring conflicts. All such open or unarticulated hostilities between individuals or groups poison social life far beyond the actual protagonists. If they continue, they can destroy social life.

Fortunately, common sense keeps most such tensions within limits and brings them to an end. The parties understand their interest in finding a constructive solution to keep their network of relations intact. One of the neighbours in a conflict decides to speak some friendly words over the fence, receives an equally friendly response and the de-escalation has begun. Disagreeing colleagues have to cooperate on a project and find the experience rewarding. People are brought to speak out constructively or to erase their mental oppositions, possibly after informal mediation by a neighbour, a common friend, a colleague, a diplomatic teacher, a member of the family or another person of confidence, or even after a de-escalating police intervention. But sometimes there is no calming down because no informal mediator is available, the tensions have escalated too far, mutual stereotypes block constructive communication or simply because of stubbornness. The tension rises, mutual bullying gets out of hand and may escalate into serious crime.

Where there are no natural mediators, an impartial third person must be found. Examples abound in restorative justice literature of mediation and conferencing in schools, in neighbourhoods, in welfare work and so on. While these are not included in my strict definition of restorative justice, they are clearly vital foundations for a community and society climate in which restorative justice responses to crime can thrive. To extend a generalised approach to conflict resolution which is based on a philosophy of participation and inclusion, agencies must be available and accessible in schools, neighbourhoods and other local community levels. They must be supported, but not steered, by the authorities.

Such community practices can best be based on a network of community development initiatives in neighborhoods and other territorial entities (Blad 1996b, 1998; Peper and Spierings 1999; Pranis 2001). The staff need not be highly professional, but can consist of guided volunteers, comparable with the 'peacemakers' in the South African Zwelethemba project mentioned in Chapter 1 (Shearing 2001). Such proximate centres may respond to the requests of local citizens or offer their services proactively. They work with a broad scope of daily frictions, misunderstandings and conflicts, such as quarrels between neighbours, tensions in families, conflicts between ethnic groups or annoyance caused by youths hanging around.

The initiatives are also available for settling benign local offences if victim and offender agree to participate. Many relatively non-serious offences, such as vandalism, fighting or theft, involve victims and offenders who live in the same area. While a police or judicial response may be counterproductive for local social life, a possible local agreement between the stakeholders can be much more constructive. Mediation by the local community centre can help to reach such an agreement. But if a deliberative solution cannot be reached, referral to the police remains possible. Conversely, if the police are informed about a local offence, they should consider referring the case down to the local mediation initiative, possibly after consulting the victim. Such a referral will usually be more effective in preserving social peace in local communities and is in line with the parsimony principle: in the type of society we advocate, the use of (judicial) force should be strictly limited to what is necessary.

One of the considerable advantages of locating this offer in proximate community centres is that it can be integrated into a more comprehensive initiative of community development. As seen in the Zwelethemba modal (Shearing 2001), its activities are not limited to resolving conflicts, but can focus even more on revitalising community life and empowering the population. In Pranis' words, conflict-resolving dialogue may become community dialogue, make links to larger community responsibility and increase the sense of community capacity (Pranis 2001). In that sense, what starts as negative tensions or conflicts can be transformed into positive forces for community-building.

Finally, expanding the offer for deliberative conflict resolution in communities may help to develop the overall mental and social capacities for dialogue, listening with respect and seeking consensus in conflict resolution. In the longer term, it could contribute to a shift in the cultural climate, from using force and threats to using diplomacy and constructive dialogue. It would decrease improper appeal to societal institutions for trivial matters and increase the search for autonomous conflict resolution. It would favour the discovery of the common self-interest in taking active responsibility in the development of respectful communities, driven by solidarity.

Restorative justice processes

The most common restorative justice processes were briefly described in Chapter 1. Restorative justice advocates agree that these inclusive deliberative responses to crime in order to achieve the best possible reparation of the harms caused form the core of restorative justice in practice.

The main difference from the earlier stage is that the focus is now on settling the aftermath of an offence. Dominion has been intruded on and public interest is involved. In addition to being an arrangement with the victim, the response needs to reassure the public that rights and freedoms are taken seriously. The intrusion even qualifies for a coercive judicial response if necessary. But the dominion concept imposes parsimony, meaning that priority must be given to the less intrusive responses. That is why the police, for example, or the public prosecutor in continental European systems must consider referring registered crimes to the local community centres described in the previous section.

The police or the public prosecutor can also refer a case to more specialised agencies for monitoring restorative justice processes. In contrast to the local community centres, the specialised agencies will have the capacity to work with crimes for which the main stakeholders do not live in the same area and with more serious crimes, and will operate in parallel or in conjunction with the police and the justice system. It should be a rule that no judicial procedure should be initiated without a previous attempt at, or at least consideration of, a restorative process. Such an obligation has been specified in the New Zealand CYPFA since 1989, and in the new Belgian Juvenile Justice Act 2006.[2] The principle is that victims are entitled to an opportunity for restoration, and that the need for restoration certainly pertains after serious crime. Like Braithwaite and Dignan, I assume that a great proportion of crimes will be resolved by such voluntary restorative processes. It is expected that this proportion will increase as the agencies monitoring restorative encounters become more skilled and more widespread and available, and as the public gets more used to this way of working.

Besides these specialised agencies for monitoring restorative encounters, specific victim support is needed as well. Indeed, as advanced in the first chapter, victim support on its own is the first concern in a consequential restorative justice approach. The local community centres are able to deal with many of the victim's needs, but not all, and not always. Some victimisations are so traumatising, for example, that they require a more specialised response. Hence the need to develop a network of accessible centres for victim support. The network must operate autonomously, but be able to work in close relation with the police and the justice system. Its tasks are to provide welfare-oriented assistance to victims, possibly to advise victims in restorative processes and to help them through complicated judicial procedures.

Both agencies for monitoring restorative processes and agencies for victim support are (financially) supported, but not steered, by administrative and judicial authorities. Their cooperation with the police and the judiciary will be most effective if done from a position of autonomy, because their inclusive, bottom-up approach is fundamentally different and cannot be inserted into the top-down coercive apriorism in the control institutions.

But the state cannot withdraw completely. The complete absence of the state from the process would leave the parties on their own to find a solution. State authorities would not be guaranteeing respect for rights and freedoms and would thus not be assuring dominion. To give this assurance, the state must guarantee that everything possible will be done to respect and restore the intruded-upon dominion. Leaving space for, or referring to, a voluntary restorative deliberation does not mean renouncing a response to the offence. The state remains present, at least in the background, and has a number of responsibilities.

First, the state verifies that the deliberation actually takes place and results in an acceptable outcome; it provides an opportunity for the parties to leave the deliberative process and turn to the traditional judicial response if one of them feels that their interests are not adequately acknowledged in the deliberative process. In this way, the authorities demonstrate that they take dominion seriously, not only with regard to the victim's rights and freedoms but also as a guarantor of the offender's rights and as a safeguard for the collectively assured set of rights and freedoms.

Second, the state must in the background safeguard the power balance in the deliberation. Despite a high degree of deliberative accountability in conferences and other restorative processes, there is a considerable risk that such meetings turn into serious abuses of power and unreasonably punitive outcomes (Dignan 2002; Roche 2003). Several mechanisms are possible to check the power balance, on top of which state guarantee is needed.

Third, some pressure on the offender may be needed. Though voluntariness is said to be crucial in restorative processes, one must not be naïve. Offenders do not ask to participate in a conference or to be involved in mediation. The great majority of them probably seek to get away with the least possible sanction. They accept participation because they are under pressure from their family or from other members of their community of care, or even from the threat of being referred to court (Boyes-Watson 2000). Restorative justice processes leave a broad space for free choice and deliberation, but they have also a margin of social pressure. The more pressure is needed to bring the parties to meet, the closer is the eventuality that the case will need to be referred to court.

Judicial pressure and reparative sanctions

The parsimony principle in the use of judicial coercion requires that all options for a non-coercive response are thoroughly explored and given a full chance. As noted before, diversion from the judicial procedures is obligatory whenever possible. Hence the criminal investigation is not only focused on establishing the facts and guilt, but also on finding out the personal, relational and social prejudices caused by the offence. It includes considerable opportunities for input by victims and others affected by the crime. It also explores the potential for negotiation, and thus for diversion towards restorative deliberations or for possible restorative sanctions if a deliberative response is not possible.

In principle, every prosecution is preceded by or done in parallel with a referral to a restorative process agency situated at the second level, as described in the previous section. This is not only because of the parsimony rule to try all non-coercive options thoroughly, but also because of the victim's overall entitlement to a restorative option, if relevant. In the exceptional cases where the prosecutor does not refer to the restorative processes, he must justify why he did not. Successful mediation does not preclude possible prosecution. Otherwise, the seriousness of the crime would be for many prosecutors a reason to insist on prosecution and to not give mediation a chance. Moreover, mediation deals only with the victim–offender controversies, while the public dimension may also have to be addressed.

There are several reasons why an appeal to the public juridical system may be necessary. Often, the voluntary process cannot be achieved, because the victim or the offender refuses to participate in the encounter or because an agreement cannot be reached. Some particular offences may provoke such public turmoil because of their seriousness, repetitiveness or other circumstances that a public response is considered vital to restore social peace.

The decision to prosecute in court must be justified with positive arguments, i.e. by demonstrating that it is in the victims' interests or necessary to preserve community peace or for safety or public order. The simple observation that the law has been broken is insufficient to start up a judicial procedure.

Once the procedure has started, it should at all stages allow easy exits towards voluntary informal crime regulation. For example, the offender may accept participation in a mediation process after having experienced judicial pressure, or the victim may accept meeting the offender once the initial emotional reaction has passed or because he has received financial compensation for his material losses.

Judicial interventions lead to sanctions including obligations and deprivation of liberty. How restorative justice relates to these sanctions is a matter of debate. Adherents of the process-based definition of restorative justice hesitate or even refuse to include them in the restorative approach (McCold 2000). Maximalists try to reform the judicial intervention itself in a restorative direction.

The differences between Braithwaite's and Dignan's pyramids are illustrative of the divergence. When restorative justice processes fail, Braithwaite (2002b) abandons restorative justice in favour of punitive and deterrent reactions. He maintains, however, that restorative values should be given as much space as possible within the punishing environment, and he favours de-escalation down the pyramid towards restorative processes whenever possible. Dignan (2002) sticks to the restorative primacy at court level, and advances court-imposed restoration orders and restorative punishments for recalcitrant and persistent offenders.

I am sympathetic to Dignan's option. First, because I share his concern that Braithwaite's position would lead to a two-track model and that it leaves unanswered the instrumental and ethical problems with the punitive responses (see Chapter 2). Secondly, it seems to be inconsistent in principle to give up the socio-ethical added value of the restorative approach if resistance is met. Also for non-cooperative offenders, the reason for rejecting their behaviour is that they harm victims and assurance of dominion; the social response must therefore express that as far as possible by aiming at maximum possible reparation of that harm. As stated by Blad: 'For restorative justice, punishment orientated law is not a backup; it is a contradiction' (Blad 2003: 206). I argued in Chapter 2 that only the need to repair harm – not deterrence – justifies the possible use of coercion. The deterrent impact of the judicial intervention comes not from the infliction of pain, but from the certainty that a sanction will follow (Braithwaite 2005), even if it is not intended to be painful but an unavoidable obligation.

Contrary to Dignan, however, I do not speak of restorative punishments but of reparative sanctions. The main reasons for that have been explained previously. Dignan himself specifies that the restorative punishments he has in mind are not 'conceptualised in an unambiguously punitive manner', but 'in a straightforwardly reparative manner as a more constructive and meaningful undertaking' (Dignan 2002: 225). That is exactly where I make the difference between punishment and restorative sanction. Whereas Braithwaite backs priority for restorative justice processes with a punitive criminal justice system, Dignan opts for a back-up from a criminal justice system, imposing punishments that are not really punishments. The ambiguity is probably due to the lack of distinction between coercion and the deliberate imposition of pain. Backing up deliberative restorative justice processes by the possibility of judicial coercion is necessary, but intentionally imposing pain is ethically rejected. That is why the criminal justice system has to be reformed into a primarily restorative one.

Reparative sanctions are not punitive because they are not meant to intentionally inflict pain but to serve as much as possible the reparative goal. So, for example, if negotiated restorative actions cannot be reached, reparative gestures can be imposed. They will probably be limited to material restitution or compensation to the victim, or at the maximum consist of a letter of apologies to the victim. Another possibility is the reform of the system of fines, so that it becomes a financial contribution to a victims' fund or to another social agency. Community service can be imposed and understood as a symbolic compensation for the harm caused to social life. These judicially imposed obligations have a primarily reparative aim, though their restorative impact will almost always be less than after a deliberative process. That is why I call these sanctions 'reparative' and not 'restorative'.

Even at that level, a space of deliberation remains, but it is limited. The offender can try to negotiate with the judge and decide to comply or not. To enforce compliance with these primarily reparative sanctions, additional pressure may be exerted by (threatening or carrying out) explicitly unpleasant deprivations of liberty, such as a curfew or forced stay in a closed facility. In principle they last only until the offender accepts the reparative sanction. A maximum limit is, however, needed to ensure that very resistant or stubborn offenders do not undergo a disproportionately long sentence while not representing a serious threat to public safety (Dignan 2002; Walgrave 2002a). The next main section deals with the limits of possible judicial coercion.

Incapacitation

Finally, some irrational or fanatic offenders clearly represent a serious threat to public safety. They have committed serious crimes and there is a justified fear that they will reoffend, causing new severe victimisations. Or they appear to be incorrigible and continue to commit moderately serious offences after several interventions. Deliberative restorative actions have had no effect, and reparative sanctions seem not to offer a reasonable expectation that the threat will end. In such cases, restorative justice has reached its limits. Priority must then be given to incapacitation to preserve dominion. That is important for the potential victims, who might otherwise undergo further serious suffering from new crimes, and for the public assurance, so that the authorities are seen to be taking the preservation of dominion seriously.

From another point of view, taking away the offender from his 'natural' environment may also be necessary to protect the offender from being victimised by revenge or vigilant actions.

Both Braithwaite and Dignan call the top triangle of their pyramid the space for incapacitation of 'incompetent or irrational actors' (Braithwaite 2002a: 32, 2002b: 159) or 'actors who are likely to inflict serious physical harm on others' (Dignan 2002: 180). It is unclear whether they consider it a punishment or a security measure.

There is a theoretical difference between incapacitation and punishment. In punishment, an offender is locked up because *he* has committed a crime; in incapacitation, the offender is confined because *we* are afraid. The examination of the reasons for confining an offender focuses on different issues. In the case of punishment, the examination looks at whether guilt is established and the offender thus deserves imprisonment; we ask questions about the offender's behaviour. In the case of incapacitation, the question is why we conclude that locking up is necessary for security; we ask questions about our own appraisal of risks. The decision to incapacitate depends on the assumed dangerousness of the offender, and the assumption itself has to be questioned. In Christian Debuyst's words 'When I say "this man is dangerous", I say in fact "I am afraid".'[3]

In principle, the choice here is for incapacitation because of the rejection of punishment as an intentional infliction of pain. However, estimating danger is an intrinsically prospective move because it tries to assess possible future risks, and we have already seen how unsteady a basis this is for constructing decent and controllable legal safeguards. What evidence do we have to assess the danger? How long will the incapacitation last? Current practice with incapacitating the dangerous insane is not encouraging. Blad, in favour of marginalising punishment as an ultimate remedy, wrote: 'If we can imagine that there *could* be only one crime per year so horrible ... that we could accept the state's right to punish, we should want it to be punished in a framework that guarantees due process' (Blad 2006: 111).

In fact, we must probably fall back on traditional punitive principles to be applied to serious offenders who are unwilling to participate in deliberation, and who are likely to reoffend seriously. I must admit that such an incapacitation model looks very much like the actuarial justice model described by Feeley and Simon (1992). But I do not see any other solution.

Even here, priority for security concerns does not completely exclude tentative actions in view of reparation. If possible, mediation can be tried in detention and inmates may be encouraged to undertake reparative efforts or to work for a victims' fund, for example.

The question of juridical safeguards

As long as restorative justice practices were carried out by advanced practitioners, framed – often at a distance – by thoughtful lawyers and enlightened judges and followed by committed academics, one could expect that the lack of formal legal rules would not lead to catastrophes regarding the rights of the stakeholders. But as restorative justice seems to be moving towards the mainstream, more is needed. Certainly the maximalist ambition imposes a careful scrutiny of the relation between restorative justice and the law. The basic question is how to combine the informal flexibility (crucial in the participatory priority of restorative justice) with the formality needed to control the balances demanded by the principles of the democratic state. The question is far from being resolved, and a general solution cannot be advanced because of the different legal, judicial and social traditions. But some lines can be drawn to orient reflection.

Punitive criminal justice is guided by a series of principles that are supposed to safeguard the legal rights of the defendant and other players in the procedure. Some have examined whether restorative justice would meet these requirements, such as equality, presumption of innocence, due process, right to a defence, proportionality of punishment, etc. (Ashworth 1993; von Hirsch 1998; Feld 1999; Van Ness 1999; Eliaerts and Dumortier 2002; Skelton and Frank 2004). These studies address relevant questions, but their conclusions – which are not unanimous – cannot be decisive. It is difficult to transfer unchanged the deontological principles of a punitive criminal justice system to a restorative justice system. Restorative justice is based on a different paradigm, inspired by a clearly distinct philosophy; it conceptualises the essentials of crime differently, aims at different goals, involves other key actors, uses dissimilar means and operates in a different social and juridical context. It is not possible to judge different paradigms with the same criteria, just as it is not possible to play American football with the rules of soccer.

Law and legal rules are not the inviolable rulers of society; they are servants to the quality of social life. Hence, if a socially constructive practice appears to be at odds with legal constraints, one should not delimit the practices but rather change the constraints. The questions about juridical principles must be turned around. Instead of trying to submit restorative justice to traditional criminal justice principles, the legal criteria need to be revised and reformulated in line with the restorative justice philosophy (Blad 2003: 202). This does not mean abandoning the values behind the traditional principles, but adapting their interpretation to preserve the socially constructive potential of restorative justice. 'Judges have an important role to play in monitoring restorative justice programmes, but should approach this role in a new way' (Roche 2003: 4). What that would look like is currently the subject of reflection and discussion.

A justice system that is primarily oriented towards restoration has some commonalities with the traditional criminal justice system, and also some crucial differences. In Chapter 2, restorative justice was presented as inversed constructive retributivism. Both the criminal justice and the restorative justice systems clearly blame the (harmful) norm transgression, hold the offender responsible for his behaviour and seek to restore a kind of balance. Moreover, where necessary, both use coercion according to legal standards.

The retributive character of both punitive and restorative justice provides retrospectivity of the intervention, which is crucial for the development of legal safeguards. Both the blame for the harmful norm transgression and the responsibility of the offender refer to an event and to behaviour in the past, and therefore offer a controllable yardstick for the intervention in the present. In traditional sentencing, it is the basis for two crucial questions (Ashworth 1986): have the facts been established and has the (degree of) guilt been established? Sentencing in view of reparation adds a third question: how can the sanction best contribute to reparation? This question is not asked in punitive retributive justice, because of the a priori option for punishment and because it is not prospective. Restorative justice, on the contrary, aims at repairing the harm and is therefore also prospective.[4]

In both approaches, sentencing is not a purely automatic process. Both punitive and reparative sentencing are nuanced. The amount of punishment or obligation to compensate is defined not only by the seriousness of the crime or the harm, but also by the offender's mental capacities and material resources, the degree of premeditation or intentionality, and the social and situational particularities of the event.[5]

The challenge to the traditional legal constraints comes from the key difference between the two visions of justice: the punitive apriorism vs the aim at restoration. To attain the restorative goal, ample space must be allowed for informal deliberations including all stakeholders, which is contrary to the strict formalisation in the hands of professionals in the penal system. It puts pressure on the traditional legal principles. The following subsections illustrate this for a few: equality of all citizens before the law, presumption of innocence and proportionality of sanction.

Equality

If one of the main stakeholders refuses to participate in a restorative process, the likelihood of a constructive encounter is lost or drastically reduced. Both offenders and victims thus depend on the willingness of the other, and this creates inequality (of opportunity). Moreover, the deliberations are not guided by general standards, so that both the processes and the outcomes may vary greatly. It is feared that the result is 'likely to be a form of "justice by geography" or "postcode lottery"' (Ashworth 2001, in McLaughlin *et al*. 2003: 169).

The objection is valid, but is not decisive. Equality of citizens before the law is a valuable good to aim at, but complete equality of citizens is unrealistic in a society where inequality is endemic. The claimed equality in the face of traditional criminal justice procedures is mostly rhetoric, as seen through huge differences in sentences for the same offences which cannot be explained by juridical qualifications only. It helps to have the smartest (often the most expensive) lawyer, to be confronted with a less smart public prosecutor and to have a lenient judge. Research shows that judges pass considerably differently sentences, depending partly on their 'penal attitudes' (Hogarth 1971; de Keijser 2000), but also on the race, sex, social status and attractiveness of the defendant and on other non-juridical attributes. Wealth, status and power even influence the legislative process of criminalising or not certain behaviour. Some people are better able than others to get the state power on their side, including the power of the criminal justice machine.

One might wonder whether equality of citizens would in general not be better achieved if the protagonists were stripped of their power and status and met each other in a personal face-to-face dialogue, as proposed in a restorative encounter.

It is inconsistent to refuse all citizens the possible benefits of restorative processes under the argument that it might lead to inequality for some while the equality principle is poorly achieved in penal justice itself. Moreover, the possible inequality created by unequal access to a restorative justice process can be mitigated by the consistent restorative orientation of the whole system, as well as in court. Victims who miss the restorative dialogue can benefit from a judicial sentence focused on reparation. Offenders who have to deal with a victim refusing to take part will still have an opportunity in court to show their willingness to make up, by complying with orders for material compensation and community service, for example.

A more fundamental problem is that equality is often misunderstood in legal rhetoric. If an illiterate person is subject to the same complicated judicial rules as a defendant with a diploma in law, if the rich pay exactly the same fine as the poor, if the desperate victim is offered the same support as the one who does not care, this kind of equality is 'a travesty of equal justice' (Braithwaite 2002a: 160). It is like organising an 'equal' tree-climbing contest between a cat and a dog. Legal practice mostly understands equal as identical, whereas it should be understood as equivalent, being of equal value (Claes 2004). People should have equal access, equal rights and be guaranteed equal possibilities before the judiciary, which means that their personal differences should be taken into account in assuring these equalities. The rules of the current justice system do not guarantee this equivalence any better than the informal restorative justice processes.

Presumption of innocence

Promoting voluntary participation in deliberative responses to crime is often assumed to threaten the principle of presumption of innocence, according to which people are innocent unless a due criminal procedure has established guilt. Offenders who accept at an early stage of the procedure participation in mediation or conferencing seem to implicitly admit their guilt. It is feared that this could cost them dearly if a court procedure follows.

Four possible situations are imaginable.

1 The offender denies his guilt and wishes to go to court. In fact, a considerable proportion of suspects currently refuse to participate because they claim their innocence. Nobody will deny their right to a fully fledged criminal procedure to assess guilt or innocence. Once guilt been established by a court, the offer for mediation or another restorative process can (and should) be repeated (as is the case in the New Zealand juvenile justice system).

2 An innocent person could be pressurised to participate and thus to implicitly – and falsely – admit guilt. I do not know of any case in which an innocent person was involved as an offender in a restorative process and accepted an agreement that charged him with additional constraints. But the possibility to consult a lawyer could be an additional guarantee.

3 The presumed offender has actually committed the crime. In that case, an early restorative dialogue is far preferable, as has been argued throughout this book.

4 The most delicate situation is where the presumed offender has indeed committed the crime and is prepared to participate in a restorative process for the victim, but refuses to admit guilt juridically because he would not accept punishment. Such situations occur. There is evidence that the restorative process itself can help to overcome the initial defensive attitude of the offender (Wright 2003; Braithwaite 2005). Considering participation as an implicit admission of guilt would deprive the offender of the possibility of taking advantage of all juridical opportunities to deny the facts.[6]

Legislation can help to cope with the last problem. In the New Zealand CYPFA 1989, for example, the family group conference does not depend on the juvenile admitting the facts, but simply that he does not deny them. Not denying sounds more provisional, and can be retracted if the conference comes to nothing. The new Belgian Juvenile Justice Act 2006 also does not require a confession by the offender for a mediation or a conference. The referral is possible if there are 'serious indications of guilt'. The Belgian Act also clearly stipulates that participation in a mediation process cannot be used as an admission of guilt in a further stage of the procedure.

All in all, the problem seems chiefly theoretical. My hypothesis is that a good legal text and good lawyers can reduce very much the risk of participation being used as an admission of guilt. Rejecting the possibility for a restorative justice dialogue at an early stage simply to preserve the principle of presumption of innocence is like throwing out the baby with the bathwater.

Proportionality

In penal justice, the seriousness of the crime committed is the yardstick for deciding on the proportionate amount of pain to inflict. It is considered an essential principle for assuring legal protection (von Hirsch 1993). Many penal theorists doubt that proportionality is feasible in a restorative justice procedure. Certainly in processes like mediation or conferencing there is no guarantee that the resulting obligations will be proportionate to the seriousness of what the offender has done. Not only could the processes yield disproportionate outcomes, but also a great variety in the outcomes, which would – again – lead to inequality among offending citizens.

In addition, imbuing judicial sentencing with restorative justice philosophy would render the seriousness of the crime invalid as the basis for assessing proportionality. Sentencing in a restorative justice system would address first of all the prejudices caused. The judge would exploit to the full the remaining opportunities for deliberation and persuasion in the court session, and even refer the case down to restorative justice processes if the protagonists finally were willing to join in such a process. The reparative calibre of the sanction is essential. It thus refers to the harm caused rather than to a pre-existing tariff of punishments for the type of offence.

Proportionality in penal justice is much less evident a concept than is suggested in penal theories. In its absolute dimension, there is no natural link between, for example, embezzling a million euros and spending two years in prison, committing a street robbery with physical violence and serving five years, or stealing a bicycle and being on probation for a year. In its relative dimension, classical research in criminology may reveal some consensus on the classification of a number of crimes on a scale of seriousness (Sellin and Wolfgang 1964), but it is not decisive, and the consensus certainly does not apply to all crimes. In particular, the ranking of white-collar crime is doubtful. While there is no question that physical violence is more serious than a cloakroom theft, the rank order between fraud and burglary is less clear cut.

It all amounts to social convention. While they are not purely arbitrary, the tariffs in the convention are variable over time and space, which makes it difficult to keep it as an absolute criterion (Wright 2003). Hence, it is not surprising that comparative surveys of actual sentencing practices do not demonstrate coherent proportionality. The quality of the top-down imposed proportionality is low.

Nevertheless, it remains unacceptable that, for example, a juvenile who stole a bicycle would spend a long period in a closed facility for this, even if this is part of an agreement after mediation or family group conferencing. So far, such kind of disproportionally severe outcomes are not observed after restorative processes. On the contrary, courts are generally more repressive (Braithwaite 2002b). Moreover, Maxwell and Morris (1996) found that family group conferences seemed to be guided by a kind of intuitive proportionality, so that the most serious offences were followed by the most onerous agreements.

Hence also the proportionality argument seems not to be a reason to reject restorative processes. On the contrary, it is worth exploring whether grass-roots assessments of what is a reasonable response, based on the main stakeholders' appreciation, would not be more appropriate than a preconceived imposed tariff. The deliberative way of relating the offence to the response is probably more related to what happened and to what is felt as 'just' in real life than it is in judicial sentencing.

Public nature

Restorative justice encounters are supposed to be confidential in order to ensure genuine communication which cannot be abused outside of the encounter. Therefore most of the dispositions to locate restorative processes within the legal frame admit that only the formal agreements be communicated to the judiciary, not the content of the discussion. From a purely juridical standpoint, it may be difficult to accept, because it keeps away the dialogue from juridical checks (Hildebrandt 2005). In the juridical rationale, all elements and procedures which lead to a judicially imposed deprivation of liberty must be public so that they can be controlled with regard to their legal and human rights merits.

The need for publicity to check respect for legal safeguards may be overstated. Currently, 'the public' has access to criminal justice procedures and sentences through the possibility of attending public court sessions and through the media. The information obtained is far too incomplete to allow effective public control. It is the professionals and especially the lawyers who take care of controlling the respect for legal safeguards, and publicity is a very marginal condition only. The advantage of making public restorative encounters does not counterbalance the detrimental impact it would have on the quality of the deliberation.

Additionally, it is feared that shielding the restorative dialogue from publicity strips it from a crucial mission of criminal justice: providing a public censure of offending behaviour. This issue has already been commented on in Chapter 2. Public censure speaks through the public mandate of the response to the crime. It makes clear to the public that the act is not tolerated and that the authorities sanction a solution. But the message is different if it comes from a public degradation ceremony ending in a top-down inflicted amount of pain as in current criminal justice, or from a request to make up in dialogue with the victim as in restorative justice. The content of this dialogue does not need to be publicised to inform the public that the act is not tolerated.

Respect for human rights and a legal frame

The legal constraints, such as equality of citizens before the law, presumption of innocence and proportionality, are intended to protect valuable human and democratic principles throughout the preconditioned coercive judicial procedures and sentences. But they appear to be mainly paper tigers, hollowed out as they are in current judicial practice. It is therefore difficult to maintain them as decisive criteria to restrain the potential of restorative responses to crimes.

Restorative processes

Giving priority to restorative processes for all offences where victim and offender are willing to take part in the process is not contradictory to the concern for the values in the legal constraints and for citizens' democratic rights. On the contrary, there are reasons to believe that well conducted mediations or restorative conferences come closer to promoting true equality of citizens and a more meaningful relationship between the offence and the restorative action than judicial sentences do. Submitting such processes to strict juridical rules would strip them of their huge potential for communication and promotion of peace.

But they cannot take place in a juridical vacuum. How restorative justice relates to the legal frame is a matter of debate. Based on what is currently known, a number of options point to possible ways of ensuring respect for legal safeguards.

1 Facilitators must be educated to be aware of human rights, to ensure a balance of power in the encounter and, if necessary, to help orient the agreement towards a reasonable relationship between the act and the restorative action.

2 All participants must have the possibility of consulting a lawyer before or after the encounter. In family group conferencing in New Zealand (and, conditionally, in Belgium), the lawyers are even allowed to be present in the meeting.

3 Citizens who do not want to participate must have the option to go through a traditional judicial procedure; all participants

who estimate that they cannot obtain what they consider as their legitimate rights and interests must have the option to step out of the restorative process and go to court.

4 The new Belgian Juvenile Justice Act 2006 adds another juridical safeguard: it stipulates that the outcome of mediation or conferencing must be submitted for confirmation to the public prosecutor or the judge; they can, however, only reject the outcome if it clearly endangers public order.

Whereas restorative justice is currently practised mostly at a developmental stage, conducted by committed and well informed teams guided by renovating ideals, it is yet to be seen what would happen if restorative justice moved into the mainstream. What would happen if referral to a restorative justice process was an evident daily action, taken with no more reflection than putting cream in your coffee? Or if facilitating a conference became a routine job and part of a heavy caseload? Some pushy professionalism, inaccuracy, cynicism and loss of patience may then threaten respect for the rights of the stakeholders. Hence there is a need for checking continuously the respect for human and legal rights in the follow-up to the gradual mainstreaming of restorative justice.

Juridical procedures in view of reparation

When no deliberative agreement can be achieved, the judicial procedure which may be started up in view of reparative sanctions or incapacitation must allow the checks and balances that always apply to judicial decisions in a constitutional democracy – clear procedural rules, full involvement of lawyers, a restricted range for sentencing and, above all, respect for human rights.

I do not speak of proportionality, because this concept suggests not only an upper limit but also a lower one. On the contrary, I have argued for parsimony in using coercion and sanctions. There is thus no reason to maintain a lower limit. Mercy can be more constructive for social life than an imposed minimal sanction (Braithwaite 2002b). If, for example, the offender shows clear repentance and the victim is vindicated, the mere fact of appearing before court and hearing the public rejection of the offence can carry a stronger message than the additional imposition of a (reparative) obligation because it is mandatory by law.

An upper limit is needed, but setting it for reparative sanctions cannot rely on the tradition of the punitive relation between seriousness of crime and amount of pain inflicted. In an earlier article, we proposed a kind of restorative justice proportionality which would relate the seriousness of the harm caused to the restorative effort (Walgrave and Geudens 1997). But it is not certain that this makes sense. The difference between the seriousness of a crime, as in punitive proportionality, and the seriousness of the harm, as in restorative understanding, may be purely theoretical. Indeed, we saw in Chapter 3 that criminalisation of behaviour should not address moral wrongfulness but social harmfulness. Attempts to estimate the seriousness of a crime appeared to amount to estimating the prejudices caused to victims and social life. The difference supposed between the seriousness of a crime and its harmfulness is thus not clear. Hence it is difficult to use it as a criterion on its own to set out a particular upper limit for the admissible amount of reparative efforts. In fact, the setting of reasonable upper limits for reparative sanctions needs to be based on experience. The publication of jurisprudence is the best way to achieve this.

Lawyers as partners of restorative justice

Throughout the procedure, the role of lawyers is of crucial importance (Shapland 2003). Lawyers of victims and offenders are often seen as the ultimate and most important guarantees of their clients' legal rights. It is no different in a restorative justice context. Rather than banning them from restorative justice through fear of them taking over or controlling what happens in the restorative processes, restorative justice should reflect on how to involve lawyers constructively as partners in the actions with a view to the best possible restoration.

However, their mission in a restorative justice environment is different from that in the current penal justice system. It is not to help the 'lone powerless defendant confronted with the mighty power of the coercive state' (ibid.: 208); it is also not bluntly trying to make the juridical procedure the most beneficial (or the least disadvantageous) possible for their client. Instead, lawyers must reconsider what is in their clients' best interest. It is to see their new 'role to support, rather than to challenge obstructively, restorative justice processes' (ibid.: 210). In terms of what is advanced in Chapter 3, lawyers must advise their clients on finding their way to the common self-interest within the boundaries set out by human rights and legal rules. The question is how their clients can take up their active responsibility while protecting their legitimate rights.

This may require a shift in mentality among many lawyers. Lawyers are currently educated primarily as fighters, aiming to win a battle; now they will have to learn to make peace. That is something quite different, as can be observed on the international scene from the interventions in Afghanistan and Iraq. Such a change in mentality is actually possible; it becomes clear through the role most youth advocates play in the New Zealand CYPFA (Morris 2004); it could also be observed in the pilot project with family group conferencing in Belgium (Vanfraechem 2006). If lawyers can make the shift from the traditional narrow view of their role in the punitive criminal justice system to a more open view of what really is in the best interests of their clients, lawyers can make a major contribution to the development of a functioning restorative justice system that respects human rights, procedural guarantees and sentencing limits.

Conclusion

The pyramid of restorative law enforcement in Figure 5.1 illustrates that restorative justice gives priority to voluntary deliberation with decisive participation by the stakeholders to resolve problems in the aftermath of crimes, but also that coercion and even public security are indispensable complements, and that a legal system is needed to frame the entire construction. Distinguishing restorative justice from punitive criminal justice does not mean totally abandoning coercion and legalism. Restorative justice deals with a particular kind of problem behaviour which has a formal public dimension, contrary to torts or improper behaviour for example, hence the need to keep a criminal justice system, which is, however oriented primarily towards doing justice through restoration, and not through punishment. In the longer term, the criminal justice system should evolve towards being a fully fledged restorative system and adapt its rules accordingly.

Interacting levels

The pyramid provides for the possibility of increasing pressure and coercion gradually. But even at the lowest level, the possibility of coercion must already be implicitly present. Yet the knowledge that the community of care, the local and wider community, the public authorities and finally the criminal justice system may expect, demand and if necessary enforce a gesture of reparation has an influence on even the most freely accepted deliberative level. For the victim, it is reassuring that victimisation is not tolerated and must be repaired. For the offender, it makes clear that he will in any case not escape his responsibility. For both, it is reassuring and moderating to know that the legal frame keeps the action within limits. For the community at large, it is a confirmation that the authorities take dominion seriously. In the pyramid, 'the rights/procedural justice discourse percolates down into restorative justice conferences' (Braithwaite and Parker 1999: 116). After all, such deliberation is never completely free of pressure and it would be unworldly to expect that it could be.

But conversely, the most powerful and coercive intervention systems must be permeated by the parsimony principle. Wherever and whenever favourable for restoration and possible in terms of public security, 'de-escalation back down the pyramid' (Braithwaite 2002b: 167) is needed. When the offender – after careful investigation or after a certain time – appears to represent a lesser danger to public security than was originally feared, when he finally agrees to comply with reparative sanctions, when social or judicial pressure has brought the victim and the offender to accept work towards a constructive agreement through an inclusive dialogue – each time, the cases should be left with, or given back to, the less coercive levels. This, of course, presupposes a moderated and reserved attitude in the more coercive agencies, and especially in the justice system. Not only must the rule of law 'percolate down into restorative justice', as stated above; restorative justice concerns must also 'bubble up the pyramid into legal discourse and procedures' (Braithwaite and Parker 1999: 116). As said earlier: the criminal justice system must transform its punitive apriorism and procedures with regard to proportionate punishments into a coherent priority for restoration in processing and in sanctioning.

Imitator paradox?

Let me end this chapter with a self-critical reflection. Does what I have proposed in this chapter go too far in enhancing 'the attractiveness of RJ for policy-makers in the criminal justice system', as Aertsen and his colleagues warned (Aertsen *et al.* 2006: 288)? In Pavlich's terms, have I walked into the trap of the 'imitator paradox', whereby 'restorative justice defines its governmentalities in opposition to basic concepts within the criminal justice system, but it does so by founding itself on many of those self-same concepts (e.g. crime, victim, offender and community)' (Pavlich 2005: 14)?

Obviously, I deal with the same world as does the current criminal justice system, in which part of the population does not see any common self-interest but pursues individual self-interest and behaves disrespectfully and in opposition to solidarity, taking no active responsibility for other citizens. At first sight, what I propose has a lot of resemblances to the traditional criminal justice system. As in that system, I do not contest 'the law's right to define crime' (ibid.: 35) and address the handling of legally defined crimes (though the reasons for criminalising behaviour are different); the proposal works with 'victims' and 'presumed offenders' (while accepting that these roles may become blurred during the deliberation); legal rules are accepted to steer the handling of the crimes (but the rules are more open for inclusive deliberation); the response is called retributive (turning the retributive action around, though); and it is hoped that reoffending is decreased by the restorative intervention (although this is a secondary objective only).

The main difference is the content of the crime concept. Probably not surprisingly, I am in favour of a collectivity where it is forbidden to take away other people's property, to hit or shoot each other. This is not only because, otherwise, I would risk losing my comfort or my life, but also because, without such rules, society would be a jungle. Rules are necessary to organise social life into a liveable collectivity. There is no good reason to reject the word 'crime' to refer to behaviours that are forbidden in order to preserve social life.

But the reason for criminalising such behaviour matters. The only acceptable reason is, as argued in Chapter 3, to preserve the quality of social life. Thinking this through logically constitutes another paradigm and yields several consequences for the criminal justice system.

1 Much behaviour of which the social harm is unclear, such as the use of drugs, should be decriminalised.

2 The objectives of enforcement must focus on repairing the harm, and restoring the victim and the quality of social life, rather than on inflicting a proportionate punishment on the offender.

3 The procedures must allow ample space for inclusive, deliberative solution-finding at the grass-roots level, and not be bound by a set of top-down imposed strict rules.

4 The current punitive apriorism is rejected.

Is this still too much of an imitation, as Pavlich might find? In my view, it is a step towards 'an alternative vision of justice aspiring to challenge the punitive, guilt-seeking, violent, pain-inflicting practices of justice calculated around criminal law and philosophies of the *lex talionis'* (ibid.: 106). But it is not 'justice as a never closed, never fully calculable, open and infinite idea that promises new ways to be with others' (ibid.: 115). I read Pavlich's book as a reminder that we will, like Sisyphus, never reach our utopian ideals, that we will never see 'the non-definable idea that forever calls us from the mists of what is to arrive' (ibid.: 115), but that we have to continue trying to move things as far as possible. Many will find that I have already gone too far.

Notes

1 In more recent publications, dominion has been renamed as 'freedom as non-domination'. This may make it easier to oppose it to the liberal concept typified as 'freedom as non-interference', but I see no other advantage in complicating the wording. I will therefore stick to the old naming, dominion.

2 'Law on Youth protection, on the taking in charge of minors who committed an act qualified as an offence, and on the reparation of the losses caused by that act' (15 May 2006). Restorative justice practices are largely introduced and promoted in the Act, but courts can still impose purely rehabilitative measures on youth offenders under 18.

3 Oral communication at the K.U. Leuven, 1990.

4 It must be noted here that genuine dialogue in deliberative processes is more adequate to assess the harm and to consider possible reasonable reparation, but we are considering here judicial proceedings with a view to reparation when these processes appeared not to work.

5 Again, such elements are evidently considered more adequately and thoroughly in deliberative conditions, such as the voluntary processes, but they are also crucial in the judicial sentencing discussed here.

6 Let me add that the juridical possibility of falsely denying the facts seems to me counterproductive to a constructive solution of the problems created by the offence and should therefore not be propagated. But we have to keep this possibility to ensure that true denials do not become impossible. Is it naïve to suppose that a non-punitive, reparation-oriented system would produce fewer such false denials?

Chapter 6

Democracy, criminology and restorative justice

This final chapter addresses the wider significance of restorative justice. It goes beyond the promotion of doing justice differently after a crime has occurred, and locates restorative justice into a larger movement for a more just and more participatory democracy.

The basic idea is that a restorative justice system, as described in Chapter 5, will function best in a societal context that presupposes active participation by responsible citizens, and is steered by socio-ethics, as described in Chapter 3. Conversely, restorative justice itself can considerably stimulate the emergence of such a social context. As Pelikan writes, traditional criminal justice is the 'apex of an authoritarian mode of conflict regulation, ... restorative justice being established and promoted as a countervailing force – striving for dominion and aiming at peace-making' (Pelikan 2007b: 1).

The idea is developed in three steps. First, an account will be given of the functioning of our democracies nowadays, with special attention to the way they deal with crime, justice and (un)safety issues. It will be a pessimistic story, but the reader should not become too depressed. Indeed, the second part positions social sciences, and especially criminology, as crucial contributors to the movement for more participatory and inclusive democracy. By feeding the democratic debate with methodologically well documented data and options, they can enhance the quality of that public debate and help to avoid populism. The third section then looks for the role of restorative justice in all this. Its indirect impact is that theoretical and empirical exploration of restorative justice is a great opportunity to release criminology from its 'embedded' position and to reposition it as an autonomous social science in the service of the quality of social life. Its direct impact is that the increased use of participatory practices to resolve the aftermath of a crime, and their extension to other fields of conflict, can be expected to promote citizens' self-confidence, so that they may more easily take up active responsibility and accept deliberative decision-making in all realms of social life.

Democracy endangered

A restorative justice system, as envisaged in the previous chapter, can function only if the powerful, potentially coercive institutions make parsimonious use of their power, limiting it to what is strictly necessary. This requirement goes beyond the criminal justice institutions. It supposes a responsive type of state power, sensitive to what is oriented, decided and resolved at the grassroots of society (Braithwaite 2002a). But the state can be responsive to the grassroots only if the grassroots do indeed orient, take decisions and resolve problems. A good society with a responsive state power and committed citizens taking active responsibility for the good functioning of society are mutually dependent.

The search is for a societal organisation which favours the achievement of common self-interest, based on the acknowledgment of the particular interests and needs for fulfilment of the individual citizens; it is framed into a motivating, developmental and responsive structure oriented to bind individual citizens' self-interests into a common project of common self-interest; it encourages citizens to participate so as to make their interests known and to deliberate on how they will see their self-interests associated in a project for common self-interest. If participation is lacking, the authorities decide upon what is, in their view, the common interest, which may alienate them from citizens' interests and needs. If deliberation is lacking, different self-interests confront each other and are not synthesised into a common project.

We have learned that democracy is the best possible state model to assure the well-being of the citizens. This seeming consensus hides extensive debates on how democracy can and should work (Barber 2003). Liberals or communitarians, advocates of representative or of direct democracies and others present different visions on the binding element(s) and driving forces in social life and on the balance between the individual liberties and state power; they have different opinions on how to govern social life and to enforce its rules; they advocate different positions on the tension between individual interests and the needs of community.

As an amateur in political theory, I cannot participate meaningfully in the debate. But, based on what I have written so far, it must be clear that the democracy I favour is one that fully serves quality of social life as the common interest, which is viewed as an association of individual interests. Such an association is possible only through continuous deliberation, driven maximally by intensive citizens' participation. Full and direct participation of all citizens in all governmental decisions cannot be absolute. But, Braithwaite writes, '... republics need constantly to nurture interest in participation, feelings of obligation to participate where one can and resources for participation by the resource-poor' (Braithwaite 2000b: 92).

Nowadays, such an ideal democracy is far from being achieved. A pessimistic story points to shrinking participation by the citizens, which endangers the quality of democracy as a whole. An optimistic version indicates active citizenship as it appears through engagements in NGOs, associations and local activities. I believe in a combination of both. While the current quality of our democracies is not good, there is a promising basis of civic commitment to develop a strong countervailing power.

Shrinking participation of citizens

Putnam (2000) gives a compelling account of the decline of social capital in the United States. Social capital 'refers to connections among individuals – social networks and the norms of reciprocity and trustworthiness that arise from them' (Putnam 2000: 19).[1] Social capital, the 'conceptual cousin' of community (2000: 21), is a private as well as a public good. 'The touchstone of social capital is the principle of generalized reciprocity' (2000: 134).

In reciprocity we expect that if we do something for our neighbour, our neighbour will do something for us. In generalised reciprocity, we do not necessarily expect that our neighbour will do something for us, but we believe that doing good in general will provide returns in the form of a peaceful and constructive social environment from which we will draw many benefits. We abide by the law, not because we obey 'some impossibly idealistic rule of selflessness, but rather because we pursue "selfinterest rightly understood"' (Putnam 2000: 135). We are committed to social life in general, because we expect reciprocity from the community and the society we live in. This presupposes honesty and trust in the honesty of others. 'Thick' trust is attributed to those we have good personal experiences with – our family and good friends. 'Thin' trust is given to the 'generalised other'. Thin trust is an attitude by which we give other people, including foreigners, the benefit of the doubt. Thin trust 'lubricates' social life and makes democracy work smoothly (Putnam 1993).

The concept of trust comes close to what is for Braithwaite and Pettit (1990) the assurance dimension in the dominion, i.e. the confidence that the others and the authorities will respect rights and freedoms (see Chapter 4). It should also be noted at this point that Putnam does not oppose individual self-interests to the obligations of social life. On the contrary, he sees social and individual interests as closely intertwined. This, of course, fits in well with the idea that individual self-interests are associated into a common self-interest.

Putnam describes how social capital has recently declined drastically in the USA, as expressed through less mutual confidence in business and other relations, less political and civic participation, decreasing commitment in the workplace, declining voluntary work and other indications. The loss of social capital has consequences for the quality of politics. 'Politics without social capital is politics at a distance' (Putnam 2000: 341). Civic participation in democracy fades away. Common-sense bottom-up input from everyday life gets lost and gives way to extremist, technocratic or professionalised options and decisions, making participation and control from the grassroots still more difficult.

There is no reason to believe that the USA has the monopoly on this deteriorating tendency. The decline in civic engagement and in mutual trust and the rise of lawyers and other professional experts in welfare agencies and in the governance of social life seem to be typical Western phenomena of recent decades. The distance between governments and citizens is increasing, the democratic deficit increases and the discontent of citizens grows.

Globalisation and uncertainty

What has happened? Putnam attributes the decline in civic engagement primarily to 'pressures of time and money ... suburbanization, commuting, and sprawl ... the effect of electronic entertainment – above all, television – ... and generational change' (Putnam 2000: 283). The question remains, however, how these dynamics came about. They can be seen as intermediate factors between the citizens' disengagement and fundamental macro-sociological developments that corrode the quality of social and democratic life. It is surprising that Putnam, commenting on a number of realms of social and economic life to document the loss of social capital, does not include dynamics in the field of crime, justice and safety. If he had done so, he would have seen that perception of more crime and less safety is probably the nucleus of infection which is gradually contaminating the overall quality of social life, civic commitment and democracy. And the basis for the deterioration of the perception of crime, justice and safety is capitalist globalisation.

In recent years, the relations between global socio-economic change, existential fear, politics in crime and justice issues and the decline of participatory democracy have been the subject of many debates and publications.[2] It is not my intention to discuss the variations on this theme here, but rather to present what I make of it.

In my view, it all began at the end of the 1960s, when activist movements spread over the Western world. What were originally student protests against concrete local and global policy issues (for example, the Vietnam war in the USA, the De Gaulle policy in France, language issues in Belgium) gradually broadened to contest the organisation of societies and the cultural hegemony as a whole. From demonstrating against war and warmongering governments, they began to attack all political and moral authority. Bourgeois society was reproached as oppressing the free deployment of individuals in all aspects of life.

The movement also penetrated developments in social sciences, especially those dealing with deviance. Traditional clinical sciences were stigmatised as being one-sidedly used and ideologically mis-used in order to attribute deviance to individual deficiencies. 'Anti-psychiatrists', such as Laing and Cooper, challenged the traditional categorisations of normal and abnormal. Radical and critical criminology saw crime as a normal response to an abnormal and unjust world and to its institutional interventions (as described in Taylor *et al.* 1973).

The movement was very influential. Within a decade, its ideas had seeped into mainstream culture, politics and the messages of moral authorities. It held the seeds of the so-called postmodernist and deconstructivist philosophy, announcing the end of the great religious, moral, nationalist and cultural stories, deconstructing the authority of churches and governments. People had to construct their own lives and to make decisions on the basis of their own moral code.

However, what was meant to be an emancipating movement actually detached people from a solid structure and moral and cultural frames. Appeals for greater responsibility of the individual actually led to selfish, hedonistic attitudes and a loss of binding elements in social life, causing cultural anxiety and uncertainty. This was not helped by the explosion of mass media – first television and later the Internet – which brought cultural globalisation. While relaxing in our armchair in front of the screen, we are confronted in our living-room with strange lifestyles, different morals and provocative opinions that challenge our own frame of moral, cultural and political beliefs, evidence and standards. The solid ground of our life is affected.

In the same period, capitalist globalisation boosted the financial and economic power of multinational enterprises, beyond the power of governments (Baumann 2000a). Finances move to where the most profit can be made. Multinational capitalist interest groups delocate investments, play the social models in different countries off against one another to keep down wages, social advantages and certainties, move employment to regions where the exploitation of labour forces is easier and more beneficial, manipulate the prices of crucial raw materials, destroy the environment, even promote war or peace. Moreover, legal and illegal immigrants, seeking some crumbs of Western wealth, add to the confrontation with cultural heterogeneity and the breakdown of the world with its familiar stakes and predictabilities.

The more capitalist interests are spread worldwide, the less local governments are able to control the basic conditions on which to develop their social, economic, welfare and cultural policies. On the contrary, governments have to accommodate capitalist interests to keep the economy going, which is needed to get the means to implement their policies. And so, capitalist globalisation tightens its grip on the world. Global economic, social and safety developments, with direct impact on citizens' living conditions and opportunities, have far transcended the decision margins of individual governments. Impotent to control the capitalist forces, governments submit their citizens to the market rhetoric through a discourse of responsibilisation. It is up to the citizens themselves to find their way around the mushrooming opportunities and offers, including the risks of being defrauded or cheated; they are primarily responsible for their own security. It leaves the citizens alone with their fear of being misled and misused (Karstedt and Farral 2004).

Both the cultural and moral fluidity and the socio-economic uncertainty are the basis for the overall *Unsicherheit* (Baumann 2000b: 137), an existential feeling of insecurity that affects all aspects of life – our relationships, our socio-economic position, our environment, our food, our health. We are living in an era of 'liquid modernity' (Baumann 2000b), in which nothing is fixed and nothing is predictable.

In principle, uncertainty is not necessarily negative. It can create new opportunities to break through the old rigid structures. This is, indeed, the case for the few best-off in societies, who profit from the deregulation of the markets. They have the power to 'steer the boat on the lake of liquid modernity'. Most citizens, however, are happy that they caught the boat, but are powerless to steer it. They row where the powerful tell them to row, but are uncertain about where that will bring them. Finally, those who missed the boat have to swim on their own, or drown.

The uncertainty is perceived by the mainstream as risk. We are obsessed with risks (Beck 1992; Giddens 1998). It is likely that, objectively, risks have not increased. We are currently, more than ever, pampered by *des protections civiles'*, as guaranteed through legal rights, and by *des protections sociales'*, as provided by the social system (Castel 2003). But we are very sensitive now to new 'humanly manufactured uncertainty', such as terrorism, global warming, unemployment, disrupted relations, dangerous traffic and 'predatory criminals' (Stenson 2001). Uncertainty makes us more sensitive to such risks. 'Dangerization is the tendency to perceive and analyse the world through categories of menace. It leads to continuous detection of threats and assessment of adverse probabilities, to the prevalence of defensive perceptions over optimistic ones and to the dominance of fear and anxiety over ambition and desire' (Lianos and Douglas 2000: 110–11).

These developments have initiated the tendencies for citizens to become increasingly cynical consumerists and for governments to focus ever more on crime, unsafety and punishment and to give in to penal populism. Both tendencies are mutually reinforcing.

Consumer democracy

What can citizens do? In the pessimistic version, citizens are increasingly aware of their powerlessness and understand that their governments have, at best, only marginal impact on social and political developments. Governments try to cope with the globality and complexity of matters by appealing increasingly to the expertise of economists, jurists, engineers (and 'embedded' criminologists). This creates a playground for self-interested lobbying by powerful groups in back rooms, which mostly results in the capitalist market being presented as a natural thing that cannot be avoided, so that the labour market must become more flexible, the wages of employees lower and the taxes for employers also lower.

Technical expertise is beyond the understanding and control of citizens, and thus increases still more the distance between the citizen and his government. The more citizens lose their grip, directly and indirectly, on the conditions of their existence, the more they find it impossible to contribute significantly to their own conditions of life and the more they reduce their social commitment. Many citizens no longer take any responsibility for the quality of social life. They try to hide away from insecurity by withdrawing into fortresses of cynical self-interest and retreating into a postmodern reconstruction of self-serving norms and values. 'Deciding what is illegal, or simply unfair or unethical, becomes idiosyncratic and personalised' (Kardstedt and Farrall 2007: 5). Social life is characterised by 'market anomie ... an increasing erosion of legal norms, moral standards and trust, culminating in a climate of mutual suspicion and rampant moral cynicism' (ibid.).

The democratic game has lost a great deal of its relevance for citizens' lives. It is hollowed out as a kind of shadow play. Elections are rituals with almost ornamental issues only, looked at like sports events. 'What does it matter ... if the crucial decisions that affect their destiny are no longer being made by democratic government at all?' (Barber 2003: xiii).

Indifference in democratic life is complemented by consumption of democratic institutions. Citizens consider the social institutions and the law from the point of view of consumers: they try to get the most possible benefits at the lowest possible price. Social institutions are consumed: rights and offers are exploited to the full and obligations are avoided or circumvented as far as possible, even if this leads to so-called 'everyday crimes of the middle classes' (Karstedt and Farrall 2007). 'Freedom becomes indistinguishable from selfishness, and is corrupted from within by apathy, alienation, and anomie; equality is reduced to market exchangeability and divorced from its necessary familial and social context; happiness is measured by material gratification to the detriment of the spirit' (Barber 2003: 24). In electoral campaigns, profits are offered as bargains and many citizens behave like bargain hunters: they do not vote for the candidate who proposes the best option for social life but for the one who is expected to defend best their own selfish interests. Democracy becomes a consumer democracy, an arena of struggle for the maximum possible consumption of rights and opportunities at the lowest possible price.

Penal populism

What can governments do? In a consumerist democracy, governments must deliver goods in a balance between three spheres of interest: (1) the demands of the capitalist groups, which governments need to humour to maintain an attractive investment climate and to keep the economy going; (2) the pressure of the consumerist citizens, who want to maximise their share of economic benefits and to consume the maximum possible of the available offers of goods and social institutions; (3) the needs of those who have 'missed the boat' and are living in poverty at the margins of society. They risk drowning.

To get the means to produce their goods (economic facilities, social, educational, welfare and culture policies), governments must please the capitalists; to be re-elected, they must please the mainstream consumerist citizens. A compromise between these two spheres of interest is possible. But saving the drowning people is more complicated. As globalisation has moved much unskilled work to the Third World, unemployment of the unskilled in Western societies is creating a growing underclass, with no realistic prospects for integration in economic and social life. These people live at the margins of or completely outside the integrated society: '[they] have nothing to lose: they have "fallen below the threshold of deterrence"' (O'Malley 2006: 220). Governments can either let them drown, which would shock the moral values of a considerable proportion of the mainstream voters (as we shall see, ethics have not been completely lost) and would be very risky for public safety (it pollutes the lake[3]); or they can give the 'swimmers' a hand to get on board, which would cost money (to the detriment of the first two groups) and delay the boat.

Delivering existential safety by focusing on the fundamental causes of the *Unsicherheit* among citizens and their cynical defensive attitudes is beyond governments' capacity. But doing nothing is not an option. And so governments focus on 'pseudo-causes' of fear: criminality, for which the responsibility is mainly attributed to those without defence, those who missed the boat. It has become a central issue in national politics: 'We are increasingly governed through crime and insecurity' (Crawford 2002b: 1). Because 'unpredictable "market forces" … are far beyond the reach of … territory bound governments' (Bauman 2000a: 36), those governments address local crime and safety problems. For the impotent governments, 'doing something, or being seen to be doing something, about fighting the crime which threatens personal safety is a realistic option – and one containing a lot of electoral potential' (ibid.). 'Fear and angst push the search for a suitable and visible target or ... for "convenient enemies"' (Albrecht 2002: 163).

Focusing on crime has the advantage that the existential anxiety is projected onto concrete objects, which creates the illusion that the problems can be tackled. The message 'we know what the problem is, we know how to tackle it, and we can do it' is a more comforting and electorally rewarding message than admitting that 'all we can do is tinker a bit at the margins of the problem, as we are unable to change the causes of your fundamental uncertainty and anxiety'.

The media fuel anxiety and focus on concrete crime topics (Roberts *et al.* 2003). As commercial enterprises, they have subjugated their overt aim of informing the public to their actual objective, which is to make profits for their owners. The media want to sell their products, and they therefore produce popular, smoothly receivable messages. Following the consumerist mood in the public, they amplify the pursuit of easily accessible safety. Complicated reality is reduced to simplistic articles. Juicy stories are more important than good information. Sensational events are highlighted and normal daily reality is under-reported. Media coverage of crime and justice issues is an essential actor in what Kutchinsky (1979) called the 'crime carousel', a complex of mutually strengthening social forces, activated by the media, the interest groups of professionals, right-wing politicians and the private security industry, which together contribute to the myth of an ever-increasing and ever-more violent crime wave threatening our lives and property and those of our loved ones. The myth is currently presented as indisputable fact, in as much as those who express doubts about it are outcast (Kappeler *et al.* 2000).

All this feeds the penal populism of governments. Consumerist democracy runs on populism. Populism follows the superficial sentiments of the population, aiming to provide immediate comfort and benefits without caring about adequate information and without ethical reflection. Populist politicians, for example, promise fewer taxes but do not balance this with realistic plans for savings or do not care about the consequences for those who are hurt by the savings. They lash out at immigrants but do not have feasible, ethically well thought-out proposals to deal with immigration. They advertise more punishment but do not say how they see that working in practice or what would be the consequences for the punished, and do not advance any good ideas about the effects of more punishment on public safety. Populism has a narrow perspective on short-term benefits in selfish terms because of its lack of information and ethical reflection. It is barefaced consumerism of social institutions, a travesty of democracy.[4] Populists think with their belly rather than with their head.

'Penal populism ... is defined ... as a punishment policy developed primarily for its anticipated popularity' (Roberts *et al.* 2003: 64–5). 'A populist penal agenda emerges not from a set of political beliefs about the nature of people and society but from the preferences of political "consumers" – the electorate' (ibid.: 66). And the consumerist citizens' request is that the authorities deliver total security at the lowest possible price. They demand a safe environment in which to do their business undisturbed and enjoy their immediate comfort unhampered. The means used for this end do not matter, as long as the investment is the lowest possible in terms of finance and civic commitment. Decreasing solidarity and shrinking civic commitment lead to a shift from concern for social problems and poverty to 'dangerisation' and criminalising of poverty (Wacquant 1999; Young 1999). The easiest response is the punitive one, because it does not ask uncomfortable questions about the social living conditions of those punished. Incapacitation delivers more immediate security than does social work.

Governments' penal populism is, however, counterproductive. It does not create more security. On the contrary, 'the expansion of security ... promises reassurance but in fact increases anxiety ... security promises freedom but erodes civil liberties ...' (Zedner 2003: 157–8). The 'war against crime and incivilities' focuses on the citizens' insatiable need for safety. Paradoxically, because these needs are insatiable, the 'war' in fact demonstrates the actual incapacity of governments to satisfy the consumerist citizens' demands. On the contrary, 'The unfulfillable promises of a crime-free society, the unwarranted promises to victims, the installing of fear: these are all palpable effects of the populists' discourse on punishment' (Daems 2007: 24). Hence the increasing disenchantment with democratic institutions (Stenson and Edwards 2001) and the growing attractiveness of authoritarian politics.

Submitting welfare work to safety conditions

We now begin to temper the pessimistic story. The evolution described is indeed not a simple one-track downward spiral leading to complete cynical selfishness and punitiveness. While the consumerist tendency is gaining considerable support in the public mentality, it is curbed and corrected. As argued in Chapter 3, all humans are moved by a fundamental inter-human sympathy, and this also applies to mainstream citizens in their relation to the poor and marginalised. A considerable number are still driven by socio-ethical reflection and do feel solidarity. We have also seen that, while 'the public is unlikely soon to abandon the notion of punishment', they support 'more creative non-carceral alternatives', including restorative responses (Roberts and Hough 2002: 6).

How can the pursuit of safety be combined with some support for the poor, who are considered by many as the cause of unsafety? 'How to include the "truly disadvantaged" minority without alienating the contented majority who constitute the political base of support for parties ...' (Stenson and Edwards 2001: 70)? The answer is to include welfare policy in the security rhetoric, as displayed in the British 'third way', or in the 'integrative prevention-strategies' on the European continent (Hebberecht and Sack 1997; Goris 2001). Police forces and welfare workers are supposed to work together in local community development and to enhance the reintegration of families and young people at risk as a way to promote safety for all. It is the ideal compromise for governments that are trying to restore their legitimacy by fighting crime, but still want to keep an ethical dimension in their policy, in reality or as a kind of image building. Conditional support for the marginalised is told to enhance their motivation to behave in an orderly way, and hence enhance public safety. Linking the 'tough on crime' policies with those that are 'tough on the causes of crime' (Stenson 2001: 25) seems to satisfy both the safety-seeking and the socio-ethical citizen. Social work and community development in deprived neighbourhoods, youth work, monitoring the school careers of young people at risk, observation of parenting performance in families – all can be part of the array of 'progressive' welfare schemes, but all can be inserted into a safety policy as well.

And the latter is what mostly happens in political rhetoric. Welfare work is submitted to the security rationale, which is, in fact, a betrayal of the original socio-ethical motives and a perversion of welfare work. Welfare work was originally driven by a genuine ethical solidarity with the poor and other people in trouble, but it is now reframed as a means of enhancing safety for the better-off. People in trouble are not recognised as needing help, but as possible risks for others. Support for their welfare and integration is submitted to the condition of not disturbing the well-integrated citizens (Goris 2001). It is a way of controlling and disciplining the poor and marginalised, under the threat of the greater punitiveness just described. Solidarity with the poor and marginalised, advanced in Chapter 3 as one of the basic ethical guidelines, is subversively replaced by calculation in the service of the rich and the well-integrated citizens.

Penal populism and restorative justice?

At first sight, these developments seem to be opposed to the obviously growing interest of governments in restorative justice practices. On the one hand, it indicates that the pessimistic approach has to be complemented by more optimistic views: constructive forces remain active, even in the administrative, political and judicial authorities. On the other hand, restorative justice can also be reformulated so as to fit better in the safety rhetoric.

Indeed, like welfare work, restorative justice practices are also reformulated as security-serving techniques. As described at the beginning of Chapter 5, institutionalising restorative justice holds risks, and they actually seem to be partly realised. Paradoxically, the thoughtless enthusiasm of policy-makers, police, magistrates, judges and social workers for integrating a few techniques into the traditional criminal justice systems may be the greatest threat to restorative justice. A touch of mediation, a bit of conferencing and a pinch of community service are added to the system, without questioning the fundamentals of the traditional way of functioning. Restorative justice practices are then stripped of their philosophy and reduced to being pure techniques, serving as ornaments of a system that essentially remains unchanged. The success of these practices is judged by the judicial gatekeepers using their traditional criminal justice criteria. They value, for example, mediation because it may have a strong influence on the offenders; they promote respect for the victim to underline the guilt and the punishability of the offender; they refer to restorative processes to deal with benign cases so that the 'hard-core' business of justice is unburdened. Genuine restorative values are not recognised and not valorised. Restorative justice is used to justify an extension of control under a punitive mandate, and included as part of the punitive rhetoric.

Moreover, some dimensions of the predominant focus on risk are in line with restorative justice (O'Malley 2006). Using the example of harm reduction programmes for illicit drugs, O'Malley argues that both restorative justice and the risk focus consider crime, not as a moral wrong or as an illegal act, but mainly as behaviour that causes harm to the victim, to the community and to the offender.

Both also appeal to the responsibility of the offender and the other stakeholders considered 'normal' individuals. Finally, both also orient responsibility towards the future, i.e. by seeking to avoid or minimise future harm.

While some commonalities among the welfare orientation, the risk focus and the restorative justice approach may attract policy-makers and practitioners to restorative justice, the three remain clearly distinct. First, the focus of the first two is much narrower. They are not conceived as an alternative way of doing justice after a crime has occurred, but are seen as complementary to the traditional punitive criminal justice system, which remains unchanged or even reinforced. As a consequence, they contribute to the bifurcation in the way those who offend are dealt with. Those who play the game will be 'saved' and offered better opportunities to avoid or obtain a reduced punishment. The others will be handed over to a system penetrated by penal populism. Seeing restorative justice as a complement to penal justice would lead to the same bifurcation.

Second, the involvement of the stakeholders, especially of those who actually suffer the harm of the crime, is less decisive – or sometimes even absent – in harm-reduction strategies and welfare-oriented interventions. They are focused on the offenders and clearly directed by professionals. In restorative justice practices, the concern for the victim is balanced with working for the offender's reintegration and the active participation of both is a prerequisite.

It is these potential reductions, co-options and reformulations of the original restorative justice philosophy that clearly point to the risk of restorative justice being 'gobbled up' into the repressive rationale (Pratt 2006). It is why I have underlined throughout this book the – in my view – crucial differences, and even contradictions, between restorative justice and punishment. Restorative justice is not an alternative punishment; neither can it be considered a complement to the punitive justice system. It must be considered as a fully fledged alternative approach on its own. Only then can it keep its renovating force, as will be seen in the next two sections.

Social sciences and criminology as democratic forces

If the story ended here, the only perspective would be capitalist forces further enslaving people, more punitiveness and the co-optation of attempts at improvement through social welfare or restorative justice in the punitive rationale, ending in a catastrophe for democracy and for the well-being of people. The shortage of possible 'exit scenarios' on offer (Daems 2007) could indeed lead to depression and immobilism, or to, cynical, pure self-interest in an increasingly consumerist democracy. But exits there are. The socio-ethical motives of citizens and groups are not completely overwhelmed by consumerism and are not entirely co-opted in ambivalent 'social' safety promotions. They keep their genuine force, and may alter developments in the direction of a more just, more solidarity-driven, more participatory social life.

Countervailing forces are based on inter-human sympathy and the ethical forces it engenders. They find their way in civil society, among aware citizens and enlightened politicians, as can be observed in the political resistance against war, the rebellion against purely capitalist globalisation,[5] the civic actions to curb global warming and the voluntary commitments in local and international NGOs. Inspiring pieces of art bear witness to hope and the rejection of war. Schiller's *Alle Menschen werden Brüder*, the movement on these words in Beethoven's Ninth Symphony and Picasso's *Guernica* are stronger appeals to keep hope and reject the atrocities humans do to one another than any rational analysis. Social sciences make critical studies of macro-social developments and warn of the human and social disasters they may produce.

All these expressions are inspired by a common intuition that is opposed to rampant market individualism. They 'reject the banal, neo-liberal tendency to view the human subject in narrowly economic terms as a consumer/non-consumer or wealth creator/drone' (Stenson 2001: 24). They do not see individual profits as the basic drive in society. Rather, they are motivated by a desire for a community based on social justice and respect for pluralism driven by solidarity and individual active responsibility. Utopian models of such societies are presented by socio-political sciences and social ethical philosophies. They are beacons for those who reflect intellectually and scientifically on the future of our global community, and they offer a vision for a scientific approach to more concrete social problems.

Social sciences as a socio-ethical activity

Some scientists behave like chickens. Chickens lay their eggs without any concern about how they will be used. People can make an omelette of them, boil them hard, scramble them, lay them out to hatch or simply throw them away. Chickens do not care. That is how some scientists behave. They produce their 'truth', lay their 'egg of knowledge' and do not worry about how it will be used. Whether it can be used to produce more energy or a bomb, to cure people or to torture them more efficiently, to improve living conditions for all or to increase individual profits of the rich, to increase the understanding of people in trouble or to provide new labels to justify their social exclusion – these scientists do not consider it as their business, because their only mission, they claim, is to produce knowledge. Just as the chicken's mission is to produce eggs.

I view scientists' mission as higher than laying eggs. It is not because they are members of the scientific community that scientists stop being members of the human community as a whole. As such, we may ethically expect that they care about the way their work is integrated into social practice, that they reflect on how their activity may contribute, directly or indirectly, to a more liveable world and a higher quality of social life. Ideologically, they may hold very different, even opposing, views on how this better world is to be conceived, but socio-ethically, they have to take active responsibility for the possible impact of their work.

Social sciences have a special role to play in the pursuit of more participatory democracy. If they conceive their social position and role adequately, social sciences can make the key difference between populist and really participatory democracy.

Not that social sciences produce objective knowledge from which to deduce irrefutable political options. Some colleagues claim they do, but it looks like being a kind of charlatanism. They promise what they cannot deliver. Social sciences operate in the real world, with a plethora of variations in situations, individual histories, personalities, experiences, influences, motivations and prospects, where the objects of study are humans with needs and rights (and, some will say, a free will). Scientific research cannot but fatally ignore a part of this complex world. It is oriented by concepts and theories which are social constructions, not objective data, and by hypotheses which are inspired by – hopefully – original personal views; it designs a research methodology, constructs variables and makes instruments to measure these variables, which are at their best creations by good scientists, accepted by the scientific community; the collected data are processed to draw conclusions, and we must hope that this is done with the original personal insight of an intelligent scientist. This pathway is not at all pre-ordained by 'the objective reality' or 'objective facts'.

The sciences cannot be objective because they are carried out by subjective humans. A fortiori, social sciences cannot be objective because they study human subjects. Even the most complicated and admirable statistical arabesques cannot prevent the pathway of social sciences being paved with subjective inputs, which at their best lead to intersubjective constructions, i.e. that transcend the purely subjective intuitions and suspicions of the researcher and are (provisionally) accepted as 'knowledge' by the scientific community and other 'consumers' of the results.

Yet, like Sisyphus, social scientists cannot give up the ultimate ambition. If they did not continue trying to approach objectivity in their findings, they would risk sinking into impressionist intuitive statements only, without a real added value. That is why adequate scientific methodology is crucially important. Methodology is meant to channel the researcher's intuitions and suspicions through a systematic and controllable procedure of thinking and collecting data: a well considered, open problem analysis, and a step-by-step account of all moves in the process of constructing data and drawing conclusions. If well done, the outcome of scientific methodology transcends the subjective vision; it provides a transitional platform of provisional knowledge, which offers a ground for reflection and common action.

The added value of scientific research lies not in delivering objective grounds for decision-making, but in its 'responsible speech', taking 'great care to distinguish – in a fashion clear and visible to anybody – between the statements corroborated by available evidence and such propositions as can only claim the status of a provisional, untested guess' (Bauman 1990: 12, cited in Daems 2007: 438). Results and views based on good scientific research are systematically investigated, contextualised and controllable. They yield data and views that transcend the more limited, short-term-oriented and biased views that prevail among the uninformed public, electorally vulnerable politicians and interest-guided practitioners. And that is of huge benefit for democratic debate in view of democratic decision-making.

Consequently, social sciences cannot be limited to informing the authorities. In our more or less democratic regimes, governments do not use social sciences as a whole, but they use scientific data as a menu. They select – or manipulate through selective financing – the research that fits best in their political options, and then present its results as objective grounds for policy options. Authorities use scientific conclusions to justify their policies, to suggest that their options are beyond any doubt and that they can do no other but decide as they do. They present scientific results as irrefutable in order to avoid democratic debate. They try to behave as if their decisions are dictated by 'independent grounds for judgment' (Barber 2003: 120, 129–31).

But democracies are at their best in the absence of independent grounds for judgment because such grounds exclude democratic debate. 'We do not vote for the best polio vaccine ... nor has Boolean algebra been subjected to electoral testing' (ibid.: 129). In totalitarian regimes, only the truth advanced by the dictators or religious leaders is accepted as independent grounds for judgment, so that any public debate is excluded. We would have an equally non-democratic technocracy if scientific results were used as independent grounds for judgment. It is only where there is room for conflicting views, which are to be resolved 'responsibly, reasonably and publicly without the guidance of independent consensual norms' (ibid.), that democracy has vigour.

'Social scientists and political elites have all too often indulged themselves in this form of hypocrisy' (Barber 2003: 154). Abuse of social sciences as pseudo-independent grounds infects democracy. Social sciences cannot be independent grounds for judgment, given their intrinsic characteristics, and they should not aim to be, given the pursuit of participatory democracy.

Besides informing the authorities on the conditions in which they can take their decisions, social sciences must first of all inform the public about the conditions, possible options and their eventual consequences, so that the options and decisions are based on the best possible information. It is the difference between populist decision-making based on a narrow view of short-term benefits with a lack of information on the broader context and longer-term consequences on the one hand, and truly participatory democratic decision-making based on an informed public debate with regard to an overall picture of the conditions and longer prospects on the other. Note that I did not write 'the' overall picture, because social sciences can offer only 'an' overall picture. But at least an overall picture, and often even several different overall pictures, based on different scientific approaches.

Criminology as a possible safeguard against penal populism

Cynically, the increase in anxiety and the focus on crime as the main cause for unsafety are excellent boosts for the criminology business. Governments commission criminological research and hire criminological expertise; swelling labour markets for criminologists and media attention to crime attract more and more criminology students; universities invest in profitable criminology programmes. All over the world, institutes for education in criminology and for criminological research are emerging. New criminological journals are launched. Research is expanding, and methodological quality is improving.

At the same time, however, criminologists deplore their loss of influence on policy-making (Haggerty 2004; Chancer and McLaughlin 2007). Indeed, it looks like a paradox that criminology is currently a flourishing business in an epoch characterised by penal populism taking over criminal policy. What was commonly accepted in, say, the 1980s as a patrimony of criminology-based knowledge on crime and adequate crime policy seems to have been swept away in two decades by poorly thought-out, short-term-oriented punitiveness. What happened? Of course, it is possible that the global socio-economic and political developments have led to intrinsic changes in crime problems, so that the earlier criminology may have lost some of its relevance. In addition, the former criminological positions are clearly not in accordance with the climate of populist punitiveness, so that they probably have lost their utility for politicians.

Some criminologists attribute their loss of influence to the ideological bias in the criminological theories and the methodological inaccuracy of criminological research. In their opinion, criminology should become a database of expert knowledge to inform policy-makers (Wiles 2002, cited in Chancer and McLaughlin 2007). Others stress the need for autonomous development of criminology based on purely scientific criteria (Austin 2003, cited in ibid.). It is not an evident option. While the quality of methodology is of course crucial for the credibility of all intellectual activities claiming to be scientific, it is equally crucial to remain modest about the status of the knowledge social science can achieve. The impact on policy cannot be direct, because policy is not a technocratic game but a matter of moral and political ideological preferences, which, in a democratic regime, must be submitted, not to scientists, but to citizens.

The discussion confronts criminology with questions about its social responsibility (Daems 2007). Basically, two options are possible. 'It can see itself as a kind of specialist underlabourer, a technical specialist … Or it can embrace the world in which crime so loudly resonates and engage the discussion at this level too' (Garland and Sparks 2000b: 18). The choices are typified by Sparks (1997, cited in Aertsen *et al*. 2006: xv) as 'floaters' versus 'players'. Players try to play as 'useful' actors in the criminological field, to find solutions for the problems defined by the mainstream public and government. Floaters try to float over the field and to observe the broader panorama, including the problem definitions themselves.

Current developments in criminology seem to be dominated by the playing orientation. There is a tendency to see usefulness through the eyes of the consumerist public and the electorally interested government. Criminology activities become merged into the 'criminality complex' (Garland 2001) by accepting the crime problems as they are defined by the authorities, the public and the media and by keeping possible solutions within the traditional pathways. There is a lack of wider theoretical reflection and ethical awareness; the evidence-based indications are illusions because research is limited to factors and dynamics that can only be grasped by positivist methodology.

Such an approach is attractive because it leads to the rewarding experience of having some influence on policy and because it is easier to find funding for research. It must be taken seriously because of its often admirable methodological discipline leading to provisional beacons of knowledge as mentioned earlier. It is respectable, and even necessary, that criminological research also yields technical reports that are mainly relevant to colleagues, practitioners and policy-makers. But its reach is limited and is not the only scientific approach possible.

If it were limited to such contributions, criminology would become 'domesticated' and vulnerable to being misused as a technical science of social exclusion. It would mainly contribute to more technocratic crime control, justified by criminological scientific expertise presented as objective facts and beyond democratic control and participation. Just as embedded war journalists report within the limits defined by the military and accept military statements as truth, 'embedded criminologists' work within the limits defined by mainstream populism and accept the government-defined problems as the real ones. Such criminology supports the official policy but does not inform the public on other possible views and options in the field of crime, justice and safety. Presented as 'independent ground for judgment', such criminology empties the realm for democratic debate on how society can and should cope with the existential anxiety and its multilevel causes. It does not feed the democratic debate. On the contrary, it keeps the public uninformed and contributes to punitive populism and to a general consumerist attitude in the population, accelerating the negative spiral in the quality of democracy.

Criminology must do much more. It must, indeed, 'float' also. A socially responsible criminology includes questions regarding the definitions of crime and the fundamental options in crime control; it uses its expertise not only to inform governments, but also to address the public so as to contribute to a more informed public debate on crime and security issues. There is a great need for an 'assertive public criminology' (Currie 2007) to add scientific results and questions to the public discourse on crime and crime policy. The enrichment of the intellectual-cultural patrimony will improve the quality and intensity of the democratic debate and thus also the social constructiveness of political decisions (Walgrave 1998). While 'academic criminology may appear ... to be a weak competitor with corporate interests, the vengeful, punitive tabloid press and populist politicians ... we should recognize that criminological ideas and broader social science theories ... have contributed to the discourses through which debate is conducted, problems conceptualized and solutions proposed' (Stenson and Edwards 2001: 69). It is clear that many now common (not always commonly accepted) opinions on crime and crime control are deeply rooted in criminological research, such as, for example: the inaccuracy of recorded crime as an estimate of real crime; social exclusion as a breeding-ground for criminality; the disastrous impact of negative prejudices and stigmatisation on crime and crime control; the poor efficiency of the punitive apriorism in responding to crime; the need for social policy in radical crime prevention; or, in direct relation to this book, the potential of restorative justice.

I am not presenting a simple opposition between the good floater and the ugly player. Both are necessary and both may go wrong. Floaters may choose an easy life. They can stay on the sideline and keep their hands clean. In the worst case, they become unworldly, irrelevant constructivists or sceptical negativists, condemning all attempts to act as insufficient, wrongly conceived, serving a hidden agenda, co-opted by authoritarian forces or produced by simpletons. In the best case, they offer thoughtful analyses, broad visions or motivating utopian views which offer significant intellectual references for those who act in the real world, the players who make necessary compromises to realise changes.

Players get their hands dirty, but they can play dirty as well. Some indeed act as cynical careerists, seeking the money wherever it is to do embedded research, without any concern for its potential counterproductive effects on a considerable part of the population. Other players, however, try to conceive and carry out the best possible experiments resulting from well thought-out compromises between ideals designed while floating and reality observed while playing.

The need is for balanced scientific criminology, which combines both floating and playing, and delivers strong empirical work to avoid criminological evangelism (Pratt 2006) and well thought-out wide social theory to avoid charlatanism.

Criminology is not a laboratory science. It operates in the delicate field where people and societal institutions confront each other, people victimise other people, citizens' rights and liberties are at stake, families are torn apart and some people are even brought to death. All this is carried out with the use of power, which carries the risk of abuse of power (van Swaaningen 1999). Recent developments increasingly position democracy at odds with its own principles: with a view to 'preserving democratic liberties', liberties are cut. The populist obsession with crime, justice and (un)safety entails an increasing appeal to criminological expertise. But in a world dominated by a ruthless struggle for individualistic power and wealth, criminology cannot just sit aside and count the strokes. Even the option to work within the official chalk marks and 'to stay away from politics' is an ideological and political choice: to accept the problems as they are defined by the powerful and to contribute to their more efficient functioning. A so-called value-less criminology is worthless.

By doing good and autonomous scientific research and also by addressing its findings to the public forum, criminology can take on active responsibility in the pursuit of a more just, more solidarity-driven and more participatory democracy. In the next section, I shall argue that one of the major opportunities to do so is by taking the theme of restorative justice very seriously in criminological reflection and research.

Restorative justice as an upheaval for criminology and for democracy

Restorative justice can contribute to the quality of democracy, both directly as a participatory philosophy and practice that can expand the potential for participation in all aspects of democratic life, and indirectly through its reinforcement of criminology as a socially responsible science.

Restorative justice in criminology

Historically, criminology is rooted in critical reflections on the way crime was responded to. First, the Enlightenment aimed to liberate citizens from the authoritarian and arbitrary punishment regimes that were predominant at the time. Beccaria (1747), for example, promoted rights for citizens which the punisher had to respect. By the end of the nineteenth century, a new perspective on punishment emerged. The *Défense Sociale* movement stated that the ground rule of penal justice should not be proportionate retribution but rather the protection of society against 'ill' criminals (Ferri 1905). It favoured the origins of criminology as a science to try to understand clinically the ill-minded criminals and to identify the social environments that provoked the development of such illness. Criminology fed the tendency to treat offenders rather than punish them, or to reconsider punishment as an opportunity to further the offender's rehabilitation. It was the soil in which the huge penal-welfare complex flourished for many decades (Garland 1985).

By the end of the 1960s, critical and radical criminology were voicing severe criticisms of this set of penal-welfare institutions. Criminal justice and its treatment extensions were reproached as labelling machines and tools in the service of the interests of the powerful and the wealthy. Criminology proposed diversion as a way of avoiding as much as possible judicial and welfare interventions ('Leave the kids alone, whenever possible', Schur 1971). But the diversionist programmes were integrated into the criminal justice system and mainly resulted in widening the penal-welfare net (Lemert 1981).

Other criminologists pleaded for the abolition of the criminal justice system but could not at that time formulate a credible alternative. This did not enhance the status of 'floating criminology'. While some tendencies indeed landed in purely academic exercises with little or no relevance, social critical criminology as a whole was sidelined. It was probably the weakness of the alternatives that made this approach defenceless against the punitive wave of recent decades. Criminology was 'depicted as academic dilettantism, witnessing fuzzy morals and flaky politics' (van Swaaningen 1999: 15). Opting for radical non-intervention or abolishing the system is indeed not an answer to the rampant fear of crime. Doing social work or promoting community development in urban areas hold only vague promises for possibly less offending in the long term, but does not respond to the suffering and social unrest caused by crimes committed. It brought some to plead for 'left realist criminology' (Young 1997).

Restorative justice research explores the potentials of a socio-ethically better way of responding to crime which increasingly appears feasible and which seems to avoid many of the drawbacks of the punitive apriorism. In doing so, it develops a credible alternative to populist punitivism and, at the same time, a constructive complement to abolitionism. More than earlier critical criminology, criminology nourished by restorative justice is becoming a real challenge to penal justice. If it communicates its messages well, it can help to develop a serious countervailing power to the unrestrained, thoughtless, selfish, disastrous increase in punitivism. Criminological research demonstrates that increasing punitiveness adds to the problems that it seeks to resolve; restorative justice research confirms that other and better responses to crime are desirable and possible. Such criminology can be extricated from its embeddedness in the mainstream, while offering an alternative and remaining a socially constructive science. It can float while remaining a player.

The condition for this is, however, that criminologists involved in restorative justice research keep a clear vision of restorative justice as an alternative to punishment, and not as an alternative punishment. While they must cooperate, as good players do, with all kinds of restorative justice experiments and practices, and learn from them in order to improve those practices, they must at the same time remain floaters to safeguard the truly renovating and challenging force of the restorative justice philosophy.

Another spin-off of restorative justice for criminology is that the conceptions of crime, criminals and crime-fighting are stripped of their exceptional character. Mainstream criminology is predominantly what Garland (2001) calls a 'criminology of the other'. Such criminology considers those who commit offences as another kind of human, intrinsically different from law-abiding citizens; it focuses on particular risk groups, such as immigrants, drug users or youths in deprived neighbourhoods, which it presents as threats to the existing social order. The criminology of the other aims to produce theoretical, empirical and practical knowledge that will allow better control of risk groups or render them less harmful for the average citizen. In doing so, this criminology delivers expertise that further excludes and controls the poor and marginalised; it becomes a technology of social exclusion and thus significantly advances dualisation in society.

'Criminology of the self' (Garland 2001), on the contrary, considers those who commit crime as normal people. The person who offends is one of us, someone who, because of circumstances, has ended up in a position that caused him to act illegally and to harm others. It could have happened to any citizen. But criminology of the self can 'normalise' the criminal in two different ways. It can bring the level down, by regarding all humans as potential criminals. The consequence of such approach is that we live in mutual distrust and protect ourselves against one another through, for example, situational prevention strategies based on rational choice theories (Felson 1994). In Putnam's terms, social capital is then drastically degraded, which, as I have described briefly, is disastrous for the quality of social life and for democracy.

But the level can also be brought up, by considering those who commit a crime neither as a peculiar type of dangerous individual to be outcast, nor as a bad person (like we all are supposed to be), but simply as a person with particular strengths and weaknesses who basically seeks a good life in harmony with his social environment, but who, through unfortunate conditions, came to act as he did. It is how, for example, the Good Lives Model of offender rehabilitation looks at the 'fellow human travelers that are labeled "offenders"' (Ward and Maruna 2007: 176). Its fundamental question is not 'what works?' (i.e. which technique works to remodel the offenders?), but 'what helps?' (i.e. how can we help the offender in his quest for rehabilitation through a personally meaningful and socially acceptable life?).

It has been argued in Chapter 4 that a restorative process offering the offender the opportunity to make up for the harm caused may be a major help in the offender's quest for rehabilitation. Basically, restorative justice has this normalising approach to all those involved in the aftermath of crime and looks at both the victim and the offender as normal, reasonably responsible persons. It presupposes that, in the right conditions, both victim and offender will be prepared to try to find together a solution that is acceptable for all parties, including the interests of the larger community and public safety. As we saw in the preceding chapters, this trust is not naïve, but is sufficiently supported by experience and empirical data to justify it as the starting point in considering what should and can be done once an offence occurs.

This de-dramatising, normalising 'trust' approach to victims and offenders is, in my view, an important input to criminology as a whole, where variations on the statement that 'bad parents living in bad circumstances produce bad kids who will cause bad experiences for the good ones' are more or less running out. It can also strengthen criminology in its social role of reducing the crime and safety problems to realistic dimensions. It can help to restrain the obsession with risk and to restore trust among citizens, which is, as we saw, crucial for democracy to work smoothly.

Hence, restorative justice is a marvellous vehicle through which criminology can play a socially responsible role by feeding the debate on how to respond to norm transgression while promoting better democracy. But restorative justice can also make a direct contribution to democracy.

Restorative justice and participatory democracy

Throughout this book, restorative justice has been presented as a participatory practice based on mutual respect and solidarity and aimed at restoring the quality of individual and social life. It transforms the offender's passive responsibility in the face of punishment into an active responsibility with a view to reparation. These values, attitudes and processes are crucial for democracy as a whole. Most restorative justice advocates have a broader agenda than just changing the way justice is done after a crime. They see restorative justice as part of a larger ideological movement aimed at restoring the quality of our democracies as a whole. Roche, for example, believes that 'By bringing participatory deliberative democracy back into the centre of the criminal justice system, restorative justice offers a possible route for restoring not just victims and offenders, but also for restoring citizens' faith in governments perceived to be unresponsive to their concerns' (Roche 2003: 238). Braithwaite locates restorative justice within the concept of a responsive regulatory state. 'Law enforcers should be responsive to how effectively citizens or corporations are regulating themselves before deciding whether to escalate intervention' (2002a: 29). 'What we want is a legal system where citizens learn that responsiveness is the way our legal institutions work. Once they see the legal system as a responsive regulatory system, they know there will be a chance to argue about unjust laws' (ibid.: 34).

Restorative justice is one of the driving forces in a broader movement for more participation by actively responsible citizens in all decision-making processes that concern them directly and indirectly. I have mentioned earlier the broad spectrum of deliberative conflict resolution practices in many fields: community mediation is used for settling disputes in (increasingly multi-ethnic) urban neighbourhoods (Merry and Milner 1993; Peper and Spierings 1999); conferencing and other restorative programmes are increasingly being used to deal with bullying and other discipline problems in schools (Ahmed 2001; Morrison 2007); deliberative processes including parents and other family members have been developed in child welfare (Fraser and Norton 1996; Pennell 2006). Before restorative justice was known as such, alternative models for dispute regulation and corporate regulation reflected the belief in deliberative ways of dealing with conflict and norm transgression in the fields of economics and business (Roche 2006). At the global level, the principles of restorative justice appear increasingly in peacemaking initiatives after gross violations of human rights and collective armed violence (Braithwaite 2002a; Sullivan and Tift 2006b: Section V; Weitekamp *et al.* 2006).

Some include these practices as part of restorative justice, but I explained in Chapter 1 why I do not. They are nevertheless crucial parts of the wide-ranging social movement for more, better and more inclusive democracy. They all rely on citizens' capacity and willingness to take active responsibility to find satisfactory solutions to injustices and other conflicts, through respectful dialogue. Theoretical reflection and research develop conceptual and instrumental strengths, enhancing credibility and thus the steady diffusion of such approach. It is gradually penetrating all aspects of everyday life.

Participation in restorative justice and other deliberative practices is, in itself, a pedagogical exercise. As argued in Chapter 3, seeing self-interest through adhering to the project of common interest is not evident. Morality and ethical attitudes are learned from parents, and through education and acculturation. Being involved in a restorative justice process is a revealing learning experience. Participants face their opponents, who appear not to be enemies but 'fellow travellers'; they experience the power of mutually respectful deliberation, and they feel satisfaction in an outcome that may be less materially profitable but more personally and relationally beneficial. They understand that promoting the common interest can be rewarding for self-interest. They also experience that what they say matters and really makes a difference in the decision. This may enhance their confidence and their motivation for civic commitment in other realms of social life.

Learning experiences are of course crucial in schools (Morrison 2007). Restorative school programmes emerged almost at the same time as restorative justice took off (Claassen 1993). From the beginning, they focused on more than simply seeking constructive solutions to concrete disciplinary problems and creating safer and more peaceful schools. Operating in an explicitly pedagogical environment, all school interventions also aim to build competencies in the students, such as skills in constructively resolving conflicts and social and emotional intelligence. The evidence available so far is promising, as is clear, for example, from the intensive evaluations of school bullying programmes (Morrison 2006). Schools not only have to deliver useful and well adapted labour forces but also have a huge impact on improving the quality of social life by the formation of well-rounded citizens who are capable of taking and willing to take active responsibility, and driven by respect and solidarity. 'In schools we have society in miniature and persons in the process of learning to become citizens ... How well we manage our schools will determine how well our society works a generation later' (Marshall 1997, cited in Morrison 2007: 325). Schools have a multitude of tools at their disposal to favour such development, through specific school programmes as well as the general school climate, by promoting cooperation rather than ruthless rivalry, and also by dealing constructively with conflicts and injustices. Restorative practices are key in such schools.

The wider transformative potentials of restorative justice have caused some people to place restorative practices at the core of what Shearing and Wood (2003) call 'nodal governance'. Because governments' steering cannot (and should not) reach into all aspects of local life, they 'mobilize individuals, families, groups, corporations and other collectivities into their own governing agenda' (Froestad and Shearing 2007: 541). Citizens take their fate into their own hands. The risk is, however, that such decentralised initiatives lead to more disparity in governing, with the rich and powerful taking advantage of such opportunities and the poor lacking the material and social resources to organise themselves into such nodal committees. Indeed, the poor run the risk of additional stigmatisation as incapable and unwilling groups (Crawford and Clear 2001; Pelikan 2007). Principles of nodal governance therefore need to be framed by a state commitment to provide methodical and organisational support. The Zwelethemba model, described in Chapter 1, is an example of such a model. Committed citizens are encouraged and helped in their attempts to find deliberative and constructive solutions to local security problems. In doing so, they become aware of both the wider causes of their problems and their power to address them. This provides an opportunity to enhance the participation of citizens in a bottom-up decision-making process.

All in all, the widening river of restorative justice is becoming a delta, which irrigates the parched democracy with the participatory potential of citizens who take up their responsibility to find constructive solutions. Its proliferation may advance belief in the potential of deliberative and inclusive conflict resolution, and in the capacities of citizens to contribute constructively to decisions in difficult social situations. In addition, restorative practices may by themselves advance self-confident, responsible citizens who understand the intrinsic interwovenness of self-interest with common interest. The quality of democracy is dependent on such citizens.

Conclusion

This chapter has explored the extended potential of restorative justice to be a significant factor in the pursuit of better and more participatory democracy. The current tendency for citizens to shirk their duties in relation to the quality of social life and social institutions and to withdraw into a selfish consumerist attitude is a threat to the democratic calibre of our societies. The obvious attractiveness of the restorative justice philosophy, as witnessed by the rapid dissemination of its practice and ideas and by its penetration in all aspects of social life, indicates that people at the grassroots are not completely in thrall to capitalist globalisation. What appears to be possible in the response to crime must also be amplified and valorised in other aspects of social life.

If the original concept of democracy is taken seriously, its institutions must be as responsive as possible to the incentives coming from the grassroots. But the responsiveness depends largely on the democratic quality of these incentives, which is itself determined by three characteristics:

1 They should be based on broad and respectful deliberation, including all possible stakeholders (all citizens).
2 The deliberation should be documented with adequate information about possible options and their consequences.
3 Participants in the deliberation should be committed to seeing their self-interest as being at least partly conditioned by common interest.

That is where social sciences and criminology come in. By providing the democratic debate with better documented and broader visions and options for the longer term, social sciences can nourish the quality of the democratic debate and play a crucial role in restraining the downwards spiral towards populist consumerist democracies.

Criminology, operating in the field of crime, justice and (un)safety, deals with one of the key issues in democracy and in the quality of social life: where dominion is intruded upon and where the mainstream punitive response to the intrusion risks degrading dominion still more. A criminology that takes on its social responsibility will avoid becoming embedded too deeply in mainstream conceptions and punitive populism and keep its 'floating' dimension. It will concentrate on addressing the public debate with scientific data and scientifically supported visions on crime and unsafety, the (macro)social context of their origins and the way they are one-sidedly defined; it will inform the public about the potential benefits and risks of the current policy orientations and about possible alternative approaches and responses. Crime, justice and (un)safety issues are too serious to be left to judicial and police professionals, electorally vulnerable politicians, populist media and self-oriented consumerist citizens. They need input from floating criminology committed to the quality of social life and of democracy.

Restorative justice is one of the social forces that can contribute to redressing the current dualisation and weakening of democracy in societies. It can both indirectly promote the democratic role of criminological sciences and directly contribute to the development of participatory practices and attitudes in the population. Its potentials for that are:

- its objective of restoring individual and social life if a crime has occurred;
- its focus on what binds us (common self-interest, dominion, quality of social life) rather than what divides;
- the reconception of the response to crime from a top-down sentencing machine to a bottom-up problem-solving system;
- the priority for inclusive deliberation, reducing the use of coercion to the strictest minimum;
- the expansion of deliberative practices to other fields that deal with conflict and injustice;
- the chance it offers for citizens to experience the power of respectful dialogue and the benefits of investing in common interest;
- its basic trust in the constructive potential of people to take their responsibility actively in crime and justice matters and in other fields of social life.

All this, it is believed, will contribute to a more participatory and committed attitude in all aspects and institutions of social life, which would augment social capital. It can add significantly to the movement for a higher quality of social life, governed through a better, more participatory, more inclusive, more responsive and more just democracy, promoting the cohesion of individual self-interests into a common project.

Notes

1 It should be noted that this conception of social capital is different from those of Coleman and Bourdieu, for example, who see social capital as a possession of individuals or individual groups (see, for example, Field 2003).

2 As, for example, in (the contributions in) Wacquant (1999), Young (1999), Bauman (2000a), Garland and Sparks (2000a), Karstedt and Bussmann (2000), Garland (1996 and 2001), Stenson and Sullivan (2001), Crawford (2002b), Hughes and Edwards (2002), Wood and Dupont (2006), and many others.

3 Baumann (2004) speaks of 'wasted lives'. If you drop waste in a lake, it pollutes the lake.

4 I am not pleading for the opposite of populism, which would be elitism, disdaining emotions and selfishness in the public. Emotions and self-interested views are crucial in a good working democracy but it is equally crucial that information and ethical debates give these emotions a more considered and – hopefully – a more constructive content.

5 Some of the activists are anti-globalists *tout court*, while others accept globalisation as an irreversible development, but pursue an essential social-cultural complement to it.

Epilogue: a list of to-do's

There is no need to add a long conclusion to what has been written so far. Writing this book has been an adventure, with both a 'playing' dimension when I tried to find out the essentials of restorative justice and what it can offer, and a 'floating' dimension when the socio-ethical foundations and the socio-political potentials were explored.

Restorative justice has been found, not as a diversionary addendum to penal justice, but as an ambitious renovating project, based on a new paradigm on doing justice after the occurrence of a crime. Like the existing penal theories, the option for restorative justice is also primarily a normative theory on how justice should be done. It is based on an ethics of social life, serving what I have called 'common self-interest', and embedded into a broader movement for improving participatory democracy.

To date, the ambition is not crippled by systematic empirical research. On the contrary, evidence available so far suggests that the victims are better off with restorative responses than with both the rehabilitative or punitive approaches to crime, that it is more satisfying for both victims and offenders, and more effective even for reintegrating offenders. Restorative justice also appears not to provoke destructive consequences for public safety, and to hold good intrinsic potentials for public law enforcement and for developing legal safeguards.

This encouraging state of affairs explains the growing interest in restorative justice and its expansion towards other fields of dealing with conflicts and injustices. In view of the wider social, economic and political developments, restorative justice comes at a timely point, and its potentials must further be explored. The exploration must be carried out along four large and mutually dependent lines of attention, which together form an extremely fruitful field of interaction between 'floating' and 'playing' criminology.

Improving the technical and practical quality of restorative justice practice

Possible expansion of restorative principles greatly depends on the methodological quality of the practices. Not all practices called restorative are carried out well. Research has made clear that the methodological quality of the way the process is monitored often has decisive impact on the outcome and on the general degree of restorativeness.

In recent years, restorative practice has improved drastically, leading to more confidence and broader implementation. Paradoxically, this is also a threat, as it may lead to routine 'fast food' practices (Umbreit 1999), with weak theoretical and methodological underpinnings. There is a need for ongoing attention to the quality of what is done under the label restorative justice. Continuous care of the methodology of restorative practice is based on permanent interaction between advanced practitioners, evaluative research and theoretical reflection. It must further improve the processes and the outcomes, leading to more satisfaction among the participant victims, offenders and communities of care; it must extend the scope of restorative justice to more difficult and more serious cases and thereby gain credibility among the criminal justice professionals and with the public.

Exploring thoroughly the relation of restorative justice to the law

The more restorative justice gains credibility and is accepted as being a part of the mainstream response to crime, the more urgent is the reflection on how to insert it into an adequate legal framework. This book has raised several questions in that regard and possible tracks for reflection have been suggested. The concrete terms of the debate are partly different in Anglo-American-based common-law countries and in countries with centralised legalistic systems on the European continent, but the basic issues are the same: how to juxtapose informal processes with formal procedures, how to rely on communities while living in organised states, how to combine the creativity and richness of the bottom-up approach with the clarity and strictness of the top-down approach, how to complement the priority for voluntariness and compliance with possible coercion. If the paradigm status of restorative justice is taken seriously, the legal safeguards of the punitive systems cannot just be reproduced. The values behind the traditional constraints such as due process, equality, right of defence, presumption of innocence or proportionality must be taken seriously, but the way they are made concrete must be revised. The construction of other legal principles which would be more appropriate for the restorative perspective must be considered.

Restorative justice literature on these questions is not abundant but increasing. It is one of the most important themes to decide how far restorative justice will succeed in penetrating the mainstream response to crime.

Developing normative and explanatory theory

The development of restorative justice theory must continue. It must first of all aim at more clarity in the concepts and the theoretical constructs around them. I have advanced a restricted definition of restorative justice and distinguished it unambiguously from the 'restorative extensions', i.e. the other fields of conflict settlement which are inspired by the same participatory and inclusive philosophy. I have also separated the socio-ethical foundations and the socio-political options from restorative justice in the strict sense. Maybe other ways to create clarity are possible, but clarity is needed. Keeping the content of the restorative justice notion too loose is a threat to the credibility of restorative justice and would leave it without defence against misconceptions and possible co-optations within other rationales and bureaucratic interests.

As most current restorative experiments take place within the frame of traditional criminal justice, there is a permanent pressure to integrate at least partly with the bureaucratic and penal justice rationales. The risks are that restorative justice practices would gradually be stripped of their philosophy and deteriorate into pure technique, serving as ornaments of a system which essentially remains unchanged. To avoid such deterioration, permanent theorising is crucial. The *technicité* of restorative justice must not be isolated from its theoretical and socio-ethical foundations, but these foundations themselves must offer strong and lucid support to frame thoughts and options.

Sloppy theorising also makes restorative justice virtually unfit for good scientific research. Much of the available research suffers from lack of clarity about what makes a series of practices 'restorative', what their objectives are and what makes them work as they do. Theorising must therefore not only develop decent normative standards but also focus on possible explanatory models.

Developing normative and explanatory theory is needed to point to the essentials of restorative justice, to bundle and interpret experience, and to build reference models to comment on, evaluate and orient the practices – together these form the best possible counterforce to avoid absorption into the traditional modes of responding to crime.

Strategy

Developments in criminal justice are a matter of criminal policy, which depends only partially on practical and scientific qualities and options, but more so on the cultural and political climate. This climate is not just an immovable given but is subject to a multitude of influences. It is here that strategy is needed.

I have pointed to the punitive populist climate but also to more respectful and solidarity-driven tendencies and movements. While simplistic repressive outcries may sound the loudest in the media, it is far from evident that they really are the mainstream. There is no reason to be pessimistic about the future of restorative justice. Restorative justice advocates have a strong case. They may have a deep impact on future developments if that case is presented well. This is partly a matter of strategy (Van Ness and Heetderks Strong 1997 and 2001; Bazemore and Walgrave 1999; Johnstone 2002). Strategy consists of quality and visibility. The full potentials of restorative justice must be exploited as much as possible by developing the three lines just described. This will improve the intrinsic quality of the restorative offer, which in itself is the most crucial strand in any strategy. But besides that, specific effort must be made to make this quality visible to policy-makers, leading professionals, the judiciary and the public. Providing these actors with complete but realistic information about what can be achieved and what cannot is a *conditio sine qua non* for motivating them to try out the restorative potentials as much as possible.

The latter is especially complicated in relation to the judiciary. Maximalist restorative justice aspires to penetrate and modify the criminal justice system itself, from being driven by a punitive apriorism to being oriented by a restorative apriorism. All institutions display some institutional inertia. This inertia is stronger in institutions with a long tradition in the centre of society, based on the use of power and bearing high social authority, for example the criminal justice system (Faget 1997). That system transforms matters of belief into irrefutable truths and juridical interpretations in coercive realities; it reduces complex human relations and experiences to simple juridical facts. The system is highly hierarchic, with many levels between the top and the fieldworkers, strict role definitions and internal sanctions. The distance from living reality is great, so that changes in real needs, problems and opportunities reach the top only in a filtered way. Hierarchy functions as the guard of conservative ideology within the organisation. It controls compliance with the rules and seeks to confirm its power.

No wonder that Sessar, for example, found that criminal justice professionals stick more to the punitive tradition than does the mainstream population (Sessar 1995). Part of the opposition to restorative justice by some penalists hides this sociological basis of resistance. The criticism they issue is indeed often so mistaken, based on such superficial knowledge of restorative justice, that it cannot be grounded on open-minded intelligent reflection.

Coping with such resistant dynamics is no simple matter. In addition to the evident efforts to improve the quality of restorative practices and make the quality visible, the approach to the criminal justice system and its agents should be oriented more by scientific 'planning of change' strategies.

... it all amounts to pushing the rock

Even if all four lines are implemented to perfection, if citizens became more aware that their self-interest is largely dependent on finding a project of common self-interest, and if they shouldered their active responsibility in the pursuit of more respect and solidarity, we shall never reach the end. Restorative justice is an ideal of doing justice in an ideal society. Both ideals are utopian views. There is nothing as practical as a good utopia, a beacon of ambition and hope and a safeguard against immobilism and despair. Even if we know that we cannot reach the top of our ideal, and even if we sometimes fall back further from the top, we cannot but keep to trying to approach the ideal as closely as possible. If not, our living conditions will deteriorate drastically. Just as Sisyphus was doomed to push the rock for eternity.

References

Acorn, A. (2004) *Compulsory Compassion: A Critique of Restorative Justice.* Vancouver: UCB Press.

Adler, C. and Wundersitz, J. (eds) (1994) *Family Conferencing and Juvenile Justice: The Way Forward or Misplaced Optimism?* Canberra: Australian Institute of Criminology.

Aertsen, I., Daems, T. and Robert, L. (eds) (2006a) *Institutionalizing Restorative Justice.* Cullompton: Willan.

Aertsen, I., Daems, T. and Robert, L. (2006b) 'Epilogue', in I. Aertsen, T. Daems and L. Robert, *Institutionalizing Restorative Justice.* Cullompton: Willan, pp. 282–304.

Ahmed, E. (2001) 'Shame management: regulating bullying', in E. Ahmed, N. Harris, J. Braithwaite and V. Braithwaite, *Shame Management Through Reintegration.* Cambridge: Cambridge University Press, pp. 211–300.

Albrecht, H. J. (2001) 'Restorative justice. Answers to questions nobody has put forward', in E. Fattah and S. Parmentier (eds), *Victim Policies and Criminal Justice on the Road to Restorative Justice.* Leuven: Leuven University Press, pp. 295–314.

Albrecht, H. J. (2002) 'Immigration, crime and unsafety', in A. Crawford (ed.), *Crime and Insecurity. The Governance of Safety in Europe.* Cullompton: Willan, pp. 159–85.

Andrews, D. and Bonta, J. (2003) *The Psychology of Criminal Conduct*, 3rd edn. Cincinnati, OH: Anderson.

Ashworth, A. (1986) 'Punishment and compensation: victims, offenders and the state', *Oxford Journal of Legal Studies*, 6: 86–122.

Ashworth, A. (1993) 'Some doubts about restorative justice', *Criminal Law Forum*, 4: 277–99.

Ashworth, A. (2001) 'Is restorative justice the way forward for criminal justice?', *Current Legal Problems*, 54: 347–76.

Bae, I. (1992) 'A survey of public acceptance of restitution as an alternative to incarceration for property offenders in Hennepin County, Minnesota, USA', in H. Messmer and H. U. Otto (eds), *Restorative Justice on Trial. Pitfalls and Potentials of Victim-Offender Mediation*. Dordrecht and Boston: Kluwer Academic, pp. 291–308.

Baehler, K. (2007) 'Justifying restorative justice', in G. Maxwell and J. Liu (eds), *Restorative Justice and Practices in New Zealand: Towards a Restorative Society*. Wellington, New Zealand: Institute of Policy Studies, Victoria University, pp. 289–99.

Barber, B. (2003) *Strong Democracy. Participatory Politics for a New Age*, 20th anniversary edn. Berkeley, CA: University of California Press.

Barton, C. (1999) *Getting Even: Revenge as a Form of Justice*. Chicago: Open Court.

Bauman, Z. (2000a) 'Social uses of law and order', in D. Garland and R. Sparks (eds), *Criminology and Social Theory*. Oxford: Oxford University Press, pp. 23–46.

Baumann, Z. (2000b) *Liquid Modernity*. Cambridge: Polity Press.

Baumann, Z. (2004) *Wasted Lives. Modernity and Its Outcasts*. Cambridge: Polity Press.

Bazemore, G. and Bell, D. (2004) 'What is the appropriate relationship between restorative justice and treatment?', in H. Zehr and B. Toews (eds), *Critical Issues in Restorative Justice*. Monsey, NY/Cullompton: Criminal Justice Press/Willan, pp. 119–32.

Bazemore, G. and Day, S. (1996) 'Restoring the balance: juvenile and community justice', *Juvenile Justice*, 3 (1): 3–14.

Bazemore, G. and Elis, L. (2007) 'Evaluation of restorative justice', in G. Johnstone and D. Van Ness (eds), *Handbook of Restorative Justice*. Cullompton: Willan, pp. 397–425.

Bazemore, G. and Maloney, D. (1994) 'Rehabilitating community service: sanctions in a balanced justice system', *Federal Probation*, 58 (2): 24–35.

Bazemore, G. and O'Brien, S. (2002) 'The quest for a restorative model of rehabilitation: theory-for-practice and practice-for-theory', in L. Walgrave (ed.), *Restorative Justice and the Law*. Cullompton: Willan, pp. 31–67.

Bazemore, G. and Schiff, M. (eds) (2001) *Restorative Community Justice. Repairing Harm and Transforming Communities*. Cincinnati, OH: Anderson.

Bazemore, G. and Schiff, M. (2005) *Juvenile Justice Reform and Restorative Justice*. Cullompton: Willan.

Bazemore, G. and Walgrave, L. (eds) (1999) 'Restorative juvenile justice: in search of fundamentals and an outline for systemic reform', in G. Bazemore and L. Walgrave (eds), *Restorative Justice for Juveniles. Repairing the Harm by Youth Crime*. Monsey, NY: Criminal Justice Press, pp. 45–74.

Beccaria, C. (1747) *Dei Delitti e delle Pene*, Dutch trans. J. Michiels (1982) *Over Misdaden en Straffen (About Crimes and Punishments)*. Antwerp: Kluwer.

Beck, U. (1992) *Risk Society*. London: Sage.

Bell, D. (1993) *Communitarianism and Its Critics*. Oxford: Clarendon Press.

Bentham, J. (1823) 'Punishment and utility', reprinted in J. Murphy (ed.) (1995) *Punishment and Rehabilitation*, 3rd edn. Belmont, CA: Wadsworth, pp. 21–35.

Bianchi, H. (1994) *Justice as a Sanctuary. Towards a New System of Crime Control.* Bloomington, IN: Indiana University Press.

Blad, J. (1996a) *Abolitionisme als strafrechtstheorie* (*Abolitionism as Penal Law Theory*). Amsterdam: Gouda Quint.

Blad, J. (1996b) 'Neighbourhood-centered conflict mediation. The San Francisco example', *European Journal on Criminal Policy and Research*, 4 (1): 90–107.

Blad, J. (1998) 'Buurtbemiddeling en strafrecht' ('Neigbourhood mediation and criminal justice'), in G. van den Heuvel and R. van Swaaningen (eds), *Criminaliteit en sociale rechtvaardigheid*. Nijmegen: Ars Aequi Libri, pp. 200–15.

Blad, J. (2003) 'Community mediation, criminal justice and restorative justice: rearranging the institutions of law', in L. Walgrave (ed.), *Repositioning Restorative Justice*. Cullompton: Willan, pp. 191–207.

Blad, J. (2004) 'Herstelrecht en generale preventie. De normbevestigende werking van herstelrecht en herstelsanctie' ('Restorative justice and general prevention. The norm confirming function of restorative justice and reparative sanctions'), in B. Van Stokkom (ed.), *Straf en Herstel. Ethische Reflecties over Strafdoeleinden* (*Punishment and Restoration. Ethical Reflections on the Objectives of Punishment*). The Hague: Boom, pp. 91–112.

Blad, J. (2006) 'Institutionalizing restorative justice? Transforming criminal justice? A critical view on the Netherlands', in I. Aertsen, T. Daems and L. Robert (eds), *Institutionalizing Restorative Justice*. Cullompton: Willan, pp. 93–119.

Bloomfield, P. (2008) *Morality and Self-Interest*. Oxford: Oxford University Press.

Bonta, J., Jesseman, R., Rugge, T. and Cormier, R. (2006) 'Restorative justice and recidivism. Promises made, promises kept?', in D. Sullivan and L. Tift (eds), *Handbook of Restorative Justice*. Oxford: Routledge, pp. 108–20.

Bottoms, A. (2003) 'Some sociological reflections on restorative justice', in A. von Hirsch, J. Roberts, A. Bottoms, K. Roach and M. Schiff (eds), *Restorative Justice and Criminal Justice: Competing or Reconcilable Paradigms*. Oxford: Hart, pp. 79–113.

Boutellier, H. (1996) 'Beyond the criminal justice paradox. Alternatives between law and morality', *European Journal on Criminal Policy and Research*, 4 (4): 7–20.

Boutellier, H. (2000) *Crime and Morality. The Significance of Criminal Justice in Post-Modern Culture*. Dordrecht: Kluwer Academic.

Boyes-Watson, C. (2000) 'Reflections on the purist and the maximalist models of restorative justice', *Contemporary Justice Review*, 3 (4): 441–50.

Braithwaite, J. (1989) *Crime, Shame and Reintegration*. Cambridge: Cambridge University Press.

Braithwaite, J. (1993) 'Shame and modernity', *British Journal of Criminology*, 33: 1–18.

Braithwaite, J. (1999) 'Restorative justice: assessing optimistic and pessimistic accounts', in M. Tonry (ed.), *Crime and Justice: A Review of Research*. Chicago: University of Chicago Press.

Braithwaite, J. (2000a) 'Decomposing a holistic vision of restorative justice', *Contemporary Justice Review*, 3 (4): 433–40.

Braithwaite, J. (2000b) 'Republican theory and crime control', in S. Karstedt and K. Bussmann (eds), *Social Dynamics of Crime and Control. New Theories for a World on Transition*. Oxford: Hart, pp. 87–103.

Braithwaite, J. (2002a) *Restorative Justice and Responsive Regulation*. Oxford: Oxford University Press.

Braithwaite, J. (2002b) 'In search of restorative jurisprudence', in L. Walgrave (ed.), *Restorative Justice and the Law*. Cullompton: Willan, pp. 150–67.

Braithwaite, J. (2003) 'Restorative justice and corporate regulation', in E. Weitekamp and H. J. Kerner (eds), *Restorative Justice in Context. International Practice and Directions*. Cullompton: Willan, pp. 161–72.

Braithwaite, J. (2005) 'Between proportionality and impunity: confrontation → truth → prevention', *Criminology*, 43 (2): 283–306.

Braithwaite, J. (2006) 'Doing justice intelligently in civil society', *Journal of Social Issues*, 62 (2): 393–409.

Braithwaite, J. and Braithwaite, V. (2001) 'Shame, shame management and regulation', in E. Ahmed, N. Harris, J. Braithwaite and V. Braithwaite, *Shame Management Through Reintegration*. Cambridge: Cambridge University Press, pp. 1–69.

Braithwaite, J. and Mugford, S. (1994) 'Conditions of successful reintegration ceremonies', *British Journal of Criminology*, 34: 139–71.

Braithwaite, J. and Parker, C. (1999) 'Restorative justice is republican justice', in G. Bazemore and L. Walgrave (eds), *Restorative Justice for Juveniles. Repairing the Harm by Youth Crime*. Monsey, NY: Criminal Justice Press, pp. 103–26.

Braithwaite, J. and Pettit, P. (1990) *Not Just Desert. A Republican Theory of Criminal Justice*. Oxford: Oxford University Press.

Braithwaite, J. and Pettit, P. (2000) 'Republicanism and restorative justice: an explanatory and normative connection', in H. Strang and J. Braithwaite (eds), *Restorative Justice: Philosophy to Practice*. Dartmouth: Ashgate, pp. 145–63.

Braithwaite, J. and Roche, D. (2001) 'Responsibility and restorative justice', in G. Bazemore and M. Schiff (eds), *Restorative Community Justice. Repairing Harm and Transforming Communities*. Cincinnati, OH: Anderson, pp. 63–84.

Brunk, C. (2001) 'Restorative justice and the philosophical theories of criminal punishment', in M. Hadley (ed.), *The Spiritual Roots of Restorative Justice*. Albany, NY: State University of New York Press, pp. 31–56.

Burms, A. (2005) 'Retributive punishment and symbolic restoration: a reply to Duff', in E. Claes, R. Foqué and T. Peters (eds), *Punishment,*

Restorative Justice and the Morality of Law. Antwerp and Oxford: Intersentia, pp. 157–63.

Cario, R. (2005) *Justice Restaurative. Principes et Promesses.* Paris: L'Harmattan.

Castel, R. (2003) *L'insécurité Sociale. Qu'est-ce qu'être protégé?* Paris: Editions du Seuil.

Chancer, L. and McLaughlin, E. (2007) 'Public criminologies. Diverse perspectives on academia and policy', *Theoretical Criminology*, 11 (2): 155–73.

Christie, N. (1977) 'Conflicts as property', *British Journal of Criminology*, 17 (1): 1–15.

Christie, N. (1981) *Limits to Pain*. Oxford: Martin Robertson.

Claassen, R. (1993) *Restorative Justice Principles and Evaluation Continuums*. Paper presented at the National Center for Peacemaking and Conflict Resolution, Fresno, CA, May.

Claes, E. (2004) 'Punitieve rechtshandhaving, herstelrecht en menselijke gelijkwaardigheid' ('Punitive law enforcement, restorative justice and human equivalence'), in B. Van Stokkom (ed.), *Straf en Herstel. Ethische Reflecties over Strafdoeleinden* (*Punishment and Restoration. Ethical Reflections on the Objectives of Punishment*). The Hague: Boom, pp. 229–53.

Collins, R. (2004) *Interactional Ritual Change*. Princeton, NJ: Princeton University Press.

Crawford, A. (2002a) 'The state, community and restorative justice: heresy, nostalgia and butterfly collecting', in L. Walgrave (ed.), *Restorative Justice and the Law*. Cullompton: Willan, pp. 101–29.

Crawford, A. (ed.) (2002b) *Crime and Insecurity. The Governance of Safety in Europe*. Cullompton: Willan.

Crawford, A. and Clear, T. (2001) 'Community justice: transforming communities through restorative justice?', in G. Bazemore and M. Schiff (eds), *Restorative Community Justice. Repairing Harm and Transforming Communities*. Cincinnati, OH: Anderson, pp. 127–49.

Crawford, A. and Newburn, T. (2003) *Youth Offending and Restorative Justice. Implementing Reform in Youth Justice*. Cullompton: Willan.

Cunneen, C. (2007) 'Reviving restorative justice traditions?', in J. Johnstone and D. Van Ness (eds), *Handbook of Restorative Justice*. Cullompton: Willan, pp. 113–31.

Currie, E. (2007) 'Against marginality. Arguments for a public criminology', *Theoretical Criminology*, 11 (2): 175–90.

Daems, T. (2007) *Making Sense of Penal Change: Punishment, Victimization and Society*. PhD thesis in Criminology. Leuven: K.U. Leuven.

Daly, K. (2000) 'Revisiting the relationship between retributive and restorative justice', in H. Strang and J. Braithwaite (eds), *Restorative Justice. Philosophy to Practice*. Aldershot: Dartmouth, pp. 33–54.

Daly, K. (2001) 'Conferencing in Australia and New Zealand: variations, research findings and prospects', in A. Morris and G. Maxwell (eds), *Justice for Juveniles. Conferencing, Mediation and Circles*. Oxford: Hart.

Daly, K. (2002) 'Restorative justice: the real story', *Punishment and Society*, 4 (1): 55–79.

Daly, K. (2003) 'Mind the gap: restorative justice in theory and practice', in A. von Hirsch, J. Roberts, A. Bottoms, K. Roach and M. Schiff (eds), *Restorative Justice and Criminal Justice: Competing or Reconcilable Paradigms*. Oxford: Hart, pp. 219–36.

Daly, K. (2005a) 'A tale of two studies: restorative justice from a victim's perspective', in E. Elliott and R. Gordon (eds), *Restorative Justice: Emerging Issues in Practice and Evaluation*. Cullompton: Willan.

Daly, K. (2005b) 'Restorative Justice and Sexual Assault: An Archival Study of Court and Conference Cases'. Unpublished paper.

Davis, G., Boucherat, J. and Watson, D. (1988) 'Reparation in the service of diversion: the subordination of a good idea', *The Howard Journal*, 27: 127–34.

de Haan, W. (1990) *The Politics of Redress*. London: Sage.

de Keijser, J. (2000) *Punishment and Purpose. From Moral Theory to Punishment in Action*. PhD thesis. Leyden: University of Leyden.

de Saint-Chéron, M. (2006) *Entretiens avec Emmanuel Levinas (1992–1994)*. Paris: PUF, Livre de poche.

Debuyst, C. (1990) 'Pour introduire une histoire de la criminology: les problématiques du départ', *Déviance et Société*, 14 (4): 347–76.

Dignan, J. (2002) 'Restorative justice and the law: the case for an integrated, systemic approach', in L. Walgrave (ed.), *Restorative Justice and the Law*. Cullompton: Willan, pp. 168–90.

Dignan, J. (2003) 'Towards a systemic model of restorative justice: reflections in the concept, its context, and the need for clear constraints', in A. von Hirsch, J. Roberts, A. Bottoms, K. Roach and M. Schiff (eds), *Restorative Justice and Criminal Justice: Competing or Reconcilable Paradigms*. Oxford: Hart, pp. 135–56.

Dignan, J. (2005) *Understanding Victims and Restorative Justice*. Maidenhead: McGraw-Hill and Open University Press.

Dignan, J. and Cavadino, M. (1998) 'Which model of criminal justice offers the best scope for assisting victims of crime?', in E. Fattah and T. Peters (eds), *Support for Crime Victims in a Comparative Perspective*. Leuven: Leuven University Press, pp. 139–68.

Dignan, J. and Marsh, P. (2001) 'Restorative justice and family group conferences in England: current state and future prospects', in A. Morris and G. Maxwell (eds), *Restorative Justice for Juveniles. Conferencing, Mediation and Circles*. Oxford: Hart, pp. 85–101.

Doob, A., Sprott, J., Marinos, V. and Varma, K. (1998) *An Exploration of Ontario Residents' View of Crime and the Criminal Justice System*. Toronto: Centre of Criminology, University of Toronto.

Duff, A. (1992) 'Alternatives to punishment or alternative punishment?', in W. Cragg (ed.), *Retributivism and Its Critics*. Stuttgart: Steinder, pp. 44–68.

Duff, A. (2001) *Punishment, Communication and Community*. Oxford: Oxford University Press.

Duff, A. (2002) 'Restorative punishment and punitive restoration', in L. Walgrave (ed.), *Restorative Justice and the Law*. Cullompton: Willan.

Dumont, H. (2000) 'Le pardon, une valeur de justice et d'espoir, un plaidoyer pour la tolérance et contre l'oubli', *Revue Canadienne de Criminologie*, 42 (3): 299–322.

Duyndam, J. and Poorthuis, M. (2003) *Levinas*. Rotterdam: Lemniscaat.

Eliaerts, C. and Dumortier, E. (2002) 'Restorative justice for children. In need of procedural safeguards and standards', in E. Weitekamp and H. J. Kerner (eds), *Restorative Justice: Theoretical Foundations*. Cullompton: Willan, pp. 204–23.

Elias, N. (1994) *The Civilizing Process*. Oxford: Blackwell.

Etzioni, A. (1995) *The Spirit of Community. Rights, Responsibilities and the Communitarian Agenda*. London: Fontana Press.

Etzioni, A. (1996) *The New Golden Rule. Community and Morality in a Democratic Society*. New York: Basic Books.

Etzioni, A. (1998) *The Essential Communitarian Reader*. Lanham, MD: Rowman & Littlefield.

European Forum for Victim–Offender Mediation and Restorative Justice (ed.) (2000) *Victim–Offender Mediation in Europe. Making Restorative Justice Work*. Leuven: Leuven University Press.

Faget, J. (1997) *La Médiation: essai de politique pénale*. Ramonville Saint Agnes: Erès.

Faget, J. (2006) '"Reintegrative shaming": à propos de la théorie de John Braithwaite', *Les Cahiers de la Justice*, Spring: 59–70.

Fatic, A, (1995) *Punishment and Restorative Crime-Handling*. Aldershot: Avebury.

Fattah, E. and Parmentier, S. (eds) (2001) *Victim Policies and Criminal Justice on the Road to Restorative Justice*. Leuven: Leuven University Press, pp. 295–314.

Feeley, M. and Simon, J. (1992) 'The new penology: notes in the emerging strategy of corrections and its implications', *Criminology*, 30 (4): 449–74.

Feinberg, J. (1990) *The Moral Limits of the Criminal Law*. New York: Oxford University Press.

Feld, B. (1993) 'Criminalizing the American juvenile court', in M. Tonry (ed.), *Crime and Justice: A Review of Research*, Vol. 17. Chicago: Chicago University Press:

Feld, B. (1999) 'Rehabilitation, retribution and restorative justice', in G. Bazemore and L. Walgrave (eds), *Restorative Justice for Juveniles. Repairing the Harm by Youth Crime*. Monsey, NY: Criminal Justice Press, pp. 17–44.

Felson, M. (1994) *Crime and Everyday Life*. Thousand Oaks, CA: Pine Forge Press.

Ferri, E. (1905) *La Sociologie Criminelle*. Paris: Alcan.

Field, J. (2003) *Social Capital*. London and New York: Routledge/Key Ideas.

Foucault, M. (1975) *Surveiller et Punir*. Paris: Gallimard.

Fraser, S. and Norton, J. (1996) 'Family group conferencing in New Zealand child protection work', in J. Hudson, A. Morris, G. Maxwell and B. Galaway (eds), *Family Group Conferences. Perspectives on Policy and Practice*. Leichhardt, NSW and Monsey, NY: Federation Press and Willow Tree Press, pp. 37–48.

Froestad, J. and Shearing, C. (2007) 'Conflict resolution in Africa. A case study', in G. Johnstone and D. Van Ness (eds), *Handbook of Restorative Justice*. Cullompton: Willan, pp. 534–55.

Galaway, B. (1984) 'A survey of public acceptance of restitution as an alternative for imprisonment for property offences', *Australian and New Zealand Journal of Criminology*, 17 (2): 108–17.

Garland, D. (1985) *Punishment and Welfare. A History of Penal Strategies*. Aldershot: Gower.

Garland, D. (1990) *Punishment and Modern Society*. Oxford: Clarendon.

Garland, D. (1996) 'The limits of the sovereign state: strategies of crime control in contemporary society', *British Journal of Criminology*, 36: 445–71.

Garland, D. (2001) *The Culture of Control. Crime and Social Order in Contemporary Society*. Oxford: Oxford University Press.

Garland, D. and Sparks, R. (eds) (2000a) *Criminology and Social Theory*, Clarendon Studies in Criminology. Oxford: Oxford University Press.

Garland, D. and Sparks, R. (2000b) 'Criminology, social theory and the challenge of our times', in D. Garland and R. Sparks (eds), *Criminology and Social Theory*, Clarendon Studies in Criminology. Oxford: Oxford University Press, pp. 1–22.

Giddens, A. (1998) Risk society: the context of British politics', in J. Franklin (ed.), *The Politics of Risk Society*. Cambridge: Polity.

Gilligan, C. (1982) *In a Different Voice: Psychological Theory and Women's Development*. Cambridge, MA: Harvard University Press.

Goris, P. (2001) 'Community crime prevention and the "partnership approach": a safe community for all?', *European Journal on Criminal Policy and Research*, 9 (4): 447–57.

Green, S. (2006) 'The victims' movement and restorative justice', in G. Johnstone and D. Van Ness (eds), *Handbook of Restorative Justice*. Cullompton: Willan, pp. 171–91.

Guarino-Ghezzi, S. and Klein, A. (1999) 'Protecting community: the public safety role in a restorative juvenile justice', in G. Bazemore and L. Walgrave (eds), *Restorative Justice for Juveniles. Repairing the Harm by Youth Crime*. Monsey, NY: Criminal Justice Press, pp. 195–211.

Hadley, M. (2001) *The Spiritual Roots of Restorative Justice.* Albany, NY: State University of New York Press.

Hagemann, O. (2003) 'Restorative justice in prison?', in L. Walgrave (ed.), *Repositioning Restorative Justice.* Cullompton: Willan, pp. 221–36.

Haggerty, K. (2004) 'Displaced expertise: three constraints on the policy-relevance of criminological thought', *Theoretical Criminology*, 8 (2): 211–32.

Harris, N. (2003) 'Evaluating the practice of restorative justice: the case of family group conferencing', in L. Walgrave (ed.), *Repositioning Restorative Justice.* Cullompton: Willan, pp. 121–35.

Harris, N., Walgrave, L. and Braithwaite, J. (2004) 'Emotional dynamics in restorative conferences', *Theoretical Criminology*, 8 (2): 191–210.

Hastings, R. and Bailleau, F. (2005) 'Socio-legal regulation in a multi-ethnic society: assessing the shift to the local in France or the community in Canada', in N. Queloz, F. Bütikofer Repond, D. Pittet, R. Brossard and B. Meyer-Bisch (eds), *Youth Crime and Juvenile Justice. The Challenge of Migration and Ethnic Diversity.* Berne/Brussels: Staempfli/Bruylandt, pp. 335–56.

Hayes, H. (2005) 'Assessing reoffending in restorative justice conferences', *Australian and New Zealand Journal of Criminology*, 38: 77–101.

Hayes, H. (2007) 'Reoffending and restorative justice', in G. Johnstone and D. Van Ness (eds), *Handbook of Restorative Justice.* Cullompton: Willan, pp. 426–44.

Hayes, H. and Daly, K. (2003) 'Youth justice conferencing and reoffending', *Justice Quarterly*, 20 (4): 725–64.

Hayes, H. and Daly, K. (2004) 'Conferencing and re-offending in Queensland', *Australian and New Zealand Journal of Criminology*, 37 (2): 167–91.

Hebberecht, P. and Sack, F. (eds) (1997) *La prévention de la délinquance en Europe: nouvelles stratégies.* Paris: L'Harmattan.

Hildebrandt, M. (2005) 'Restorative justice and the morality of a fair trial: a reply to Brochu', in E. Claes, R. Foqué and T. Peters (eds), *Punishment, Restorative Justice and the Morality of Law.* Antwerp and Oxford: Intersentia, pp. 89–99.

Hirschi, T. (1969) *Causes of Delinquency.* Berkeley, CA: University of California Press.

Hogarth, J. (1971) *Sentencing as a Human Process.* Toronto: Toronto University Press.

Hudson, B. (2006a) 'Beyond white man's justice: race, gender and justice in late modernity', *Theoretical Criminology*, 10 (1): 29–47.

Hudson, B. (2006b) 'Balancing the ethical and the political: normative reflections on the institutionalisation of restorative justice', in I. Aertsen, T. Daems and L. Robert (eds), *Institutionalizing Restorative Justice.* Cullompton: Willan, pp. 261–81.

Hudson, J., Morris, A., Maxwell, G. and Galaway, B. (eds) (1996) *Family Group Conferences. Perspectives on Policy and Practice.* Annandale, Australia/ Monsey, NY: Federation Press/Willow Tree Press.

Hughes, G. and Edwards, A. (2002) *Crime Control and Community. The New Politics of Public Safety*. Cullompton: Willan.

Hulsman, L. (1979) *An Abolitionist Perspective on Criminal Justice and a Scheme to Organise Approaches to 'Problematic Situations'*. Paper presented at the University of Louvain-La-Neuve, Belgium.

Hulsman, L. (1982) 'Penal reform in the Netherlands. Reflections on a White Paper proposal', *Howard Journal of Penology and Crime Prevention*, 21: 35–47.

Hulsman, L. and Bernat de Celis, J. (1984) *Peines perdues. Le système pénal en question*. Paris: Centurion.

Jaccoud, M. (1998) 'Restoring justice in native communities in Canada', in L. Walgrave (ed.), *Restorative Justice for Juveniles. Potentialities, Risks and Problems for Research*. Leuven: Leuven University Press, pp. 285–99.

Jaccoud, M. (2006) 'Les cercles de sentence au Canada', *Les Cahiers de la Justice*, 1 (1): 83–94.

Johnstone, G. (2002) *Restorative Justice. Ideas, Values, Debates*. Cullompton: Willan.

Johnstone, G. (2004) 'How, and in what terms, should restorative justice be conceived?', in H. Zehr and B. Toews (eds), *Critical Issues in Restorative Justice*. Monsey, NY/Cullompton: Criminal Justice Press/Willan, pp. 5–15.

Johnstone, G. and Van Ness, D. (2007) 'The meaning of restorative justice', in G. Johnstone and D. Van Ness (eds), *Handbook of Restorative Justice*. Cullompton: Willan, pp. 5–23.

Kappeler, V., Blumberg, M. and Potter, G. (eds) (2000) *The Mythology of Crime and Criminal Justice*, 3rd edn. Prospect Heights, IL: Waveland Press.

Karp, D. and Walther, L. (2001) 'Community reparative boards in Vermont: theory and practice', in G. Bazemore and M. Schiff (eds), *Restorative Community Justice. Repairing Harm and Transforming Communities*. Cincinnati, OH: Anderson, pp. 199–217.

Karstedt, S. (2002) 'Emotions and criminal justice', *Theoretical Criminology*, 6 (3): 299–317.

Karstedt, S. and Bussmann, K. (eds) (2000) *Social Dynamics of Crime and Control. New Theories for a World in Transition*. Oxford: Hart.

Karstedt, S. and Farrall, S. (2004) 'The moral maze of the middle class. The predatory society and its emerging regulatory order', in H. Albrecht, T. Serassis and H. Kania (eds), *Images of Crime II*. Freiburg i. Br.: Ed. Iuscrim, pp. 65–94.

Karstedt, S. and Farrall, S. (2007) *Law Abiding Majority? The Everyday Crimes of the Middle Classes*, Briefing 3. London: Centre for Crime and Justice Studies.

Kohlberg, L. (1976) 'Moral stages and moralization', in T. Lickona (ed.), *Moral Development and Behavior: Theory, Research and Social Issues*. New York: Holt, Rinehart & Winston, pp. 31–53.

Kurki, L. (2003) 'Evaluating restorative practices', in A. von Hirsch, J. Roberts, A. Bottoms, K. Roach and M. Schiff (eds), *Restorative Justice and Criminal Justice: Competing or Reconcilable Paradigms*. Oxford: Hart, pp. 293–314.

Kutchinsky, B. (1979) 'Law, crime and legal attitudes: new advances in Scandinavian research on knowledge and opinion about law', in S. Mednick and S. Shoham (eds), *New Paths in Criminology*. Lexington, MA: Heath & Co, pp. 191–218.

LaPrairie, C. (1995) 'Altering course: new directions in criminal justice and corrections: sentencing circles and family group conferences', *Australian and New Zealand Journal of Criminology*, Special Issue, December: 78–99.

Latimer, J., Dowden, C. and Muise, D. (2001) *The Effectiveness of Restorative Justice Practices: A Meta Analysis*. Ottawa: Department of Justice.

Laub, J. and Sampson, R. (2001) 'Understanding desistance from crime', in M. Tonry (ed.), *Crime and Justice: A Review of Research*, Vol. 28. Chicago: Chicago University Press.

Leest, J. (2004) 'Gevoelige zaken. Een zorgethisch perspectief op herstelrecht' ('Sensitive matters. A care-ethical perspective on restorative justice'), *Tijdschrift voor Herstelrecht*, 4 (1): 38–47.

Lemert, E. (1981) 'Diversion in juvenile justice: what hath been wrought', *Journal of Research in Crime and Delinquency*, 22: 34–46.

Levinas, E. (1966) *De totaliteit en het oneindige: essay over de exterioriteit (Totality and Infinity: An Essay on Exteriority)*, trans. from French: *Totalité et infini: essai sur l'extériorité* (1961). Rotterdam: Lemniscaat.

Lianos, M. and Douglas, M. (2000) 'Dangerization and the end of deviance', in D. Garland and R. Sparks (eds), *Criminology and Social Theory*, Clarendon Studies in Criminology. Oxford: Oxford University Press, pp. 103–25.

Lilles, H. (2001) 'Circle sentencing: part of the restorative justice continuum', in A. Morris and G. Maxwell (eds), *Restorative Justice for Juveniles. Conferencing, Mediation and Circles*. Oxford: Hart.

Loesel, F. (2007) 'It's never too early and never too late: towards an integrated science of developmental intervention in criminology', *The Criminologist*, 32 (5): 1–8.

Louw, D. (2006) 'The African concept of ubuntu and restorative justice', in D. Sullivan and L. Tift (eds), *Handbook of Restorative Justice*. Oxford: Routledge, pp. 161–73.

McCold, P. (1998) 'Restorative justice: variations on a theme', in L. Walgrave (ed.), *Restorative Justice for Juveniles: Potentialities, Risks and Problems*. Leuven: Leuven University Press, pp. 19–53.

McCold, P. (2000) 'Toward a holistic vision of restorative juvenile justice: a reply to the maximalist model', *Contemporary Justice Review*, 3 (4): 357–414.

McCold, P. (2001) 'Primary restorative practices', in A. Morris and G. Maxwell (eds), *Restorative Justice for Juveniles. Conferencing, Mediation and Circles*. Oxford: Hart.

McCold, P. (2003) 'A survey of assessment research on mediation and conferencing', in L. Walgrave (ed.), *Repositioning Restorative Justice*. Cullompton: Willan, pp. 67–117.

McCold, P. (2004a) 'Paradigm muddle: the threat to restorative justice posed by its merger with community justice', *Contemporary Justice Review*, 7 (1): 13–35.

McCold, P. (2004b) 'What is the role of community in restorative justice theory and practice?', in H. Zehr and B. Toews (eds), *Critical Issues in Restorative Justice*. Monsey, NY/Cullompton: Criminal Justice Press/Willan, pp. 155–72.

McCold, P. (2006) 'The recent history of restorative justice. Mediation, circles and conferencing', in D. Sullivan and L. Tift (eds), *Handbook of Restorative Justice*. Oxford: Routledge, pp. 23–51.

McCold, P. and Wachtel, B. (1998) *Restorative Policing Experiment: The Bethlehem Pennsylvania Police Family Group Conferencing Project (Final Report)*. Washington, DC: US Department of Justice, National Institute of Justice, National Criminal Justice Reference Service.

McCold, P. and Wachtel, T. (1997) *Community Is Not a Place*. Paper presented at the International Conference on Justice without Violence, Albany, NY, 5–6 June. Online at: http://www.realjustice.org/pages/albany.html.

McCold, P. and Wachtel, T. (2002) 'Restorative justice theory validation', in E. Weitekamp and H. J. Kerner (eds), *Restorative Justice: Theoretical Foundations*. Cullompton: Willan, pp. 110–42.

McGuire, J. and Priestly, P. (1995) 'Reviewing 'what works': past, present and future', in J. McGuire (ed.), *What Works: Reducing Reoffending*. Chichester and New York: J. Wiley.

MacIntyre, A. (1983) *After Virtue. A Study in Moral Theory*, 2nd edn. Notre Dame, IN: University of Notre Dame Press.

Mackay, R. (2006) 'The institutionalisation of principles in restorative justice – a case study from the UK', in I. Aertsen, T. Daems and L. Robert (eds), *Institutionalizing Restorative Justice*. Cullompton: Willan, pp. 194–215.

Mackie, J. (1985) 'Morality and retributive emotions', in J. Mackie (ed.), *Persons and Values*. Oxford: Oxford University Press, pp. 206–19.

McLaughlin, E., Fergusson, R., Hughes, G. and Westmarland, L. (eds) (2003) *Restorative Justice. Critical Issues*. London and Thousand Oaks, CA: Sage.

MacRae, A. and Zehr, H. (2004) *The Little Book of Family Group Conferences New Zealand Style. A Hopeful Approach When Youth Cause Harm*. Intercourse, PA: Good Books.

Marshall, T. (1996) 'The evolution of restorative justice in Britain', *European Journal of Criminal Policy and Research*, 4 (4): 21–43.

Marshall, T. (1997) 'Seeking the whole justice', in S. Hayma (ed.), *Repairing the Damage. Restorative Justice in Action*. London: ISTD.

Maruna, S. (2001) *Making Good: How Ex-convicts Reform and Rebuild Their Lives.* Washington, DC: American Psychological Association Press.

Maruna, S. and King, A. (2004) *Shame, Materialism and Moral Indignation in the East of England. An Empirical Look at Ranulf's Thesis.* Paper presented at the workshop on 'Emotions, Crime and Justice', Onati, Spain, 13–14 September.

Masters, G. and Roberts, A. (2000) 'Family group conferencing for victims, offenders and communities', in M. Liebman (ed.), *Mediation in Context.* London: Jessica Kingsley.

Masters, G. and Smith, D. (1998) 'Portia and Persephone revisited: thinking about feeling in criminal justice', *Theoretical Criminology*, 2 (1): 5–27.

Maxwell, G. (2007) 'The youth justice system in New Zealand: restorative justice delivered through the family group conference', in G. Maxwell and J. Liu (eds), *Restorative Justice and Practices in New Zealand: Towards a Restorative Society.* Wellington, New Zealand: Institute of Policy Studies, Victoria University, pp. 45–67.

Maxwell, G. and Morris, A. (1996) 'Research on family group conferences with young offenders in New Zealand', in J. Hudson, A. Morris, G. Maxwell and B. Galaway (eds), *Family Group Conferences. Perspectives on Policy and Practice.* Monsey, NY/Annandale, NSW: Willow Tree Press/Federation Press, pp. 88–110.

Maxwell, G. and Morris, A. (1999) *Understanding Reoffending. Final Report.* Wellington, New Zealand: Institute of Criminology, Victoria University.

Maxwell, G. and Morris, A. (2002) 'The role of shame, guilt and remorse in restorative justice processes for young people', in E. Weitekamp and H. J. Kerner (eds), *Restorative Justice: Theoretical Foundations.* Cullompton: Willan, pp. 267–84.

Maxwell, G., Kingi, V., Robertson, J., Morris, A. and Cunningham, C. (2004) *Achieving Effective Outcomes in Youth Justice.* Wellington, New Zealand: Ministry of Social Development.

Maxwell, G., Morris, A. and Hayes, H. (2006) 'Conferencing and restorative justice', in D. Sullivan and L. Tift (eds), *Handbook of Restorative Justice.* Oxford: Routledge, pp. 91–107.

Merry, S. and Milner, N. (eds) (1993) *The Possibility of Popular Justice: A Case Study of Community Mediation.* Ann Arbor, MI: University of Michigan Press.

Merton, R. (1938) 'Social structure and anomie', *American Sociological Review*, 3 (3): 672–82.

Messmer, H. and Otto, H. U. (eds) (1992) *Restorative Justice on Trial. Pitfalls and Potentials of Victim-Offender Mediation. International Research Perspectives.* Dordrecht, Boston and London: KluwerAcademic.

Miers, D. (2001) *An International Review of Restorative Justice*, Crime Reduction Research Series 10. London: Home Office.

Miers, D. and Willemsens, J. (eds) (2004) *Mapping Restorative Justice. Developments in European Countries.* Leuven: European Forum for Victim–Offender Mediation and Restorative Justice.

Miller, W. (1999) 'In defence of revenge', in B. Hanawalt and D. Wallace (eds), *Medieval Crime and Social Control.* Minneapolis, MN: University of Minnesota Press, pp. 70–89.

Moore, M. (1995) 'The moral worth of retribution', in J. Murphy (ed.), *Punishment and Rehabilitation.* Belmont, CA: Wadsworth; reprint from F. Schoeman (ed.) (1987) *Responsibility, Character and Emotions.* Cambridge: Cambridge University Press.

Morris, A. (2002a) 'Shame, guilt and remorse: experiences from family group conferences in New Zealand', in I. Weijers and A. Duff (eds), *Punishing Juveniles. Principle and Critique.* Oxford: Hart.

Morris, A. (2002b) 'Critiquing the critics', *British Journal of Criminology,* 42 (3): 596–615.

Morris, A. (2004) 'Youth justice in New Zealand', in M. Tonry and A. Doob (eds), *Youth Crime and Youth Justice. Comparative and Cross-national Perspectives,* Crime and Justice, Vol. 31. Chicago: University of Chicago Press, 243–92.

Morris, H. (1981) 'A paternalistic theory of punishment', *American Philosophical Quarterly,* 18: 263–71.

Morris, R. (2000) *Stories of Transformative Justice.* Toronto: Canadian Scholars' Press.

Morrison, B. (2006) 'School bullying and restorative justice: toward a theoretical understanding of the role of respect, pride and shame', *Journal of Social Issues,* 62 (2): 371–92.

Morrison, B. (2007) 'Schools and restorative justice', in G. Johnstone and D. Van Ness (eds), *Handbook of Restorative Justice.* Cullompton: Willan, pp. 325–50.

Nussbaum, M. (1993) 'Equity and mercy', *Philosophy and Public Affairs,* 22 (2): 83–125; reprinted in J. Murphy (ed.) (1995) *Punishment and Rehabilitation,* 3rd edn. Belmont, CA: Wadsworth, pp. 212–48.

O'Malley, P. (2006) 'Risk and restorative justice: governing through the minimization of harms', in I. Aertsen, T. Daems and L. Robert (eds), *Institutionalizing Restorative Justice.* Cullompton: Willan, pp. 216–36.

Parker, R. (2005) *Restorative Justice. Why Doesn't It Work in Reducing Recidivism?* Paper presented at the 7th International Conference on Restorative Justice, Canberra, 23–25 February.

Pavlich, G. (2001) 'The force of community', in H. Strang and J. Braithwaite (eds), *Restorative Justice and Civil Society.* Cambridge: Cambridge University Press, pp. 56–68.

Pavlich, G. (2002) 'Towards an ethics of restorative justice', in L. Walgrave (ed.), *Restorative Justice and the Law*. Cullompton: Willan, pp. 1–18.

Pavlich, G. (2005) *Governing Paradoxes of Restorative Justice*. London and Portland, OR: Glasshouse Press.

Pavlich, G. (2007) 'Ethics, universal principles and restorative justice', in G. Johnstone and D. Van Ness (eds), *Handbook of Restorative Justice*. Cullompton: Willan, pp. 615–30.

Pelikan, C. (2007a) 'The place of restorative justice in society. Making sense of developments in time and space,' paper presented at the COST-Workshop 'Structuring the Landscape of Restorative Justice Theory', Maastricht 26 October 2005, in R. Mackay, M. Bosnjak, J. Deklerck, C. Pelikan, B. Van Stokkom and M. Wright (eds), *Images of Restorative Justice Theory*. Frankfurt: Verlag für Polizeiwissenschaft.

Pelikan, C. (2007b) Introduction to the COST-Workshop 'Structuring the Landscape of Restorative Justice Theory', Maastricht, 26 October 2005, in R. Mackay, M. Bosnjak, J. Deklerck, C. Pelikan, B. Van Stokkom and M. Wright (eds), *Images of Restorative Justice Theory*. Frankfurt: Verlag für Polizeiwissenschaft.

Pelikan, C. and Trenczek, T. (2006) 'Victim offender mediation and restorative justice. The European landscape', in D. Sullivan and L. Tift (eds), *Handbook of Restorative Justice*. Oxford: Routledge, pp. 63–90.

Pennell, J. (2006) 'Restorative practices and child welfare: toward an inclusive civil society', *Journal of Social Issues*, 62 (2): 259–79.

Peper, P. and Spierings, F. (1999) 'Settling disputes between neighbours in the lifeworld: an evaluation of experiments with community mediation in the Netherlands', *European Journal of Criminal Policy and Research*, 7 (4): 483–507.

Peters, T. and Aertsen, I. (1995) 'Restorative justice. In search of new avenues in dealing with crime', in C. Fijnaut, J. Goethals, T. Peters and L. Walgrave (eds), *Changes in Society, Crime and Criminal Justice in Europe*, Vol. 1. The Hague: Kluwer Law International, pp. 311–42.

Peters, T. and Aertsen, I. (2000) 'Towards restorative justice: victimisation, victim support and trends in criminal justice', in Council of Europe (ed.), *Crime and Criminal Justice in Europe*. Baden-Baden: Koelblin, pp. 35–46.

Polk, K. (2001) 'Positive youth development, restorative justice and the crisis of abandoned youth', in G. Bazemore and M. Schiff (eds), *Restorative Community Justice. Repairing Harm and Transforming Communities*. Cincinnati, OH: Anderson, pp. 265–86.

Pranis, K. (2001) 'Restorative justice, social justice, and the empowerment of marginalized populations', in G. Bazemore and M. Schiff (eds), *Restorative Community Justice. Repairing Harm and Transforming Communities*. Cincinnati, OH: Anderson, pp. 287–306.

Pratt, J. (2006) 'Beyond evangelical criminology: in meaning and significance of restorative justice', in I. Aertsen, T. Daems and L. Robert (eds), *Institutionalizing Restorative Justice*. Cullompton: Willan, pp. 44–67.

Prichard, J. (2003) 'Juvenile Conferencing and Restorative Justice in Tasmania'. Unpublished PhD thesis, University of Tasmania, Faculty of Law.

Prison Fellowship International (2007) Online at: http://www.rjcity.org/the-city.

Putnam, R. (1993) *Making Democracy Work. Civic Traditions in Modern Italy.* Princeton, NJ: Princeton University Press.

Putnam, R. (2000) *Bowling Alone.* New York: Simon & Schuster.

Rawls, J. (1972) *A Theory of Justice.* Oxford: Oxford University Press.

Robert, L. and Peters, T. (2003) 'How restorative justice is able to transcend the prison walls: a discussion of the "restorative detention" project', in E. Weitekamp and H. J. Kerner (eds), *Restorative Justice in Context.* Cullompton: Willan, pp. 95–122.

Roberts, J. and Hough, M. (2002) 'Public attitudes to punishment: the context', in J. Roberts and M. Hough (eds), *Changing Attitudes to Punishment. Public Opinion, Crime and Justice.* Cullompton: Willan, pp. 1–14.

Roberts, J., Stalans, L., Indermaur, D. and Hough, M. (2003) *Penal Populism and Public Opinion. Lessons from Five Countries.* Oxford: Oxford University Press.

Roche, D. (2001) 'The evolving definition of restorative justice', *Contemporary Justice Review*, 4 (3–4): 375–88.

Roche, D. (2003) *Accountability in Restorative Justice.* Oxford: Oxford University Press.

Roche, D. (2006) 'Dimensions of restorative justice', *Journal of Social Issues*, 62 (2): 217–38.

Rorty, R. (1989) *Contingency, Irony and Solidarity.* Cambridge: Cambridge University Press.

Salas, D. (2005) *La volonté de punir. Essai sur le populisme pénal.* Paris: Hachette.

Schafer, S. (1977) *Victimology. The Victim and His Criminal.* Reston, VA: Prentice Hall.

Scheff, T. and Retzinger, S. (1991) *Emotions and Violence: Shame and Rage in Destructive Conflicts.* Lexington, MA: Lexington Books.

Schelkens, W. (1998) 'Community service and mediation in the juvenile justice legislation in Europe', in L. Walgrave (ed.), *Restorative Justice for Juveniles: Potentialities, Risks and Problems for Research.* Leuven: Leuven University Press, pp. 159–83.

Schiff, M. (1999) 'The impact of restorative interventions on juvenile offenders', in G. Bazemore and L. Walgrave (eds), *Restorative Justice for Juveniles. Repairing the Harm by Youth Crime.* Monsey, NY: Criminal Justice Press, pp. 327–56.

Schur, E. (1971) *Labeling Deviant Behaviour.* New York: Harper.

Schweigert, F. (1999) 'Moral education in victim offender conferencing', *Criminal Justice Ethics*, Summer/Fall: 29–39.

Sellin, T. and Wolfgang, M. (1964) *The Measurement of Delinquency*. New York: Wiley.

Sessar, K. (1995) 'Restitution or punishment. An empirical study on attitudes of the public and the justice system in Hamburg', *Eurocriminology*, 8 (9): 199–214.

Sessar, K. (1999) 'Punitive attitudes of the public: myth and reality', in G. Bazemore and L. Walgrave (eds), *Restorative Justice for Juveniles, Repairing the Harm by Youth Crime*. Monsey, NY: Criminal Justice Press, pp. 287–304.

Shapland, J. (2003) 'Restorative justice and criminal justice: just responses to crime?', in A. von Hirsch, J. Roberts, A. Bottoms, K. Roach and M. Schiff (eds), *Restorative Justice and Criminal Justice: Competing or Reconcilable Paradigms*. Oxford: Hart, pp. 195–217.

Sharpe, S. (2007) 'The idea of reparation', in G. Johnstone and D. Van Ness (eds), *Handbook of Restorative Justice*. Cullompton: Willan, pp. 24–40.

Shearing, C. (2001) 'Transforming security: a South African experiment', in H. Strang and J. Braithwaite (eds), *Restorative Justice and Civil Society*. Cambridge: Cambridge University Press, pp. 14–34.

Shearing, C. and Wood, J. (2003) 'Nodal governance, democracy and the new "denizens"', *Journal of Law and Society*, 30: 400–19.

Sherman, L. (1993) 'Defiance, deterrence and irrelevance: a theory of the criminal sanction', *Journal of Research in Crime and Delinquency*, 30 (4): 445–73.

Sherman, L. (2003) 'Reason for emotion: reinventing justice with theories, innovations, and research', *Criminology*, 41 (1): 1–37.

Sherman, L. and Strang, H. (2007) *Restorative Justice: the Evidence*. London: Smith Institute.

Sherman, L., Strang, H. and Woods, D. (2000) *Recidivism Pattern in the Canberra Reintegrative Shaming Experiments (RISE)*. Canberra: Centre for Restorative Justice, Australian National University.

Sherman, L., Gottfredson, D., McKenzie, D., Eck, J., Reuter, P. and Bushway, S. (1997) *Preventing Crime. What Works, What Doesn't, What's Promising*. Washington, DC: Department of Justice, Office of Justice Programs.

Skelton, A. and Frank, C. (2004) 'How does restorative justice address human rights and due process issues?', in H. Zehr and B. Toews (eds), *Critical Issues in Restorative Justice*. Monsey, NY/Cullompton: Criminal Justice Press/Willan, pp. 203–13.

Skolnick, J. (1995) 'What not to do about crime. The American Society of Criminology 1994 Presidential Address', *Criminology*, 33 (10): 1–15.

Sparks, R. (1997) 'Recent social theory and the study of crime and punishment', in M. Maguire, R. Morgan and R. Reiner (eds), *The Oxford Handbook of Criminology*, 2nd edn. Oxford: Oxford University Press, pp. 409–35.

Stenson, K. (2001) 'The new politics of crime control', in K. Stenson and R. Sullivan (eds), *Crime, Risk and Justice. The Politics of Crime Control in Liberal Democracies*. Cullompton: Willan, pp. 15–28.

Stenson, K. and Edwards, A. (2001) 'Rethinking crime control in advanced liberal government: the "third way" and the return to the local', in K. Stenson and R. Sullivan (eds), *Crime, Risk and Justice. The Politics of Crime Control in Liberal Democracies*. Cullompton: Willan, pp. 68–86.

Stenson, K. and Sullivan, R. (eds) (2001) *Crime, Risk and Justice. The Politics of Crime Control in Liberal Democracies*. Cullompton: Willan.

Strang, H. (2002) *Repair or Revenge: Victims and Restorative Justice*. Oxford: Clarendon.

Strang, H. and Sherman, L. (2005) *Effects of Face-to-Face Justice on Victims of Crime in Four Randomized Controlled Trials*. Paper presented at the 7th International Conference on Restorative Justice, Canberra, 23–25 February.

Strang, H., Sherman, L., Angel, C., Woods, D., Bennett, S., Newbury-Birch, D. and Inkpen, N. (2006) 'Victim evaluations of face-to-face restorative justice conferences: a quasi-experimental analysis', *Journal of Social Issues*, 62 (2): 281–306.

Stuart, B. (1996) 'Circle sentencing: turning swords into ploughshares', in B. Galaway and J. Hudson (eds), *Restorative Justice: International Perspectives*. Amsterdam/Monsey, NY: Kugler/Criminal Justice Press.

Stubbs, J. (2002) 'Domestic violence and women's safety: feminist challenges to restorative justice', in H. Strang and J. Braithwaite (eds), *Restorative Justice and Family Violence*. Cambridge: Cambridge University Press.

Sullivan, D. and Tift, L. (2006a) 'Introduction: the healing dimension of restorative justice: a one-world body', in D. Sullivan and L. Tift (eds), *Handbook of Restorative Justice*. Oxford: Routledge, pp. 1–16.

Sullivan, D. and Tift, L. (2006b) Gross human rights violations and transitional justice', in D. Sullivan and L. Tift (eds), *Handbook of Restorative Justice*. Oxford: Routledge, pp. 337–41.

Sylvester, D. (2003) 'Myth in restorative justice history', *Utah Law Review*, 1 (1): 471–522.

Taylor, J., Walton, P. and Young, J. (1973) *The New Criminology*. London: Routledge.

Tonry, M. (1995) *Malign Neglect: Race, Crime and Punishment in America*. New York: Oxford University Press.

Tonry, M. and Farrington, D. (1995) 'Strategic approaches to crime prevention', in M. Tonry and D. Farrington (eds), *Building a Safer Society. Strategic Approaches to Crime Prevention*, Crime and Justice, Vol. 19. Chicago: University of Chicago Press, pp. 1–20.

Tulkens, F. (1993) 'Les transformations du droit pénal aux Etats-Unis. Pour un autre modèle de justice', in UCL Law Faculty (ed.), *Nouveaux itinéraires en droit*. Brussels: Bruylandt, pp. 461–93.

Tutu, D. (1999) *No Future Without Forgiveness*. London: Rider.

Tyler, T. (1990) *Why People Obey the Law*. New Haven, CT: Yale University Press.

Tyler, T. (2006) 'Restorative justice and procedural justice: dealing with rule breaking', *Journal of Social Issues*, 62 (2): 307–26.

Tyler, T. and Huo, Y. (2002) *Trust in the Law. Encouraging Public Cooperation with the Police and Courts*. New York: Russell Sage Foundation.

Umbreit, M. (1999) 'Avoiding the "McDonaldization" of victim–offender mediation: a case study in moving toward the mainstream', in G. Bazemore and L. Walgrave (eds), *Restorative Juvenile Justice: Repairing the Harm of Youth Crime*. Monsey, NY: Criminal Justice Press, pp. 213–34.

Umbreit, M. and Zehr, H. (1996) 'Restorative family group conferences: differing models and guidelines for practice', *Federal Probation*, 60 (3): 24–9.

Umbreit, M., Vos, B., Coates, R. and Brown, K. (2003) *Facing Violence*. Monsey, NY: Criminal Justice Press.

United Nations (2006) *Handbook of Restorative Justice Programmes*, Criminal Justice Handbook Series. Vienna: United Nations Office on Drugs and Crime.

Van Ness, D. (1999) 'Legal issues of restorative justice', in G. Bazemore and L. Walgrave (eds), *Restorative Justice for Juveniles. Repairing the Harm by Youth Crime*. Monsey, NY: Criminal Justice Press, pp. 263–84.

Van Ness, D. (2002a) 'The shape of things to come: a framework for thinking about a restorative justice system', in E. Weitekamp and H. J. Kerner (eds), *Restorative Justice: Theoretical Foundations*. Cullompton: Willan, pp. 1–20.

Van Ness, D. (2002b) 'Creating restorative systems', in L. Walgrave (ed.), *Restorative Justice and the Law*. Cullompton: Willan, pp. 130–49.

Van Ness, D. and Heetderks Strong, K. (2002) *Restoring Justice*, 2nd edn. Cincinnati, OH: Anderson.

Van Ness, D. and Heetderks Strong, K. (2006) *Restoring Justice. An Introduction to Restorative Justice*, 3rd edn. Cincinnati, OH: Anderson.

Van Ness, D. and Schiff, M. (2001) 'Satisfaction guaranteed? The meaning of satisfaction in restorative justice', in G. Bazemore, and M. Schiff (eds), *Restorative Community Justice. Repairing Harm and Transforming Communities*. Cincinnati, OH: Anderson, pp. 47–62.

Van Stokkom, B. (2002) 'Moral emotions in restorative justice conferences: managing shame, designing empathy', *Theoretical Criminology*, 6 (3): 339–60.

Van Stokkom, B. (2004) 'Verantwoorden en pacifiëren' ('Explaining and pacifying'), *Tijdschrift voor Herstelrecht*, 4 (1): 52–6.

Van Stokkom, B. (2005) 'Does punishment need hard treatment?', in E. Claes, R. Foqué and T. Peters (eds), *Punishment, Restorative Justice and the Morality of Law*. Antwerp and Oxford: Intersentia, pp. 165–77.

Van Swaaningen, R. (1997) *Critical Criminology. A Vision from Europe*. London: Sage.

Van Swaaningen, R. (1999) 'Reclaiming critical criminology. Social justice and the European tradition', *Theoretical Criminology*, 3 (1): 5–28.

Vanfraechem, I. (2003) 'Hergo in Vlaanderen' ('FGC in Flanders'), unpublished research report. Leuven: Onderzoeksgroep Jeugdcriminologie, K.U. Leuven.

Vanfraechem, I. (2006) *Herstelgericht Groepsoverleg. Op zoek naar een constructief antwoord op ernstige jeugddelinquentie (Restorative Group Deliberation. In Search of a Constructive Response to Serious Youth Offending)*, PhD criminology thesis. Leuven: K.U. Leuven.

Vanfraechem, I. and Walgrave, L. (2004) 'Restorative conferencing in Belgium: can it decrease the confinement of young offenders?', *Corrections Today*, 66 (7): 72–5.

Vanspauwen, K. and Valiñas, M. (2006) 'Truth-Seeking After Violent Conflict', unpublished manuscript. Leuven: Criminology K.U. Leuven.

von Hirsch, A. (1993) *Censure and Sanctions*. Oxford: Clarendon Press.

von Hirsch, A. (1998) 'Penal theories', in M. Tonry (ed.), *The Handbook of Crime and Punishment*. New York and Oxford: Oxford University Press, pp. 659–82.

von Hirsch, A. and Jareborg, N. (1991) 'Gauging criminal harm: a living-standard analysis', *Oxford Journal of Legal Studies*, 11: 1–38.

Wachtel, T. and McCold, P. (2001) 'Restorative justice and everyday life', in H. Strang and J. Braithwaite (eds), *Restorative Justice and Civil Society*. Cambridge: Cambridge University Press, pp. 114–29.

Wacquant, L. (1999) *Les Prisons de la Misère*. Paris: Liber, Raison d'agir.

Walgrave, L. (1981) 'Recht tegenover jeugddelinquentie: beteugelen en herstellen, maar niet straffen', *Familie- en Jeugdrecht (Family and Youth Law)*, 4: 106–18.

Walgrave, L. (1995) 'Restorative justice for juveniles: just a technique or a fully fledged alternative?', *Howard Journal*, 34 (3): 228–49.

Walgrave, L. (1998) 'Criminology, criminal policy and democracy', *Criminal Justice Matters*, 34: 23–4.

Walgrave, L. (1999) 'Community service as a cornerstone of a systemic restorative response to (juvenile) crime', in G. Bazemore and L. Walgrave (eds), *Restorative Justice for Juveniles. Repairing the Harm by Youth Crime*. Monsey, NY: Criminal Justice Press, pp. 129–54.

Walgrave, L. (2000) 'Restorative justice and the republican theory of criminal justice: an exercise in normative theorising on restorative justice', in H. Strang and J. Braithwaite (eds), *Restorative Justice. Philosophy to Practice*. Aldershot: Dartmouth, pp. 165–83.

Walgrave, L. (2001a) 'On restoration and punishment: favourable similarities and fortunate differences', in A. Morris and G. Maxwell (eds), *Restorative*

Justice for Juveniles. Conferencing, Mediation and Circles. Oxford: Hart, pp. 17–37.

Walgrave, L. (2001b) *Met het oog op herstel* (*In View of Restoration*). Leuven: Leuven University Press.

Walgrave, L. (2002a) 'Restorative justice and the law: socio-ethical and juridical foundations for a systemic approach', in L. Walgrave (ed.), *Restorative Justice and the Law.* Cullompton: Willan, pp. 191–218.

Walgrave, L. (ed.) (2002b) *Restorative Justice and the Law.* Cullompton: Willan.

Walgrave, L. (2003a) 'Imposing restoration instead of inflicting pain: reflections on the judicial reaction to crime', in A. von Hirsch, J. Roberts, A. Bottoms, K. Roach and M. Schiff (eds), *Restorative Justice and Criminal Justice: Competing or Reconcilable Paradigms.* Oxford: Hart, pp. 61–78.

Walgrave, L. (2003b) 'La justice restauratrice et les victimes', *Journal International de Victimologie/International Journal of Victimology*, 1 (4) – online at: http://www.jidv.com.

Walgrave, L. (2004a) 'Restoration in youth justice', in M. Tonry and A. Doob (eds), *Youth Crime and Youth Justice. Comparative and Cross-national Perspectives*, Crime and Justice Vol. 31. Chicago: University of Chicago Press, pp. 543–97.

Walgrave, L. (2004b) 'Has restorative justice appropriately responded to retribution theory and impulses?', in H. Zehr and B. Toews (eds), *Critical Issues in Restorative Justice.* Monsey, NY/Cullompton: Criminal Justice Press/Willan, pp. 47–60.

Walgrave, L. and Aertsen, I. (1996) 'Reintegrative shaming and restorative justice: interchangeable, complementary or different?', *European Journal of Criminal Policy and Research*, 4 (4): 67–85.

Walgrave, L. and Geudens, H. (1997) 'Restorative community service in Belgium', *Overcrowded Times*, 8 (5): 3–15.

Ward, T. and Maruna, S. (2007) *Rehabilitation. Beyond the Risk Paradigm.* London/New York: Routledge.

Weijers, I. (2002) 'Restoration and the family: a pedagogical point of view', in L. Walgrave (ed.), *Restorative Justice and the Law.* Cullompton: Willan, pp. 68–81.

Weitekamp, E. (1992) 'Can restitution serve as a reasonable alternative to imprisonment?', in H. Messmer and H. U. Otto (eds), *Restorative Justice on Trial. Pitfalls and Potentials of Victim-Offender Mediation.* Dordrecht/Boston: Kluwer Academic, pp. 81–103.

Weitekamp, E. (1999) 'History of restorative justice', in G. Bazemore and L. Walgrave (eds), *Restorative Justice for Juveniles. Repairing the Harm by Youth Crime.* Monsey, NY: Criminal Justice Press, pp. 75–102.

Weitekamp, E., Parmentier, S., Vanspauwen, K., Valiñas, M. and Gerits, R. (2006) 'How to deal with mass victimization and gross human rights violations. A restorative justice approach', in U. Ewald and K. Turkovic (eds), *Large-Scale Victimization as a Potential Source of Terrorist Activities.*

Importance of Regaining Security in Post-Conflict Societies. Amsterdam: IOS Press, pp. 217–41.

Willemsens, J. and Walgrave, L. (2007) 'Section C. Europe', in G. Johnstone and D. Van Ness (eds), *Handbook of Restorative Justice*. Cullompton: Willan, pp. 488–99.

Winfree, T. (2002) 'Peacemaking and community harmony: lessons (and admonitions) from the Navajo peacemaking courts', in E. Weitekamp and H. J. Kerner (eds), *Restorative Justice: Theoretical Foundations*. Cullompton: Willan, pp. 285–307.

Wood, J. and Dupont, B. (eds) (2006) *Democracy, Society and the Governance of Security*. Cambridge: Cambridge University Press.

Wright, M. (1989) 'What the public wants', in M. Wright and B. Galaway (eds), *Mediation and Criminal Justice: Victims, Offenders and Community*. London: Sage, pp. 105–7.

Wright, M. (1992) 'Victim-offender mediation as a step towards a restorative system of justice', in H. Messmer, and H. U. Otto (eds), *Restorative Justice on Trial. Pitfalls and Potentials of Victim-Offender Mediation*. Dordrecht/Boston: Kluwer Academic, pp. 525–39.

Wright, M. (1996) *Justice for Victims and Offenders: A Restorative Response to Crime*, 2nd edn. Winchester: Waterside.

Wright, M. (2003) 'Is it time to question the concept of punishment?', in L. Walgrave (ed.), *Repositioning Restorative Justice*. Cullompton: Willan, pp. 3–23.

Yazzie, R. and Zion, J. (1996) 'Navajo restorative justice: the law of equality and justice', in B. Galaway and J. Hudson (eds), *Restorative Justice: International Perspectives*. Amsterdam/Monsey, NY: Kugler/Criminal Justice Press, pp. 157–73.

Young, J. (1997) 'Left realist criminology: radical in its analysis, realist in its policy', in M. Maguire, R. Morgan and R. Reiner (eds), *The Oxford Handbook of Criminology*, 2nd edn. Oxford: Oxford University Press, pp. 473–98.

Young, J. (1999) *The Exclusive Society*. London: Sage.

Zedner, L. (2003) 'Too much security?', *International Journal of the Sociology of Law*, 31: 155–84.

Zehr, H. (1990) *Changing Lenses. A New Focus for Crime and Justice*. Scottsdale, PA: Herald.

Zehr, H. (2002a) *The Little Book of Restorative Justice*. Intercourse, PA: Good Books.

Zehr, H. (2002b) 'Journey to belonging', in E. Weitekamp and H. J. Kerner (eds), *Restorative Justice: Theoretical Foundations*. Cullompton: Willan, pp. 21–31.

Zehr, H. and Mika, H. (1997) 'Fundamental principles of restorative justice', *Contemporary Justice Review*, 1 (1): 47–55.

Zellerer, E. and Cunneen, C. (2001) 'Restorative justice, indigenous justice and human rights', in G. Bazemore and M. Schiff (eds), *Restorative Community Justice. Repairing Harm and Transforming Communities*. Cincinnati, OH: Anderson, pp. 245–63.

Index